# My
## Small
## Country Living

# My Small Country Living

Jeanine McMullen

*Illustrated by Fiona Silver*

W · W · NORTON & COMPANY
*New York    London*

First Edition

Library of Congress Cataloging in Publication Data
McMullen, Jeanne.
My small country living.
1. McMullen, Jeanne. 2. Radio broadcasters—Great
Britain—Biography. 3. Small country living (Radio
program) I. Title.
PN1991.4.M37A35 1984 791.44′092′4 [B] 84–10104

ISBN 0-393-01900-4

W. W. Norton & Company, Inc., 500 Fifth Avenue, New York, N. Y. 10110
W. W. Norton & Company Ltd., 37 Great Russell Street, London WC1B 3NU

1  2  3  4  5  6  7  8  9  0

*For Peter and Arthur who lent me The Gypsy*
*and without Her, it wouldn't have happened!*

# My
## Small
### Country Living

# Chapter 1

The producer's voice crackled sharply through the headphones. 'We'll go ahead in one minute from now. All right?'

I nodded at him, insulated by the plate-glass window between the studio and the control room. Above it the red light was on and I knew that outside in the corridor was a panel flashing 'QUIET. ON AIR'. We weren't, actually; all we were doing was recording a pilot programme which might or might not one day be broadcast. I'd done so many programmes over the years, had sat and waited just like this when they'd really been about to go out live on the air, feeling the tight knot in my stomach as the second hand of the clock tonked its way remorselessly towards transmission time. I'd been nervous then, always, no matter how often I'd broadcast before, but this time I was terrified. There was more than my job at stake, more than the humiliation of making a public fool of myself.

A whole way of life was riding on this programme. It was to be the proving point for a decision made years before against all reasonableness, a decision which had made me turn my back on the warm comfort of studios like this and the even greater comfort of being a professional amongst professionals and take on a tiny hill farm in a remote valley more beautiful than dreams, but cursed with eternal wind and rain. It had brought into my life animals of every kind – a huge, neurotic draught horse and her foals, a bunch of highly individual sheep, a herd of goats in urgent need of a psychoanalyst, an embarrassment of useless poultry, a large geriatric pig, far too many dogs and cats and more debt, despair and self-doubt than I'd thought one human being could conceivably withstand.

All of it had been a mad, defiant gesture to prove that I was a fit and proper person to research and present the programme I was now waiting to do. But perhaps it was too late; perhaps the broadcaster in me had given way to the peasant and the whole plan had gone horribly wrong. Even now, instead of concentrating on the script in front of me, half of my mind was worrying about the dreadful southerly gale which had been blowing for the past three days and which had swept me out of the farm gate only a few hours before. I could still hear the scream of the wind in my ears; could still see the big ash tree bending and twisting and threatening to unload its heavy branches onto the roof of the little white cottage; could still hear the creak and rattle of the slates on the buildings; could still see the horses standing miserably with their backs to the hedge, the black dots of the sheep lying up in the hollows, the chickens fighting their way lopsidedly across the yard with their feathers blown inside out; and above everything the huge, soaring, sandstone cliffs of the Carmarthen Fans brooding behind the flying clouds wreathing their twin summits.

The green light on the table in front of me gave an experimental flick and brought me back to the carpeted, soundproofed elegance of the studio.

'Coming up,' said the voice in the headphones and then, while the first jaunty notes of the signature tune burst out, I swallowed once, smiled up at the microphone and, with the green light now bright and steady, said for the first time the name of the programme on which I'd staked everything – 'A Small Country Living'.

10

# Chapter 2

Of course I had no idea of radio programmes or anything so practical in mind when I first saw the little white farm nestling against the hill, flanked by its long perfection of a barn and guarded by the huge ash tree standing between them. I was in love with and drugged by the sheer magic of the valley with its lush tide of green spreading up the slopes of the great bare cliffs of the Carmarthen Fans which dominated it, and was haunted by the atmosphere of the deep, silent lake lying at the foot of those cliffs with its legends of fairy brides and underwater kingdoms.

I was fascinated, too, by the mad gaiety of the people I was with: people who, in spite of the imminent threat of having everything from the phone to the electricity cut off, lived with a house full of dogs and birds and had that rare ability to create around them a glamour, a sense of the sheer excitement of being alive, which ignored anything so mundane as lack of money. In their tiny witch's cottage, almost completely hidden by a tangle of hedge from which emerged an amazing variety of tame wildlife as well as exotic parakeets and other birds flying free, I'd felt as completely at home, as completely content, as I'd thought it was possible to be.

The owners of this paradise were Gerald and Imogen Summers. Gerald was a well-known falconer and naturalist, perhaps not as well-known as he should have been because until now he hadn't gone into print. But, encouraged by Imogen, he'd finally written the remarkable story of his kestrel, Cressida, which he'd taken all through the Second World War, in and out of prison camps, and finally brought triumphantly home again. I was going down to record an interview with him about the book and decided to spend a couple of weeks in Wales by way of a holiday.

Now one of the sad things about being a broadcaster is that you meet a lot of larger-than-life characters, which tends to make you a bit blasé after a while. Even sadder, people with amazing stories to tell are sometimes pretty boring in themselves. I fully expected to find the Summers living in antiseptic luxury, existing on memories. My only hope was that Gerald's were vivid enough for him to do a decent interview. It's hard now to recapture that feeling of total indifference to the people or the place I was going to see. I've tried many times to recall it, to go back to a time when I was totally unaware of the world I was about to enter, as one struggles to regain that moment of quiet ignorance before a searing love affair.

I was querulous and bored, and so were the two dogs in the back of the car. At the wheel was the Artist, who'd been part of my life for the past three years. For some reason he'd decided to leave the A40 and take me on a scenic diversion, which would have been all right except that it was pitch-black outside and it was a filthy night anyway. We could just make out the shapes of mountains as we went on endlessly, hungry and tired, through the driving rain. At some point I was aware that we'd turned off and were travelling across open moorland, the dim forms of ponies just visible and the eyes of sheep shining in the headlamps. Every now and then a distant twinkle of light from some remote farmhouse sparked briefly, promising warmth and comfort, only to disappear at the next bend of the road.

By the time we finally arrived I was asleep, but woke to the sound of dogs barking, lights flashing through the rain, welcoming voices (two of which I later found out belonged to a parrot and a minah bird) and at last the warm glow of an open fire. A tiny blonde woman was breathlessly asking me how I liked my steak done, while making sure that our whippet and lurcher were seated comfortably in the best chairs, and a tall man with a booming voice was making us free of his whisky. I was also dimly aware of a cage full of baby budgerigars in one corner of the room, in the kitchen the sound of what must have been twenty dogs yelling up and down the register, and someone or something repeating over and over again, 'Bonjour, mon vieux. Bonjour, mon vieux.'

We never did get the steak because the dogs knocked it off while we were all being madly social in the next room and, although Imogen was in tears about it while the dogs sat around burping happily, Gerald spent the next half-hour working out how they'd got it down from a very high shelf. His speculations were assisted by a minah bird sitting by the Rayburn and assuring him in a perfect Welsh accent, 'Sure to be. Sure to be.'

'Bloody whippets probably made a stepladder out of themselves and Meece there,' Gerald finally announced, pointing to a small terrier frantically burrowing under a cushion, 'she climbed up and hoisted it down to the rest of 'em. Never mind, plenty of whisky left, eh?'

The rest of the evening was a happy blur of whisky and bizarre conversation and only ended when the bottle finally gave out and I was driven with my whippet, Merlin, to a lonely little pub to sleep. The Artist and his lurcher returned to bunk down on the Summers' well-worn sofa.

What with the journey and the whisky, I was in a state of near-paralysis as I tottered to the bathroom of the pub and flung open the window to get some fresh air. The sound of a river and an owl hooting somewhere tempted me to poke my head outside – straight into the livid face of a huge gander roused from his sleep on the roof of a shed almost on a level with the bathroom window. Merlin, whose nerves had already been severely tried that night by the Summers' motley gang of dogs and bird life, decided that enough was enough. So there I was at midnight, trying to separate a furious whippet and a gander raucously screaming the alarm while flapping its wings and endeavouring to break my beloved dog's neck in mid-air. The noise was appalling but, as business in the bar downstairs was still in full voice, no-one came to see what was happening. I tightened my grip on Merlin's back legs, hauled him, still baying his defiance, back into the bathroom and bundled him under my arm across the tiny passage to our room.

By now the whisky had evaporated from my brain, my tiredness was gone and, with the racket downstairs not promising to abate one little bit, I slipped Merlin's collar on and crept down the stairs, out into the night which was as clear and still as it had been wet and rampant only a few hours before. Now a fitful moon burst through the racing clouds, stars flickered in and out and a drift of wood-smoke floated from the pub and wreathed itself amongst the damp trees. Behind me the lighted bar still pulsated with sound. I found out later that a local murder with scandalous overtones, which rippled to the heart of London's gangland itself, had caused the police to turn a blind eye and deaf ear to things like closing hours. I think the idea was that tongues loosened by drink might remember what, when sober, they had forgotten about the strangers seen in the district who seemed to have asked the way to the isolated murder cottage from everyone they'd met.

I didn't know all this then, however, and never gave the midnight carousing a thought except to turn and see the old stone building, spearing light out onto the deserted road, as a thing apart from the wild darkness around. I made for the river which roared between tall, dripping trees so that soon even the noise from the pub was drowned out. Merlin and I walked on into a world as lost to time as I felt myself at that moment. The whole night was full of waiting, of an expectation of something or someone yet to come.

'It's real Merlin country,' I said to my dog, who was as tense and alert as I was, and I could almost imagine the wizard himself appearing out of the trees, 'all befurred in blacke shepis skynnes, and a grete payre of bootis, and a bowe and arowis, in a russet gowne, and brought wylde gyese in hys honde'.

Malory's description had been floating through my mind as we walked and indeed, one of the reasons I'd agreed to come to the Black Mountain was that it was in Carmarthenshire, Merlin's own county. The experts seem to have been able to explain who Arthur probably was in all this Matter of Britain, but Merlin is still left to the dreamers and the deep, strange places like that

14

dark ravine where the river hurtled over the great rock slabs and the moon slanted down through the trees onto the rushing water.

I'd called my dog well, for he was almost as magical in his way as the wizard whose name he bore: beautiful and intelligent far above the average, perfectly equipped for the job he'd been born to do, run fast, and a companion who could sense every change of mood like my own nerves. The night I'd found him, two years before, I'd had exactly the same odd feeling of tense expectation as on that evening when I slipped out of the pub and wandered dreaming along the river.

It had been stormy then, too, and the Artist and I had been driving through the Hertfordshire countryside, looking at whippet pups. We had several addresses of breeders who offered pups for sale and had duly inspected most of them. We had been enchanted with them all and practically decided on a little fawn dog, but still I wasn't satisfied. There was one final address miles further on but when I showed it to the Artist, he groaned. 'I thought you liked this little chap,' he said.

'Oh, I do,' I assured him. 'It's just that I've got this odd feeling we ought to go and see this other place. I might be wrong but, if you can bear it, I'd just like to have a look.'

The Artist stared at me for a moment and then sighed and got back into the car. He was used to my odd hunches by now and he was just as anxious as I was to get the right dog. It was one of the things that had brought us together, our love of greyhounds and whippets, in fact all the sighthounds, even the crosses, or lurchers.

My own passion had begun with the greyhounds themselves. I was about seven years old when my Aunt Ann had smuggled me into a Sydney dog track under her fur coat and told me to put a pound on any runner I fancied. When Digger's Hat came romping in at twenty to one, a rank outsider, I fell in love with the long, lean dogs with their bunched muscles and their heart-catching grace as they flew round the track. The fact that I'd actually won money on them helped, for I was born in Sydney of a long line of gamblers and teethed on discarded betting slips. The first horse I ever got up on was one of my uncle's flat racers and for years I thought that the radio had been invented solely to broadcast the racing commentaries.

15

Apart from the races, my only other brush with sighthounds was with the lean, ravenous dogs kept to hunt kangaroos in the Outback; they lived mostly chained to their barrels, yelling their heads off or growling horribly over vast, unnamable hunks of offal when a sheep was slaughtered. It wasn't till many years later that I connected these poor, wild brutes with the elegant, doting lurcher owned by the Artist, when an Australian woman accosted us with the cry, 'Hey! What are you doing with a kangaroo dog in London?'

By then, greyhounds to me were no longer associated with hot-eyed gamblers and arc-lit racetracks. They were creatures from Malory, the gifts of chivalric kings, prized and gilded with jewelled collars. They were the mystic shapes in the tapestries I went to gaze at again and again in the Cluny Museum in Paris; they leapt across the exquisite margins of mediaeval Books of Hours; and they were there in the big print of Pisanello's 'Vision of St Eustace' which went with me everywhere.

When eventually, after years of wandering and of living in London in a variety of bed-sits, I found a basement flat of my own for the ludicrous sum of £5 a week, and within minutes of Kensington Gardens, I thought of having my own dog. It would have to be a whippet, or 'bonsai greyhound' as I'd first thought of them when I saw a quartet mincing up Campden Grove, the light reflected from their silvery coats.

Already Elke, the Artist's lurcher, a lovely golden creature half greyhound and half deerhound, had made herself free of my new home. She was very polite and tolerated me, but was always demonstrably glad to get back to their own place in Bayswater where she could have him all to herself again. My two Burmese cats, Suyin and Pip, after an initial bout of swearing and hurling themselves onto Elke's broad back, had finally accepted her visits and I judged that the introduction of a dog of my own would be fairly easy. So, with the new flat all painted up, hot water laid on and a fence rebuilt round the tiny garden at the back, the Artist and I had set off to find the perfect whippet.

'Thought of a name yet?' he enquired as he peered through the rain at the winding lane ahead.

'Merlin,' I said promptly, having not given the matter a thought till that moment. 'Yes, Merlin, I think. You know what it says in *The Boke of St Albans*: "A Merlin for a Lady." Me, I'm

16

no lady, but you see what I mean. A whippet is to the bigger sighthounds as the merlin is to the larger falcons and hawks. So he'll be named for a wizard and a bird.'

After a great deal of backtracking and questions put to the odd wayfarer who disclaimed all knowledge of the place we were seeking, we did eventually find that last address on our list. We dashed up the path and banged on the door. A deep, steady baying and a lot of high-pitched yaps sounded from behind the door and at last a lady arrayed in carpet slippers and a deeply suspicious scowl opened the door, accompanied by a vast mastiff and a minute golden poodle.

'We've come to see the whippet pups,' I told her.

'Oh hell! I'd given you up by now. I'm afraid they're all back out in the run and the light's gone out there. I'll have to get a torch.' She retreated into the sitting room where a loud television was booming away, leaving the mastiff to make friendly overtures and the poodle to warn us not to take a step further.

A few minutes later we were picking our way across a concrete yard to a dim shed. The breeder opened the door and called. A wild rush of fat bodies poured over my feet and promptly poured back again. Only one little shape continued to dash gaily round in the gloom and I walked after it and whistled. It squatted for a quick piddle and then flung itself at my legs. I bent down and picked it up.

'Let's have a look at this one in the light,' I said, and carried the ecstatic pup down to the porch. After a few quick swipes at my nose, it settled in my arms and made a funny honking noise. 'It's a blue!' I whispered in delight to the Artist.

At that time, the deep gunmetal-blue colour was not very common in whippets, just as, curiously, black is quite rare to this day. I hadn't even dreamed that I'd be lucky enough to find a blue whippet.

'How odd,' said the breeder. 'That's the only one in this litter. You found it first go. Did you want a blue particularly?'

I did, but we'd seen a lot of pups that night and suddenly I wanted to go away and think about it all.

The Artist, sensing my hesitation, said, 'Look, we haven't had anything to eat yet and I think we'd like to discuss it a bit. Is there a pub near here where we can get some supper?'

17

The breeder regarded us cynically. She'd heard the same excuse lots of times before. Whippets then were not the easiest of breeds to sell and she was sure we'd only been wasting her time. She took the pup from me, gave us directions for the pub and turned away resignedly.

'Well, good-bye then. We really will let you know,' said the Artist as he held the door open for me.

'Actually,' I said, turning back, 'you can start writing up his pedigree now. His name is Merlin. I wonder if the Kennel Club will let me register him as that.'

The breeder stared at me in amazement. 'But I thought ... I mean, wouldn't you like to see the others?'

'No. Just make up his pedigree and particulars and I'll write you a cheque.'

The Artist nudged me and his eyes were shining. He hadn't dared to hope that I would share his feeling of absolute certainty that this was the pup we'd been looking for. Since then I've learnt a great deal about whippets, but probably never again would I be able to buy the right one straight off, just like that. Too much knowledge about what I should be looking for might make me damp down the gut reaction which has always been there when I've bought an animal which has proved perfect for me and my particular way of life.

It was long after midnight when we got back to the flat and, anticipating a sleepless night with a whining pup, I brewed up lots of coffee while the Artist introduced Merlin to his basket. Merlin struggled straight out of it again and I groaned. 'I knew he wouldn't wear that,' I said.

'Look,' said the Artist wonderingly, and I did look, fascinated, while the eight-week-old pup snuffled his way all round the outside of the basket, honked approvingly once or twice, climbed laboriously back up into it, curled himself up and went to sleep.

He never stirred nor whimpered all night. He was house-trained within two days and he spoiled me for all the times to come when a new pup would howl and piddle its way through my days and nights. Never again have I found one to settle so quickly and amiably into its new life, nor have I ever found one again which was so exactly my idea of the perfect dog.

The odd little honk he made as a puppy developed into an

amazing range of sounds which were so expressive that I even used him to co-present a little programme on children's books which I did for love and precious little money on a local radio station. When we finally took him racing, he proved to be clever at that, too, and by the time he and I were sitting beside that little mountain river in the moonlight, he'd won enough races to make him one of the stars of the whippet racing club we belonged to. Now he stood beside me, melting into my mood and the shadows.

Voices, laughing and shouting, came faintly over the sound of the river and, as Merlin pricked to attention, I realised that at last the pub was emptying. I was suddenly very tired again but, as I walked slowly back to the light and warmth, something of the wildness of the river went with me. If I was still wondering, as the sound of it lulled me to sleep in the little room at the pub, what had been the sense of urgency which had sent me out to find the torrent, I couldn't know then that higher up, the very same river was soon to form the background to other and more fervent dreams.

That was the beginning of a glorious week of exploring the rich autumn valleys; of watching Gerald handling his golden eagle, Random; of listening to Imogen's hilarious stories of her adventures with all the dogs she'd owned and bred; of dinners with budgerigars and kestrels dive-bombing the soup; of sharing the chairs in front of the roaring fire with at least four dogs apiece; of being insulted by the minah bird and the parrot in three languages and of going to auction sales in the nearby market town and coming home triumphantly with a car boot full of musty books and boxes of curious objects for which no practical use could be found.

As we drifted around the area or talked to the constant stream of visitors to the Summers' cottage, we heard mention of the Lake which was somewhere up in the hills and had a famous legend about it, a legend about a Lady. When at last we went to see this Lake almost casually, Imogen and Gerald for once deserted their animals and came with us.

It was a raw day, with spatters of icy rain obscuring the bleak landscape of boulders and rushing mountain streams. After a long climb in the biting air we found the Lake itself, a grey sheet of water shivered intermittently by gusts of wind trapped between the airy red cliffs of the Carmarthen Fans above it. It was so remote, so silent that, thinking then that the Lady of the Lake was yet another version of the Arthurian one, it seemed the right sort of place for supernatural arms clothed in white samite to lurk.

Gerald, not bothering to correct us about the source of the legend, played the game with us and agreed that at any moment the distant shepherd on his pony would prove to be a dolorous knight and that the whistling wind could be the unearthly music of that funeral barge with its burden of sorrowing queens and dying king. He bent down and picked up one of the stones glittering with crystal that lie scattered by the shore of the Lake. 'Dragon's breath, solidified!' he declared with a grin and then strode off, his attention caught by a distant bird hovering over the rocks.

Imogen looked after him and sighed, but stopped on the point of saying something to us as the Artist and I stood gazing out across the water lost, as usual, in our own Malory-ridden fantasies. It wasn't until much later that she finally told us that the Lady in question had nothing whatever to do with the Arthurian legend.

'There's a farm, just over the side of that hill by the Lake,' she explained over tea back at the cottage. 'The story goes that it belonged to a widow whose only son used to herd the cattle by the Lake in summer. One day he saw a *gorgeous*-looking woman and ...' At this point a minor drama amongst the dogs caused her to leap to the rescue, only stopping to throw back over her shoulder, 'No white samite, no swords. Different story altogether. Stop it, that dog! Stop it, I say!'

After that, as was the way of life with the Summers, too much happened too quickly for us to pick up the threads of the story and in truth we were not much concerned to do so. On those first days of our visit we felt little connection with the Lake except as another beautiful place amongst the many we'd seen, and we remained content to people it with our own visions. It was Rosemary, Imogen's daughter, who finally made us listen properly to the legend on another wild night, when the wind shrieked around the yard of her own farmhouse just across the fields from her mother's cottage.

Seeing the tangles of white water crowfoot that drift on the surface of the Lake in summer, it is easy to understand the old idea that there was a wonderful garden under the water, ruled by a king whose daughter came, once every seven years, to wander on the land. Many a hopeful youth had tried to catch her and woo her, but it was the son of the poor widow at the farm near the Lake who finally enticed her, with the gift of medium-baked bread, to leave her fairy world for him. There was almost a hitch when the Lady went back to get her father, the king, and reappeared with two identical sisters. Only the fact that he'd noticed she had a shoe-lace tied crookedly helped the boy to distinguish his chosen bride.

Fairy brides always come with conditions along with their dowries (and this one had a dowry of as many sheep, cattle and goats as she could count in one breath) but the conditions laid down upon this marriage seemed fairly easy to the besotted husband. If he struck his wife three blows without just cause, she and her dowry would return to the Lake forever.

For a long time the possibility of the young farmer ever striking his wife seemed as remote as ever and she bore him three sons. By now, living prosperously with the help of that dowry, the couple owned a farm near Myddfai, several miles away from the Lake and the supernatural family of the Lady. It doesn't pay to mix with that other world, though. Its morality is simpler than ours; they're not concerned about the opinions of others and they grant our wishes for their own devious reasons.

The first blow came at last but was little more than a push. The second was rather harder and given to stop the Lady crying at a wedding 'for now they are entering upon their troubles'. The third was a real blow of anger when she laughed at a funeral because the departed was now finished with sorrow. As for the young farmer, he was finished with prosperity, for his wife went back to the Lake, calling behind her all the cattle and sheep, even the black calf which had been slaughtered that day and the two oxen pulling the plough. In places you can see the marks of that plough as they dragged it across the mountain and, some people say, if the sun is in the right position, you can follow the path they took all the way to the Lake and their hoofprints are still visible in the rocks beside the water.

The Lady did come back, though. She came to see her three sons and to show them the healing plants and herbs which grew in certain places on the mountain, and she gave them the knowledge which would later make them into the famous Physicians of Myddfai. The Physicians, whether the sons of the Lady or not, seem really to have existed and certainly the village of Myddfai has had a tradition of medical people for centuries.

As Rosemary finished the story, we nodded and smiled, unable then to see it as more than just another interesting local curiosity. It was to be many years before I realised just how deep and fascinating a legend it was. For the moment, the more tangible magic of hill and cloud and the charmed circle which Gerald and Imogen seemed to live in, with their demanding, hectic crew of animals in that little witch's cottage full of warmth and laughter, was catching hold of us and making us lose all sense of time and direction. At some point the idea was born that we should buy a cottage and come and live nearby.

I suppose nearly everyone who goes on holiday to a lovely part of the countryside plays the game of make-believe which involves buying a place there and making the holiday go on forever. We were no exception, although to be honest the Artist had been trying to uproot me from London for years. He was actually a graphic designer trapped in a publishers' publicity department, but he yearned to break away and spend his days painting meaningful works of art and tramping the hills with his lurcher. When Imogen mentioned that she'd heard of a ruined farmhouse and an acre of land going for £300, and as that was about the sum total of our mutual bank balances, we rushed off to see it.

It was a pitiful sight, that old broken cottage where nothing but sheep and cattle had sheltered for years. I tried to imagine a roof where only sagging beams now framed the sky, tried to feel the warmth of a leaping fire in the cold, black chimney, tried to visualise daffodils glowing in the grass beyond the broken step where now only brambles twisted; and with it all, the echo of voices long since gone sounded mournfully in my imagination.

'We could make one enormous studio-type room out of it,' said the Artist rather wistfully. 'You know, just use it for weekends.'

'No, we couldn't,' I said. 'I'd die of melancholy.'

He nodded, and we turned away and walked thoughtfully down the crumbling path, both huddled in our coats as a sharp,

icy wind flicked over the hedge and in through the blind
doorway of the ruin, bringing with it the first touch of cold
reality we'd felt since we'd arrived.

Perhaps it was the desire to shake off those sad ghosts lingering
around the ruin that caused us to turn left instead of right when
we reached the crossroads and nose the car gently along the road
which wound high above a valley rising sharply up from the glint
of a river far below. Where the ruined cottage had been dark and
closed in, here the sense of space and light and sky was blinding.

It was one of those fickle autumn days when cloud and rain
give way suddenly to brilliant shafts of sunlight. I remember the
car stopping and both of us getting out to stand and lean on a
gate, I remember a robin piping in the hedge and I remember
the flood of gold as the sun burst out and lit the autumn trees
like candles. And I remember, oh how I remember, the leaping
sense of familiarity as the cluster of white buildings clinging to
the hillside below sprang into focus and changed my whole life.

# = *Chapter 3* =

Neither the Artist nor the dogs were at all sympathetic when I insisted that we go down and take a closer look at the little farm which had caught my attention. The Artist having uplifted his soul enough with the spectacular view, and the dogs being by now quite satisfied that the hedge held nothing more fascinating than the pungent smell of sheep, they were all united in their desire to get back to the warm chaos of the Summers' kitchen and the massive tea that awaited us. I swept aside such base arguments with a determination which had about it all the inevitability of an Alice following the White Rabbit down his hole – and what happened next was just as illogical.

To reach the farm we had to put the car into first gear to negotiate a perfectly homicidal hill, but presently we were walking through the gate onto a muddy yard where a slim woman carrying a basket of eggs was loudly exhorting a mob of hysterical geese to shut up. They didn't, so in order to hold some kind of reasonable conversation, we retreated to the house and were ushered into a room that looked like a Tunnicliffe drawing

24

of a classic farmhouse kitchen. There was an enormous red-tiled grate framing an open fire on which a vast black kettle was steaming imperiously; hams hung from hooks on the beams in the ceiling; on their shelves on the old dresser, blue and white plates and Staffordshire figures winked in the glow from the fire; there was a roll-top desk in one corner and a table set for tea under the tiny paned window which framed a view of the old plum tree outside on the lawn.

We stood there taking it all in as our new friend bustled about stacking her eggs away and talking breathlessly all the while. Incredibly, the farm was for sale but her husband hadn't come back from the mountain yet, although he'd be in any minute now and meanwhile what about a cup of tea and she had some Welsh cakes just fresh made and would we excuse her for a minute while she went and sorted those old geese. There was a slight movement from under the table and she leapt forward and dragged out a small blonde child bashfully hiding his head against her apron.

'Now then, Terry,' she shrilled at him as he made a dive for the legs of the table again, 'don't be like that. These nice people have come to buy our farm. Trouble with him is,' she said as the boy finally wriggled under the table once more, 'he don't see many people up here. Now you just make yourselves comfortable and I'll be back in a minute.' And she hurried out of the room, supremely unaware of the bombshell she'd just delivered.

The Artist looked at me appalled. '*Have* you come to buy their farm?' he murmured.

'Do you know,' I said thoughtfully, 'I've got an awfully funny feeling I have.'

Funny feeling or not, finding out how much the Griffiths wanted for the farm took a lot of sitting around that fireplace, vast quantities of tea and an absolute mountain of Welsh cakes. As her husband didn't return then, we told Kathleen Griffiths we'd come back that night and we did so, reinforced by Meurig Jenkins, Rosemary's husband. Meurig, who was then the local Milk Inspector, had assured us that they couldn't want more than £6000 for the whole forty acres, but that if I wanted less, then we'd have to do some steady bargaining.

Cliff Griffiths beamed at us as we arrived. He was a complete contrast to his wife, as broad as he was long and thinking very

25

carefully before he moved or spoke. His son had emerged at last from under the table and stood hiding his head in his father's lap as we sat around talking about everything and anything except the actual price of the farm. We did find out that it was for sale because the Griffiths had bought a larger place and that Cliff would prefer to keep most of the land and just sell me the house, the buildings and.... There we stuck, on the question of how much land I could have and how much it would cost.

As we left, Kathleen Griffiths switched on the outside light and the long, fine shadow of the plum tree leapt out and etched itself across the whitewashed wall of the long barn. It was that exquisite image, as delicate as any Japanese flower painting, which sustained me during the long weeks of bargaining that were to follow as the Griffiths havered endlessly about the price and I tried to raise whatever it was from a variety of sources in London – not an easy thing to do for a single female who earned as precarious a living as I did.

Gerald and Imogen never doubted that all would be settled eventually because, showing little or no interest in anything but the view, they'd seen a merlin fly straight over the cottage.

At last, after endless trips up and down the A40, Cliff and I shook hands on thirteen acres and a sum of £3500, and a few weeks later, on the very day they opened the M4 into Wales, the contracts were signed and I found myself in possession of what was to prove a paradise, a hell on earth, an absorbing passion and a thundering great millstone round my neck.

It may seem odd, but until that actual moment of owning the farm, I really had no firm idea of what I'd bought. The whole process of bargaining and borrowing and rushing up and down from London had somehow blurred the edges of the place itself. The cottage I knew well enough by then: a little doll's house affair of whitewashed stone with four windows and a door all picked out in bright blue with an old cowshed, now used for poultry, tacked on at one end. All this was set in a long, sloping lawn surrounded by a low wall topped by a clipped hedge which also flanked the path up to the cottage and put me in mind of the picture of Kelmscott in William Morris' book, *News From Nowhere*.

On the yard there was the long white barn which incorporated a stable and hid from view a new brick cowshed and a ramshackle tin shed where Cliff's ponies lurked knee-deep in mud. There was also a stone pigsty and a dovecote, but standing right by the entrance to the yard was a huge rusting hay barn which obsessed us with the desire to knock it down so that we barely looked at anything else, unless it was the even more irritating sight of two old railway carriages rotting under the ash tree. As for the land, that comprised three fields around the house and below it a large meadow bounded by a river on one side and a small wood on the other. Apart from the meadow everything, including the house, was on a steep angle which was to make even the simplest task an arduous climbing matter.

A surveyor had come in to look at the cottage and buildings and had pronounced the new cowshed to be the only decent thing on the place. That didn't worry me a bit because as far as I could see, the cottage at least was warm and dry, even if it didn't have a bathroom and the only loo was another tin shed straddling a stream and placed strategically in a sea of mud over by the gate. But the little, obscure building society which finally agreed to lend me the £3500 at well over the going interest rates was impressed enough by his report to withhold half the money until I'd 'improved' the living quarters.

That such improvements were necessary came home fully on the bitterly cold night in January when, with Cliff and his family finally gone, we came to take formal possession. We arrived full of almost hysterical excitement, ignoring the vicious flurries of sleet and snow, and opened the blue door on a scene of complete desolation. With the fire dead for only a few days, the damp had begun to peel the bright wallpapers away to expose crumbling plaster and mildew beneath, the big flagstones were slimy with wet and a howling draught was hurling itself across the room and banging furiously at the window. We slept that night on the wet floor, each clasping a dog in our sleeping bags for warmth because every attempt to light the fire with the few sticks of damp wood we'd found only resulted in billows of foul smoke and every now and then a spiteful shower of tar and soot.

I lay there feeling as if a real-life horror story had caught up with me. Apart from the bone-biting cold and the depressing state of everything, I began to panic. One thing I've always had a horror of is debt; even owing a fiver gives me sleepless nights and that story of the Russian mystic, Gurdjieff, who once made a woman pupil of his get into debt needlessly in order to cure her of such a horror, gives me nightmares. Now here I was, up to my eyes in debt for a place that looked as if it would collapse in a heap any minute and no more money to do anything about it.

If it hadn't been for the optimism of the Artist, who promised me that he'd work his fingers to the bone to get everything to rights while I got on with earning the cash to pay for the mortgage and the materials, I'd have had us all back in the car and driven through the night to London. As it was, he reminded me that the value of the place had already doubled now that the M4 was opened and that whichever way I looked at it, buying it had been one of my better ideas. Next morning, before I had time to sit around and dissolve into despair again, he whirled me off to an auction of furniture in a huge, unheated barn of a saleroom in the town.

There's something very special about a country auction, or there was in those days before too many dealers moved in on the act. What began as a collection of vaguely curious bystanders, most of whom had come in from the cold to see what was going on, became a furiously partisan audience. We sat, huddled against the cold, on chairs which until then had stood in farmhouse kitchens and had been polished by generations of behinds to a dull shine. We waited in whispering anticipation for the auctioneer to begin the entertainment, to acknowledge those he knew by calling their bids by name and to acquaint us more fully with these relics of other people's lives which he'd come to sell.

The Artist and I had nosed around earlier and, keeping firmly in mind our requirements for something to sit on, something to sleep on and something to cook on, had selected various likely things. But neither of us had bargained for the intense excitement of the auction. As the auctioneer got into his stride and the jokes began to flash back and forth, or a deathly hush settled over the room while we watched, enthralled, a couple of farmers bidding furiously for a really hideous three-piece suite which neither of them wanted but was determined not to let the other have, and as one by one the various treasures were held up to our view and their marvels extolled and the audience breathed deep at the sheer magnificence of the oratory, we ceased to have any definite object in mind and got completely carried away.

28

Before long the auctioneer knew my name and that of my new property, and heads began to turn. We caught whispers of 'That's who's bought it, then', and people smiled at us and cheered when we won a bid and all the horror of the night before vanished.

They're still here, all those things we bought so recklessly more than ten years ago. The dreadful old moquette settee is now draped with a woven rug, but the big square table still stands where we put it under the window, the beds are the very same ones we struggled through the door with, and the same threadbare carpet still covers the flagstones. The four chests of drawers still haven't been stripped, but the three enormous grandfather chairs have come up wonderfully with linseed oil and beeswax. The huge brass plate still hangs over the stair-well and the candles I light when the electricity fails still stand in the same long, curly, wooden candlesticks. The beautiful old chair, with its carved skirts coyly hiding its secret, is still used by visitors who can't face the nighttime trek downstairs to the bathroom, just as we used it when we couldn't face the cold journey out to the tŷ bach by the gate.

The little electric stove has been reinforced by a Rayburn, but the ancient rolling pin and the blue and white plates and the curious old knives and forks and spoons are still used in the kitchen. The wall-high gilt mirror is still much admired for all that it cost only 50 pence, and so are the brass fenders which cost even less in one job lot. I found that first bill the other day and discovered that I had furnished the entire cottage for less than £90.

We lived for the next few weeks in a kind of wonderland of our own dreams, getting to know at last the fields and woods, or sitting snug by the roaring fire as the gales shook the very bones of the cottage, for in those days of innocence we didn't know that barn roofs could fly away so easily and there were no animals to rush out and rescue from the bitter rain. If we doubted what we were doing at all, we only had to go and see Imogen and Gerald, who still gave us an uproarious welcome and fed us with piping hot meals and enthusiasm.

Up and down from London we came every week, battling through blizzards and braving the motorway skimmed with ice, till eventually the spring came and we arrived to the haunting cries of newborn lambs echoing around the valley and watched in delight as the sun warmed the earth back into life and a faint haze of green blurred the sharp silhouettes of winter.

By now the Artist had given up his London job. In late April he and his lurcher took up permanent residence in Wales, and I had to face the long journeys alone with Merlin. It was on one of my lonely trips from London that I stopped off in a dreamy Cotswold village of mellowing stones and visited a blacksmith, a man famous not only for the way he'd maintained the old family smithy but for his creative wrought iron work. There, amidst racks of horseshoes and the sections of a pair of heraldic gates he was engaged upon, I handed him a design, made by the Artist, for a weathervane in the shape of a unicorn flying before the wind.

The blacksmith, a tall, craggy man with the penetrating gaze, slightly misty round the edges, of the true creative craftsman, looked at the unicorn with its intricate mass of feathering on legs and tail and head and pursed his lips.

'Going to be tricky, that is, to get cut out in steel and then balanced so it turns properly. Trouble is, I've got about two years' commissions waiting already, see.'

I looked at him anxiously, knowing that I should have been spending my borrowed money on more practical things but also knowing that that unicorn was just as important, to us anyway, as a septic tank. We were both prepared to go on stomping through the mud to the tŷ bach, to live with sagging walls and wet flagstones, but we felt it would all be more bearable with our lucky symbol, the unicorn, keeping watch up there in the winds above the cottage.

The unicorn has many legends about it, but the one we loved best was that which told of it as the protector of all the smaller beasts. It is also, equally, the symbol of pure and profane love, and after years of adding to my collection of unicorns in glass and wood and bronze, it proved a pretty good test of the way people's minds worked. Some would come into my flat, glance around and then sniff, 'Unicorns, eh? Very Freudian, my dear', whilst others would look slightly embarrassed and then ask tentatively, 'Do you think it just possible that unicorns ever existed?'

The Artist had done neither: he'd simply sat down and quietly

30

drawn me a picture of one in full gallop. It was on the strength of that that we became friends and found that we shared many other interests, all of them equally unlikely, but somehow the unicorn remained as our lucky symbol. Now, with our new chancy venture on hand, we felt we needed every bit of luck we could find and nothing less than a unicorn up there above the slates seemed good enough – silly, but there it was.

The blacksmith was still poring over the drawing I'd given him and I stood there, feeling ridiculously that what he said next would be a kind of mystic pronouncement on our future, giving all my own doubts into his hands like a gambler throwing everything on one turn of the wheel.

He looked up at last. 'I've never made a unicorn weathervane before. They usually want foxes and horses and cockerels. Will you be passing this way in about a fortnight?'

A fortnight later I drove triumphantly onto the yard with the long stem of the weathervane poking out of one of the Volkswagen's windows and at once the Artist was up on the roof, banging and hammering away to set it in place. As he finished, the spring sun flickered for a moment before sinking behind the forestry, one last ray catching the unicorn on the roof as it began gently turning in a breeze that bore with it the scent of hawthorn and honeysuckle and dogrose, and we knew that at last the warm days were really here.

Gerald and Imogen came to see our unicorn and understood perfectly why it meant so much to us and why it had taken priority over all the other boring realities we had to face up to rather quickly. They were the only people who even recognised it for what it was; mostly it was remarked on as a rather odd-looking horse.

But it took Gwyn, a farmer friend of theirs, to slap us right down to earth. Gwyn had been fascinated all through our negotiations the previous winter and he came at last, hands deep in sagging pockets and cap pulled over his sparse hair, to see what we'd ended up with. He stomped all over our hard-won fields and pronounced them mostly rock and swamp. Finally he put a question we hadn't considered till then.

'Now then,' he demanded, 'what will you be doing with this land?'

We looked at him in amazement. Do with this land? Nothing

like that had even entered our minds. This was our private world where we could walk at liberty with our dogs, my escape from the pressures and cynicism of the competitive world I worked in, the Artist's base from where he could dream up his pictures, our haven from – well, just about everything!

Gwyn was waiting for an answer. We smiled at him facetiously. 'Why, we're going to breed pedigree unicorns, Gwyn,' we said.

Instead of laughing, Gwyn looked puzzled. He pushed his cap onto the back of his head and thoughtfully scratched an ear. 'I don't know,' he said at last. 'I can't be keeping up with all these new foreign cattle. Unicorns, you say. Would they be something the same as a Charolais then?'

But whatever confusion the unicorn caused in the minds of our human neighbours, for the animals in the vicinity there were no such doubts. If we had hung out a large sign marked 'Vacancies', they could not have responded more eagerly. Almost as soon as the weathervane was installed they began to arrive – the halt and the lame and the homeless, sure of an easy berth in the place where their mythical protector swung its horn round the compass of the welcoming fields.

They came, were succoured and at once began to lay the foundations of tyranny with which to rule our lives. And, to make quite sure of our total submission, they started whole dynasties of their own kind.

# Chapter 4

The next few years drifted away: happy, optimistic years. Even the dramas we endured with the Council Planning Department, who were determined that the cottage would be 'improved' into a boring suburban affair of picture windows and tidy grates and hideous synthetic tiles on the floor, we treated like a game. It was a game we more or less won, even though the cottage still raged with draughts, the enormous open fireplace we'd unearthed behind the red-tiled stove smoked abominably when there was no wind and the stone slabs we replaced after the damp proof course was laid were bone-chilling under our feet. Builders came and went and we ended up with the only dud Rayburn in the district, a septic tank that overflowed in all the wrong places, more holes in the walls and a highly erratic hot water supply.

We didn't seem to mind too much at the time, being far more concerned with putting up shelves for all our precious books and

33

slapping on white paint everywhere. Besides which, the animals had already begun drifting in and we spent the greater part of our time fussing over our waifs and strays.

If my friends and colleagues in London were amazed at my sudden decision to buy a few acres of rock and mud a couple of hundred miles away and to spend every spare moment I had rushing off to see what was happening on them, my family in Australia took it as a matter of course. They'd been surprised, if anything, that I'd left it so long and that for the past few years I'd had nothing more remarkable than a pair of cats and one small dog in the way of livestock. My mother in particular had learned very early on that she'd have to find room somewhere in our luggage for anything from a goat to a large duck with a whole newly hatched brood.

'In our luggage', because all her life my mother has been travelling on and, one way and another, I went to seventeen different schools ranging from the most expensive boarding ones to little bush places where the kids came thundering up on their tough ponies just as the bell rang. Sometimes we lived in hotels with long wooden verandahs, a hard-drinking, laconic clientèle and more often than not a cook who didn't mind me sitting in her kitchen as she sweated over a big stove in the heat; sometimes we put up at remote sheep stations where the stockmen encouraged me to ride and then swore at me when I pinched their horses; for a while we lived in a tiny ramshackle hamlet in the middle of a flat, arid plain where my mother had taken a job as a bush nurse and had to cope alone with everything except major surgery, when the Flying Doctor came in to airlift the patients to hospital 120 miles away.

Mrs P, as everybody knows her these days, has an ancestry like a patchwork quilt and our family is a mongrel combination of most of the Celtic races with a leavening of Anglo-Saxon and a dash of Spanish blood to liven things up again. Legend has it that the Spanish blood came by courtesy of a highborn Spanish lady who was abducted over her convent wall by a dashing Irish officer, but my mother has always sworn that the lady in question was in truth a gypsy and that by some odd genetic freak she herself is a throwback to that colourful ancestor. Thus, she is fond of explaining, her own predilection for brilliant colours and bright, gaudy things like spangles and, above all, her dislike of

34

settling in any one place for more than a few months at a time.

Two husbands haven't made a great deal of difference to her desire to keep on the move. The second, my stepfather Arthur, a tall, rangy man who looked like Gary Cooper and came from one of the big sheep stations she'd visited in her wanderings, didn't even try at first. For a couple of years they roamed all over New South Wales in an incredible vehicle named 'the Billy' which was an old converted Chevrolet. My young brother and I, when I was released from boarding school for the holidays, were simply parked in the back of the Billy as Arthur and my mother went wherever the fancy took them. Finally, however, Arthur put the Billy, which had taken us through flood and fire and blizzard and drought without a hitch, out to grass and settled down, to my mother's undying frustration.

Naturally, when I began to wander on my own account, she was never far behind, using my welfare as an excuse to hit the road again. As I expected, not long after I bought the little farm, she arrived from Australia to find out what was going on. Mrs P took the primitive state of things in her stride, cast a philosophical eye over our mounting collection of animals and then decided she would be of more use in London where she could keep the little flat warm and make soothing noises to radio producers when they demanded to know where I was. It says much for my stepfather that he understood perfectly, although he still couldn't make out what I intended to do with such a tiny place, his own idea of a small farm being something in the region of 10,000 acres of dry land and scrub.

I wished I could have told him that we did have some kind of plan in mind, that we'd determined to grow all our own food or even to breed some particular animal really well. Oh, we had all kinds of ideas, from fish farming to a home for retired greyhounds or the setting up of a miniature farm park. Much depended on what had taken our interest at the time and if, for instance, show jumping was in the news, then we'd be carried away with the thought of breeding the future winner of the Horse of the Year Show by putting our big draught mare to a thoroughbred. It was all pathetically haphazard.

A lot depended, too, on whom and where I was interviewing. As the mysteries of country life began to unfold for us, I realised that for anyone with a small property and needing information

35

badly, there was hardly anywhere then that you could go for it. I took the simple way out by finding stories and people related to what we wanted to know and going off to interview them for the radio. One thing led to another and soon I was badgering producers with the idea that I should do a full-scale programme for smallholders. The producers were very taken with the thought, but two successive Controllers of Radio 4 refused the idea and the best I ended up with was a country edition of the 'You and Yours' consumer programme every Bank Holiday.

These Bank Holiday country programmes achieved a certain success with the listeners, but for the Artist they were a nightmare because they usually meant yet another enthusiasm of mine and, worst of all, more stock arriving. When they came, however, he was if anything even more enthusiastic than I was. By now he'd found a part-time job in an Art College which specialised in wildlife and animal painting, so the animals became useful points of reference.

The first to arrive had been a pair of whippet puppies thrust at me by Imogen. Gerald, always on the lookout for homes for his growing flock of pigeons, gave us a pair of homing ones which we spent hours taking to distant places to make sure that they really did come back. The large black rabbit who'd proved too tough even for the other residents at the Summers' place was supposed to have been released in the wood, but it came back to take up quarters in the barn, from which it emerged twice a day to terrorise the whippets. A quartet of orphan hedgehogs were rescued to live in a box in the kitchen and kept the Artist busy digging up worms for them until they were old enough to fend for themselves.

The cavalcade began in earnest with Sarah, a small, speckled bantam hen complete with a clutch of chickens which the Artist kept in the living room, and she was quickly followed by a half-dead muscovy duckling that I revived with brandy and sugar.

To keep my foundling company, we invested in a knock-kneed Aylesbury drake called Stanley and yet more ducklings to keep him fully occupied one day. The whole lot promptly went down with a mysterious ailment which our neighbours assured us was 'the July sprawls' and which caused the Min. of Ag. chap in Carmarthen to despair when we kept ringing up to find out if it was a notifiable disease. A couple of geese of no known pedigree

36

and looking for all the world like a pair of odd football socks came next and, hot on their heels, a seemingly ancient cart-horse called Doli.

Doli! How can one put Doli into mere words? Doli wasn't just a horse any more than the mountain is just a mountain. Doli was a way of life, a whole history of events and people. Everyone who'd ever known her recalled her vividly – some with hatred, more with wry affection. The dealer who'd originally brought her over in a job lot from Ireland clearly remembered her from the hundreds of horses he'd handled in fifty-odd years. Lenni the blacksmith, who hadn't seen her for a very long time, shouted with glee when he saw her standing patiently in my loosebox. I heard snippets of her past from all kinds of casual acquaintances whose paths she'd crossed briefly. And no stallion, large or small, could resist her whether she was in season or not. She was a veritable Marilyn Monroe amongst mares.

In my more ambitious moments I described her as an Irish Draught, but the plain fact is that Doli was nothing more nor less than a cart-horse. Part of her was obviously Shire or Clydesdale. The other part or parts of her were quite unknown, but if Doli herself could have expressed an opinion on the matter, it would be that there was a lot of very hot thoroughbred blood coursing through her mighty veins and even years of tushing timber in the forestry had done nothing to still its urgent desire for expression.

During our first summer at the farm, the Artist and I were glad to have a few mouths around to keep the lush grass at bay and so we played host to a group of Meurig's skittish young heifers and Doli. Doli had been lent out by her previous owner to Rosemary Jenkins, who was running a trekking centre. Doli's job was to carry the heavyweight beginners, which she did with great calm and efficiency until one day Rosemary mounted an American psychoanalyst on her. What happened between him and Doli on their slow progress up the mountain is open to conjecture. Perhaps he whispered a few Freudian thoughts in her ear and awakened the darker side of her nature. The poor man was, understandably, a trifle incoherent after Doli had violently decanted him onto the rocks, leaving him to his own dreams and the thoughtful speculations of a pair of buzzards wheeling overhead.

Whatever happened, the fact remained that Doli was not deemed safe to be trusted with trekkers, heavyweight or otherwise, and Rosemary had sent her to graze my fields.

When I first saw her, Doli was not a lovely sight. Old scars from the forestry chains marked her legs and she had a way of hanging her head and posing as a picture (no doubt by Landseer) of an old, neglected horse. It was a good act; it convinced us anyway that here was a horse who needed rescuing. When the Artist began to put pressure on by assuring me that her immediate future would probably be either the knacker's or a return to hard work and misery in the forestry, ('Just look at those scars!' he kept reminding me), and when Rosemary kept sighing about what a dear old girl Doli was if kept away from psychoanalysis, I dug into the overdraft and paid out £145 to her owner. He was an Italian who kept a fish-and-chip shop in one of the villages and, being very fond of Doli, had hoped to keep her for his children to plod around on. His wife, however, wanted a new washing machine and Doli didn't stand a chance. It was the wife who came and collected the money.

The first of Doli's problems concerned her age. I had assumed that she was very old, mainly on the strength of her price and that way of drooping around over fences as if seeing the world for the last time. Several horsey 'experts' came and looked in her mouth, felt her legs and assured us that indeed Doli was pretty ancient. Doli, who'd obviously found in the past that looking old and tired was a good way to get out of work, adopted an even more pathetic pose. We consoled ourselves with the thought that we'd performed a humane act in rescuing her from the forestry and treated her as a mobile armchair, even carrying the odd whippet on board when perambulating gently round the fields on her back.

It wasn't till the Artist (who had an amazing capacity for tracking people down) discovered the dealer who'd brought her over from Ireland that both the 'experts' and Doli were confounded. According to him, Doli was just rising seven. He advised us to stop pandering to her and get her down to work. This was all very well but, the odd ride apart, neither of us knew how to work a horse, especially not on those steep fields which had already claimed the life of one farmer when he was mowing.

It must have been about the same time that the BBC asked me

to prepare a programme which would be a kind of Idiot's Guide to Show Jumping. For weeks I trailed around, tormenting the life out of people like Dorian Williams, Anne Moore, Alan Oliver and Harry Llewellyn. I even spent one hair-raising afternoon in the Course Builder's box in the middle of the ring at Hickstead. I remember that clearly for the massive beast which got out of control and came heaving and snorting towards the box. Everyone, including the Course Builder, made for the exits instantly. Everyone, that is, except me, who had some crazy idea of recording the whole thing for posterity but in my fright forgot to turn the machine on.

As it turned out, the rider got control of his horse in time to swerve it aside and I lived to tell the tale in person. And tell it I did, till everyone was bored to death with the story, but not half as bored as they were to become with my sudden, passionate ambition to breed a show jumper from Doli. I still blush (as I do when I hear the record the BBC finally made of the programme) when I think of how I outlined this preposterous plan to those busy men and women of the show jumping world who were too polite to tell me I had my own and Buckley's chance of doing anything of the kind.

The sire we found for this future phenomenon was a small thoroughbred of excellent temperament, called Dominic. His owners came and collected Doli, who found out what it was she'd been missing all these years, made violent overtures to Dominic and bossed the other mares around dreadfully. She came back, six weeks later, a changed animal. Gone was the 'twilight of her days' act. What we now had thumping about the place and churning the mud up with her big feet was the soul, if not the body, of a spirited blood mare who knew exactly how to handle the two fools who fussed over her as if she'd just been served by Mill Reef.

Of course, it wasn't certain that she was in foal at all. Even the fact that she hadn't cycled again was no proof, so we asked the vet to come and examine her. To do the job properly, he told us, would mean a rectal probe so that he could feel against the wall of the womb if she was carrying anything.

The details of that afternoon's work are seared into my brain. Islwyn Thomas, the vet, had always shown remarkable patience with our bombardment of questions about Doli. He is indeed an extraordinarily good vet and Imogen and Gerald swear that but for him, they would never have saved so many of their birds and animals over the years. He is also highly experienced with the larger farm animals. Understandably, though, he was a little nervous about Doli's coming examination – not, I suspect, so much because of Doli herself as because of the two people he was relying on to hold her steady while he probed. Apart from anything else, one of them was cheerfully brandishing a microphone at him and expecting to record the whole event.

Whether he normally took such elaborate precautions I don't know, but Doli was led out of the stable and positioned carefully on a flat stretch of concrete path in front of the cowshed. Several bales of straw were placed behind her as a barrier and at the other end, the Artist held her steady with her nose in a bucket of nuts to keep her occupied. Islwyn is not a big man and even when he donned a voluminous green parturition overall and long plastic gauntlets he didn't add a great deal to his general proportions, so Doli's large backside hid him partly from view when he began his probing. He emerged briefly a few times with handfuls of steaming dung from her bowel, which effectively put a stop to my questions and caused me to remove myself and the microphone at once.

There was a long silence broken only by the sound of Doli's steady munching, the mindless screech of a crow somewhere down in the wood and the distant droning of a tractor. The Artist and I stood rigidly tense. Neither of us had ever seen a rectal examination before and it held as much mystery to us as a heart transplant operation. Apart from which, of course, we were desperately anxious to find out if Doli had taken. We waited for the vet to speak.

At last, after what seemed a very great age, he did so. 'My God,' said Islwyn, in a voice that sounded muffled, yet curiously hollow, 'it's big in here!'

Wildly improbable visions of the small vet having gone right inside to look personally for the foetus were dismissed when I found him with his cheek pressed against Doli's massive flank, reaching forward for all he was worth. He grinned at me. 'I think there's something,' he said, 'but there's so much space in there, it's hard to say for certain. It's early days yet. You'll just have to wait and see.'

Waiting and seeing were the very least of what we did for the remainder of Doli's eleven-month term. The discussions of diet and exercise and the general care of pregnant mares finally drove friends from our side in despair. Doli herself made a big production out of her condition. Her nerves, she gave us to understand, were in a shocking state. The slightest noise, the mere glimpse of a piece of paper, were enough to send them jangling. She thought the least we could do was to refrain from riding her.

As her time grew nearer, she burped in our faces and groaned and staggered about shamefully, in case we forgot she was carrying a Little Burden. When I wasn't there to join in our endless watch on her, the Artist rang me every night to give me a minute by minute description of Doli's day, a bulletin which I faithfully handed on in detail to anyone who'd listen. Of course I arranged everything so as to be there when the foal was due and of course Doli put off the birth until I'd been forced to go back to London.

She dropped the foal out on the field on the first really foul morning we'd had for weeks. The Artist rang me at six in the morning to announce breathlessly that she'd had two foals. Then he rang back straightaway to say no, there was only one, but the rain had streaked his glasses and made him see double, and the foal had a long string dangling from its middle and what the hell was that? My mother took the phone and calmly explained about umbilical cords and that what Doli had hanging out of her was afterbirth and not another foal coming.

Moelwyn we called the foal – Mole for short. He was big and beautiful and intelligent and, although he never looked like achieving the career we'd planned for him, we wouldn't have swapped him for Red Rum himself.

Some time that summer, just after Moelwyn was born, we got the pigs. For that, Joe Henson at the Cotswold Farm Park was responsible.

I'd had an aversion to pigs ever since, when I was four, I'd tried to separate a vast sow and her litter at the Sydney Show. I can't remember much about it, but Mrs P does, vividly. She'd been hunting frantically through the crowds for her befrilled infant and found her, the centre of fascinated spectators, trying to pull a line-up of suckling piglets off their mother's side under the illusion that they were devouring their dam alive. Neither sow nor piglets were taking kindly to the separation when I myself was hauled, kicking and screaming, from their midst.

Whether it was the smack I got from my terrified mother or the subconscious memory of that white belly overrun with screaming piglets which prejudiced me against pigs I'm not sure, but nothing I'd seen or heard about them did anything to change my mind. A brief visit to an intensive pig unit only appalled me.

It was Joe, at that time still struggling to convince people that there was much to be gained by preserving the old breeds of farm livestock, as he'd been doing himself for years, whose enthusiasm caused me to look again at the case for the pig.

For a start, his own were rollicking outside and not confined in thrusting, noisome, gobbling groups in concrete pens. His pigs were all different shapes and colours: lovely golden Tamworths, black Berkshires with a white stripe up their noses and Gloucester Old Spots with black polka dots on their behinds; pigs with ears that stuck straight up and pigs with floppy ears; pigs with long, straight snouts and pigs with snub noses and squashed-up faces. Pigs were not just long slabs of waddling flesh. Pigs, as the author Elma Williams once said, were People!

The Artist was not at all enthusiastic when I told him my plan: we would do our bit towards preserving a rare breed of pig. After all, we did have a perfectly designed pigsty and for most of the time they could be out grazing like Joe's pigs, for the older breeds are on the whole very good foragers.

'They're supposed to be handy at getting rid of bracken roots,' I told him as a final inducement.

That did the trick, because keeping the bracken at bay was one of the jobs he hated most. 'All right,' he agreed, 'but just one pig. OK?'

'Oh, definitely only one,' I assured him. 'They're rather expensive anyway. I'll get Joe to keep me a weaner gilt. One of the Gloucester Old Spots, I think, because they're so hardy.' That wasn't the reason I wanted one at all; I just couldn't resist those polka-dotted behinds.

I waited impatiently to hear from Joe that my weaner was ready but stipulated that I did want one with as many spots as possible. Finally he rang to say that he had a young gilt with lots of spots and could I come and collect it soon. 'It should fit quite well on the back seat of your Beetle,' he said.

The only trouble was that I didn't have the current Beetle with me. I'd left it in Wales, and somehow I didn't fancy the idea of travelling on public transport with a small pig.

It just so happened that I was due to go and interview Fred Archer about his latest book on village life in the Vale of Evesham. When I rang him to make the final arrangements, I casually mentioned something about the pig I was buying.

Fred became very excited. 'A Gloucester Old Spot!' he cried in his rich country voice. 'The old orchard pig! Lovely fat bacon! I haven't seen one of those for years. What are you going to do with it?'

'Well, the first thing I've got to do is get it to Wales somehow,' I said with a sigh.

'Don't you worry about that, Jeanine. I'll drive you to Wales with the pig. A Gloucester Old Spot! I'll be looking forward to that, I will!' And he rang off before I had time to decline his offer.

A few days later Joe ushered Fred, his wife Joyce and myself, strung about with tape recorder and microphone, into a small shed where two deeply suspicious weaners eyed us from the straw.

'The big one is yours,' explained Joe. 'The other one is a bit of a runt and I'll send her to market when she puts on some more weight.'

Naturally, my attention was immediately riveted on the runt, even though she had hardly any spots and was half the size of her sister, who was beautifully marked all over her portly person. I switched on the tape recorder and asked Fred to pick up the runt. As he moved forward, both piglets leapt to their feet in one sudden explosive movement, oinking and squealing hysterically. Fred made a flying lunge, caught the nearest one and, as he clasped it to his chest, it let out one long, endless ululating shriek that sent the needle on the tape recorder firmly to the end of the red marker. With the level adjusted down practically to nil, Fred and I did our interview shouting above the noise. Fred gave me a potted history of the Gloucester Old Spot pig and then bellowed, 'And which of these are you going to have, Jeanine? This big one's the best but knowing you, you'll probably like the little runt there!'

43

Laughing merrily for the benefit of the tape recorder, I agreed and then, noticing that Fred seemed to have gone oddly silent, wound up the interview and switched off. Fred, who had a funny look on his face, made an extremely uncouth remark, put the piglet down and revealed that she had peed copiously all down the front of his new suede coat.

Soon, Fred and Joyce and I were rolling along the Cotswold lanes with two subdued piglets in a cabbage crate on the back seat of the Archers' spotless car. Joe, not really wanting to keep one weaner on its own, had offered both of them to me at a bargain price and, with head and heart at variance over which one to choose, I'd closed the deal.

'I don't know what your friend'll say,' grinned a delighted Fred, 'but they'll keep each other company. A pig gets lonely, a pig does.' Joyce merely sniffed. What with the ruination of Fred's coat and the thought of two piglets fouling the seat of their car, it had been a trying day for her.

My 'friend' was not at all pleased, but it took him just twenty-four hours to fall down and worship. Within days of my return to London, he began sending sketches of the young pigs sleeping, ploughing, seeing the dogs off, trotting along the skyline, chatting up the poultry, getting the wrong end of a confrontation with the geese and sploshing about in the stream. I was so delighted with the pigs that when Fred's interview was broadcast, I followed it up by a recording of them 'singing'. It was an extraordinary noise which they made when they were deeply contented, and sounded for all the world like a pair of tuba players limbering up. It even had a bit of a tune to it.

As they grew older, it became obvious that the runt, Magnolia, in spite of being so much smaller, was the boss. Blossom, who could have flattened her sister if she'd wanted to, was far too amiable to be bothered arguing. During the colder weather, both of them grew long, woolly coats and much preferred their tin shelter up in the field to the pigsty on the yard. When it came to breeding from them, however, things didn't go so well.

Thinking that I'd only wanted a pet pig, Joe Henson had neglected to notify the birth of the litter to the National Pig Breeders' Association as all the rest of it had been males destined for market. Without that first notification, pedigree pigs good enough for breeding can't get their papers. So, in spite of their impeccable ancestry, Blossom and Magnolia had to go right to the bottom of the grading-up register. It seemed a bit pointless, therefore, to travel the many miles back into England to take them to a proper Gloucester Old Spot boar and, although nowadays there seem to be any number scattered around Wales, at that time in the early 'seventies, we couldn't find so much as a rumour of one.

The other alternative was to mate them with an ordinary white boar of some other, more common breed and produce weaners for market. Although they are a coloured pig themselves, the Gloucester Old Spots if mated to a white boar will produce pure white offspring which are much preferred in the commercial world. Still, something or other always seemed to go wrong. If we located a likely boar, we couldn't get transport or the boar went sick or some outbreak of disease somewhere put a stop to all pig movements in the area, and time passed by till Blossom and Magnolia began to get on a bit. People started to suggest that we eat them, but by then they'd become so much a part of our lives that we'd as soon have eaten one of the dogs. So the two pigs lived on, happily rootling around, doing the odd bit of broadcasting for me and enchanting everyone who met them.

It didn't stop with the pigs, of course; goats, some black sheep and three wildly independent little Dexter heifers came to divert and dismay us and, if I missed out on many of the dramatic incidents in their lives, the Artist kept a faithful record for me with his camera and his sketch-book. My planned total removal from London seemed to get further and further away as the cost of keeping so many animals housed and fed meant that I had to get more and more jobs, but somehow I believed that it would all work out in the end. It did work out all right, but not quite in the idyllic way I'd thought it would.

=== *Chapter 5* ===

The streets of Campden Hill were unusually peaceful. In the
distance the faint clatter of many hooves could be heard trotting
in unison as the Household Cavalry returned from their morning
exercise and made their way back to the barracks in
Knightsbridge. As the sound of their well-ordered retreat faded
away, the soft swish of a road sweeper made its way down
Kensington Church Street, empty in the early morning of
everyone except a few hardy dog walkers bound for the Gardens.
In a few hours that same street would be packed with impatient
cars and frantic businessmen fighting for taxis, while the less
well-heeled charged down the hill in a desperate rush for the
tube.

Now, the elegant antique shops displayed their glittering,
expensive wares to no-one but squabbling pigeons and
scavenging sparrows, and the only sign of life from the
delicatessen on the corner was the bewitching smell of newly
baked sausage rolls and fresh bread which seeped under the
shuttered door. The smell crept round the corner of Campden

46

Grove and caused the two people busily working around an ancient Bedford van, decorated with travel stickers from all over Europe, to pause for a moment in their task of stuffing as much as they could onto the already groaning springs of the van.

Inside, perched on a bundle of sheets and pillows and leaning against a sagging mattress, sat Mrs P, a point of stillness in all the bustle. Her feet were encased in a massive pair of sheepskin slippers, around her shoulders was draped a patchwork quilt of vivid, clashing reds and pinks, her hair hung down in two long, grey plaits and on her head was perched 'my Harrods Hat'. She was absorbed in the activity coming from the tea chest by her feet where a tiny whippet bitch suckled five wriggling pups, and only broke her concentration to admonish a pair of Burmese cats who were trying to escape from the cat basket behind her to the consternation of an apprehensive budgerigar suspended in a cage above.

The owner of the van stood on the narrow pavement, hands on hips, looking in disgust at the other woman struggling across the street with yet another armful of books. 'For God's sake, Jeanine,' she exploded in a broad Australian accent, 'you can't bloody fit any more in! You said only your mother and you and the pups and a few pots and pans were to go, not the whole bloody British Library Reading Room too. Here, Mrs P, tell your daughter to knock it off or we'll be spending the night in a ditch!'

'That's all, Sue, I promise,' I panted as I quickly dumped the pile on top of an unwieldy box of groceries. 'It's just that I can't bear the thought of all the empty bookshelves. The Bonneys said they look terrible now that he's taken all his books away.'

'If you ask me,' snorted Sue, 'he's taken the whole place with him the way you've stacked this van up. Right! Let's see if she starts now.' She hauled her short, muscular person up into the driving seat.

I climbed in beside her and waited anxiously while she turned the key in the ignition. A throaty roar assured us that the engine at least was willing and Sue grinned at me in triumph.

'Good grief, Mrs P, what are you up to?'

We turned to the window, which was now filled by a beautifully groomed head and, intermittently, by the masks of two whippets who were bouncing up and down in an attempt to communicate with the enticing smell of bitch and pups coming from the tea chest.

'I am going, Terence,' announced Mrs P, 'to save the farm.'

'You look as if you're going to save Wales' said Terence.

'Aye, and who better to do it,' chimed in another voice with a strong Scottish accent, accompanied by yet more Burmese cat howls from the one perched on the shoulder of another of Mrs P's fans come to say good-bye.

Before long a small crowd of neighbours and dogs and cats had gathered round the van and, above the racket of the engine and the cacophony of chatter and animal yells, Mrs P held court with great aplomb from under the Harrods Hat.

Sue sat looking at us all in amazement. She'd agreed, in a fit of Australian kindheartedness, to put off a trip to Holland for a few days in order to drive us and our animals to Wales in the old van she used as a home for her travels in between stints of working as a temporary secretary in London. She'd been filling in at the BBC when I'd met her and, curious to see the part of Wales where the farm was, she'd volunteered to get us there. Now I could see that any more noise or delay would put our benefactress into reverse with a vengeance, so I whispered, 'You'll just have to drive off, I'm afraid.'

'Right,' she said as she engaged the gears, blew an almighty blast on the horn and charged the van straight up the middle of Campden Grove. Mrs P, waving the Harrods Hat out of the window, nearly sent Sue through the windscreen and the fans ran after us, dogs and cats skirmishing as they went, till we turned into the comparative calm of a side-street and picked up speed for the A40.

We were to travel on the A40 because Sue had decided that if we broke down on the motorway, any self-respecting policeman would have jugged the lot of us on sight. 'And that would be a nice way to end the Second Coming, wouldn't it?' she smirked.

The Second Coming, but this time with no mystery, no joy, but a dread of what kind of chaos I'd find.

It was 1975, a year in which I'd come to believe fully that there really was such a thing as the Evil Eye and that it had been trained relentlessly and with the full power of its malevolence on me and mine personally. As the old Bedford van creaked and lumbered its way into Wales, I sank back into that limbo which all passengers enter who are not immediately required to navigate or give sustenance to the driver, and memories of the past four years echoed and reverberated through my weary brain.

For me, those years were a time of incredibly hard work as I fought to keep ahead of the mortgage payments, the seemingly endless demands of the stock and the repairs still urgently waiting to be done. Studios and programmes came and went, my nights were spent editing tape or researching yet more programmes, and the few days I could snatch to go to the farm became golden milestones on a long, endless road of work. I left the Artist my ancient Volkswagen to get to his job in and I took to travelling up and down by train, the guards getting to know me well with my cats in a basket and usually a couple of whippets perched on my knee. At Neath station the Artist would be waiting to drive me the thirty miles over the mountain and as we drove would bring me up-to-date on the news: Doli was in foal again to the thoroughbred, the goat needed to go to the billy, one of the hens had laid an outsize egg, the local pub had been raided after hours and everyone had tipped their beer into the tops of their wellies, we'd really have to do something soon about the wall of the cowshed....

And then came 1975, when our incredible run of luck came to a sudden and devastating end. That two such ignorant fools had managed till then to keep all the stock alive and even to see Doli through her first pregnancy is something which, now knowing how much can go wrong, still amazes me. But when the day of reckoning came, Death stalked the farm relentlessly till the drive over the mountain became a ghastly question and answer session about which animal had managed to survive the latest onslaught of disease and accident. For most of the time I had to leave the Artist to get on with things alone because my mother had suffered a stroke and was just recovering from that when she had to spend weeks in the cancer ward at Hammersmith Hospital.

Like the rest of the gamblers in our family, I knew only too well the way that old Wheel of Fortune has of sticking in one spot, so I was not altogether surprised when the other side of my life began to crumble as well. The life of any freelance broadcaster is unpredictable at the best of times and many of us go through patches when we're simply out of favour, which usually means out of work. One day you can hardly move for the

49

demands of producers, the next the phone is ominously silent and if things are really bad, even your regular stints, like the one I had presenting the daily consumer programme, 'You and Yours', can suddenly be kicked out from under you.

The news from the farm grew worse but, distracted by my mother's illness and desperately seeking for new avenues of work, I was able to get away less and less. I waited philosophically for the final blow which came, full of regrets but inevitable. The Artist had had enough. He'd found consolation with a girl in a nearby village – sorry and all that but he was off to set up a new life in a few weeks time, he wished me well and so on.

By then I was too punch-drunk with disaster to react much, but my mother, cured of her cancer although still very ill from the effects of the radiation treatment, told me not to be so feeble. 'You can think about the farm later,' she said. 'Right now you'd better attend to that bitch.'

'That bitch' was one of the pups, Bea and her brother, Bran, which Imogen had given me years before. Bea was in whelp to a dog who might be described as the then Master McGrath-cum-Mick the Miller of the whippet world. A grand champion both on the track and in the coursing field, and of impeccable breeding, Madishan Moonlake (or Luke to his friends) had mated Bea one hot summer's day and the results were due on the very day the Artist's letter arrived.

For the next twenty-four hours I was so worried about Bea, who was having great difficulty in whelping, that I hardly gave the new problem a thought. Eventually, after a mad rush to the vet and a caesarian, Bea lay with five tiny bundles in a tea chest by my bed on which reposed huge bouquets of flowers, a bottle of champagne and an amazing number of highly unsuitable dog goodies. My room was full of friends come to see the new arrivals: Terence, a designer who owned a pair of whippets himself; Joan, the Scottish nurse from next door who shared our love of Burmese cats; Howard, a professional photographer who was snapping photos as fast as he could stuff film into his camera; and many, many more. Bea was an enchanting little soul, and over the years of going into Kensington Gardens for her walks had collected an impressive band of well-wishers.

When we finally emerged from all the fuss and had settled down into a steady routine again, I set about organising some

50

temporary help at the farm. I couldn't really see how I would find someone reliable enough to pick up the pieces in a hurry, but I reckoned without the magic that even in its misery my little farm could exercise. The Bonneys, a couple whom I barely knew, were so horrified to think of it being in jeopardy that they offered to divide their time between their own smallholding fourteen miles away, for one of them to live in at the farm until I could get there, and even to continue until I could find someone more permanent.

'And I'd better go too and see you all get a square meal,' announced my mother, who was in a fighting mood by then.

Which is why the Bedford van was making its ponderous way to Wales on that bright morning in October. Apart from the fact that the cats, Pip and Suyin, escaped twice and nearly gave Oscar the budgerigar a heart attack, and Bea was sick twice all over the pups, and Mrs P nearly lost the Harrods Hat out of the window, and the van flatly refused to take a steep hill about a mile from the farm, and Sue threatened to turn straight round and go back to London, it was an uneventful journey as such journeys go.

As the old van finally puffed to a halt at the gate, the Bonneys rushed out to welcome us. Inside they'd made up a great fire in the living room and were ready to revive us with massive cups of tea and fresh scones with elderberry jam. To this day I can never think of autumn without that elusive, delicate smell of elderberry jam which pervaded the house because Meta Bonney had been up all night making it especially for us.

Bless them, they were trying desperately to hide the fact that in spite of their efforts to clear it up, the cottage had a bare, forlorn look about it still. They'd warned me as much, which was why poor Sue had had to bring so much in the van. To her disgust, the whole load had to be dragged out in the fading light, bookshelves filled, pictures hung and everything done to make it look like home again.

It was not till the next day, returning from a sad tour of the neglected buildings and the thin, despondent animals in them, that I dared look up at the roof of the cottage. What I saw froze my superstitious bones to the marrow. There was a brisk easterly breeze blowing, but the unicorn weathervane was pointing resolutely south. It had rusted solid. A long time was to pass before it and my fortunes were to swing free again.

51

## Chapter 6

'Sell it, make a profit and start having some fun, dear!'

'You could let it as a holiday cottage, rent the land out for grazing and make a tidy little living, you know.'

'For God's sake just get *rid* of it!'

The well-meant advice from friends came blowing cool sense into my fevered brain, and before I actually got back to it, to sell the farm had been my firm intention. Despite all the hard, slogging work I'd put in, there was as much debt as ever hanging over me, and the thought of the £25,000 the place was now valued at seemed a glorious and instant solution to all my problems.

I'd forgotten, though, the heart-gripping splendour of that wonderful composition of mountain and hill and field and wood and river. When I saw it again after so long away, I realised that to talk about selling was one thing – doing it was going to be quite another matter. Apart from which, the sight of those forlorn animals made the idea of sending them on to yet another uncertain future unbearable. Which was all very well, but how was I going to keep them? I certainly had no money to employ anyone and, with my work prospects at an all-time low, I wouldn't even be able to keep myself unless I was on hand in London to take any jobs offered.

'You'll give yourself a nervous breakdown if you don't quit going round in circles,' said Sue, who'd relieved her feelings during the past twenty-four hours by chopping up a great mound of wood and sorting out the rocks for a stone wall. 'Well, me and my van are off to Holland and all points east. I wonder what you'll be doing in the next few months.' And that was the last we ever saw of her except that Mrs P, who happened to be collecting Green Shield stamps, got a couple of envelopes of them from odd parts of the country.

During all my distracted meanderings around the farm, Meta and Alan Bonney had said very little, although I'd noticed them whispering quietly to each other. Now they came up with a remarkable offer. If I could leave them the use of my old car while I was back in London and Mrs P stayed to keep her company, Meta would live at the farm and get it back on its feet while Alan coped alone with their goat farm. They wanted no payment, just the assurance that I would do everything I could to keep the place and its animals intact.

'Give yourself till spring,' they urged. 'You never know what might happen then. But you can't just give up. You'll never find another place like this.'

'I know that,' I said wearily, 'but you can't live on a view. Even Cliff Griffiths, who had the rest of the land and is an experienced farmer, had to take another job to make any kind of living here. I don't mind doing that but the humiliating fact is, I'm totally unemployable outside of broadcasting.'

Meta, who has to be one of life's great optimists, then put into words something that had been lurking dangerously at the back of my mind. 'What about that country programme you've been so keen about?' she asked. 'Let's face it, at the moment you don't really know much about the day-to-day problems of running a small place. If you were to get down to it, those people at the BBC might take a bit more notice of you. The Bank Holiday programmes are all very pleasant, but they're very much a townsperson's view of what living on a farm is all about, aren't they?'

God help me, it was the very excuse I was looking for! If I'd known then how much longer it was going to take to convince 'those people at the BBC', I'd have followed Sue and her van out of the gate and never come back.

Meta might have been encouraging me to soldier on, but that her own subconscious had serious doubts about what she herself was doing became dramatically clear that very night.

The fire had been kicked into submission, the dogs settled down and we'd all staggered off to bed physically and emotionally worn out. I lay listening to the owls hooting mournfully down by the river, still going endlessly in my mind over the problems I was up against until, too exhausted to think properly any more, I dozed off into a nightmare in which I was chasing endless miles of fugitive tape down the Kafkaesque corridors of Broadcasting House, pursued by the combined forces of the bank manager, Douglas the gander and Mrs P's Harrods Hat which was laughing like a maniac. I woke, bathed in sweat, only to find the mad laughter still going on louder than ever. I now know that hair does stand up on end because mine did then as I listened to the ghastly sound of that laugh which suddenly stopped and was replaced by soft but persistent scratching from the room below.

'The poltergeist,' was the first thought I had. 'It's come back!'

The poltergeist had been a bit of a joke when we'd first moved in. It wasn't a particularly obnoxious one, but it did have a habit of chucking plates at us for about two months. It didn't do it very often and no-one had actually been hurt, although I did resent the way it only smashed the best plates and, on one occasion, a pretty china candlestick. I had mentioned it to the eminent folklorist, Dr Katherine Briggs, when I was doing a programme with her, and she'd laughingly told me that it was probably the resident bwbach making its presence felt. The bwbach is the Welsh version of the house hob or brownie and Dr Briggs, who had a great sense of humour, said it might be as well to let him know we were aware he was about and show him a few courtesies. So for years we'd got into the habit of every now and then shouting, 'Hi there, Bw!' up the chimney and even our visitors had taken to doing the same when they arrived.

Now it seemed as if something more sinister than a law-abiding bwbach was emerging from the stonework. And then the dogs began to howl.

54

Visions of some dreadful ogre tormenting my dogs got me moving at last and I hurtled down the stairs and into the big room. The light of the torch revealed a figure in long, white robes standing on the stone seat by the side of the fireplace. The three dogs and all the pups were sitting in the centre of the room, their muzzles raised to the ceiling as they howled their concern. I switched the light on and discovered Meta, her bedclothes still trailing from her shoulders as she tried with dogged determination to climb the sheer wall of the blackened chimney.

'What in the name of Heaven is going on?' Mrs P was standing in the doorway, looking particularly fetching in a brilliant orange dressing gown decorated by a panic-stricken brown cat.

Meta paused in her abortive ascent of the chimney to enquire of my mother if she didn't think this mountain just a little too difficult a climb for her.

'She's asleep,' I whispered to my outraged parent.

Meta had warned us that sometimes, when under a lot of stress, she did have a tendency to sleepwalk, but not to take any notice because she usually just went back to bed herself. I'd visualised her mildly pottering about the house, not climbing the chimney, and indeed, during the months she lived at the farm, apart from trying noisily to open a clothes-horse under the misapprehension that it was the gate of a field, her rare midnight rambles were entirely uneventful. But on that particular night she'd dreamt she was at home in her native Switzerland and had joined a jolly mountaineering party. What I'd taken for mad laughter was yodelling.

Sleepwalking apart, I couldn't have been more fortunate in having someone like Meta to take care of things while I went back to London. As well as being very knowledgeable about livestock and yet soft enough to understand how I felt about my pathetic band of refugees, Meta is happiest when she's got a tool-box in her hand and something to build. Add to that her Swiss passion for efficiency, order and cleanliness and a total dedication to what she is doing, and within a few weeks everything was looking in better repair and neater and tidier than I could ever remember it. Even in the evenings she would sit by the fire, cleaning leatherwork or brass, making goat halters or endlessly sorting out the pounds of nails and screws, which had lain littered everywhere, into specially labelled boxes. Yet she found time to take the dogs for long, rambling walks and play wild, energetic games with the pups. For all this she steadfastly refused to take any wages and when I began to insist that she accept something for all her work, she threw an almighty tantrum and followed it up by a night of sleepwalking and lamentations which would have had Lady Macbeth worn out.

'Stress,' she explained next morning. 'I simply don't want any money from you. But if you really meant it about giving me one of the pups, I'll take you up on that. And if that old battery gramophone in the tool-shed is no use to you, I wouldn't mind having that and then we're quits.'

The battery gramophone was important to Meta and Alan because they had no electricity at their farm. Meta had devised all kinds of cunning underground cool chambers for their food, they salted most of their own meat, relied on their goats for milk and cheese and grew their own vegetables. Like a lot of other people at the time, though, Alan had found his work as a freelance translator harder to come by and the small amount of money they could make from the sale of goat's milk, stud fees and the goats themselves had meant giving up anything that was not totally necessary for survival. So Meta's passionate refusal to take any money for her work was all the more remarkable. But they did miss being able to play their records and so the little gramophone was to fill a gap in their otherwise self-sufficient way of life.

Until this time Mrs P hadn't had much to do with the farm, mainly because she and the Artist hadn't exactly seen eye to eye, but now she was taking an interest with a vengeance. Only my firm orders to Meta, that my mother was to do little besides cooking and a bit of light dusting if the spirit moved her, caused any real friction between them. As it was, the phone in London rang endlessly with pleas from Meta to speak severely to Mrs P, who'd been found out on the potato patch again.

Potatoes at the time were in the news, there being a so-called 'famine' of them with people queueing and paying exotic prices for the common old spud. Now Mrs P, as a result of her years of wandering in out-of-the-way places, is able to make a really good meal out of practically nothing and, as part of our bargain, she'd seen to it that Meta was very well fed. But Meta missed her potatoes and Mrs P flatly refused to buy any even if they'd been readily available. It wasn't the cost of them, but the fact that she was convinced we had some perfectly good potatoes of our own.

When he'd left, the Artist had told the Bonneys that over by the hay barn there was a patch of potatoes he'd planted earlier in the year for the two pigs, Blossom and Magnolia.

'But we couldn't find any,' lamented Meta. 'Just a few mouldy ones in a bag and some the size of marbles out in the place he showed us.'

I began to have my suspicions that some of the Artist's wooing had been done with the elusive potatoes, but Mrs P said he wouldn't be miserable enough to take the lot and that it just required a bit of application and some really serious digging to find the ones he'd left. She became completely obsessed by those missing potatoes and whenever we took our eyes off her for a moment she'd be out on the potato patch, armed to the teeth in wellington boots and mackintosh, muttering furiously to herself as she poked about in the mud with her walking stick and a totally inadequate gardening fork.

Meta had done her best to locate the fugitive tubers and so had I, but neither of us had unearthed anything worthwhile. And then my mother, who's a subtle soul sometimes, got round to promising Meta that she'd make her some of her special rum truffles. Exhausted after a particularly gruesome journey from London on the bus in an attempt to cut down on expenses, I sat dozing in front of the fire with only one ear on their conversation.

'Truffles,' I mused. 'Truffles are things pigs hunt, truffles are. If truffles, why not potatoes?'

Meta was truly impressed with my plan next morning, and her boyish face lit up with glee as we collected wheelbarrow, spade and two bemused Gloucester Old Spot pigs and marched them out to the sodden patch which was beginning to look like no-man's-land after all the frantic digging and delving of the past weeks.

Magnolia, being a pig of little imagination, was patently uninterested and, remembering the crab apple tree at the top of that field, plodded off to see if there were any windfalls she'd overlooked in the autumn. But dear old Blossom stood stock still, quivered all over, closed her ugly little eyes and pointed her great snout into the soft mud. She prodded long and deep, a beatific grin spreading over her unlovely features and the black spots on her long body undulating wildly as she began to wriggle with delight.

'Watch her, Meta!' I yelped as the piggy grin grew broader and the grunts more gleeful. Then, with Meta pushing a surprised and indignant Blossom to one side, I dug the spade into the hole she'd excavated. Potatoes, lots of potatoes, big, round, lovely potatoes came tumbling out of the earth.

An hour and several hysterical fights with Blossom later, Meta and I stood gloating triumphantly over our loaded wheelbarrow. Magnolia, disgruntled after her fruitless apple hunt, came down to see what Blossom was doing.

And where was Blossom? Over in a corner of the patch which she'd studiously avoided all the time we'd been watching her, she was devouring the biggest potato either of us had ever seen, one of those legendary potatoes that gardeners regard as the crowning achievement of their careers. Too late, Meta, Magnolia and I rushed her as she gulped it down and burped happily. She's no fool is old Blossom, and neither is my mother.

As Meta and I staggered into the kitchen with our loaded buckets, my persistent parent looked up and smiled sweetly at us. 'I knew you'd think of a way to find those potatoes,' she said. 'Here – have a rum truffle!'

# =====Chapter 7=====

The little diesel train gave a warning toot as it came round the bend in the track. The small group of bored people, who'd spent the last fifteen minutes studiously avoiding each other as they stomped up and down the single platform trying to keep warm, turned expectantly and a couple of them waved their hands just in case the driver misinterpreted their presence and drove on.

'Wouldn't do to miss it, would it, not after all that,' cried the girl who was waving enthusiastically beside me.

'All that' had been a frantic collecting of suitcases and carrier bags and last-minute bits and pieces, followed by a wailing session in the kitchen as she wept all over Mrs P and the dogs, and a tearful dash round the rest of the animals who waited hopefully at the gates in case they were being fed earlier than usual. Finally there was a wild career along the six miles to the little railway stop with Merlin perched precariously on the luggage on the back seat, fervent prayers from me that the car would make it all the way, and my passenger repeating yet again all the reasons why she couldn't stay any longer. In between negotiating the bends and worrying about the brakes, I made understanding noises. I'd got used to making understanding noises by now, for this was the last of several would-be hermits and helpers.

After three months of Meta's devoted care, the animals looked healthy, content and sure of their place in the world again. The buildings were freshly whitewashed, their doors painted a gleaming black, and inside everything was neat and tidy. Sagging fencing had been repaired, stone walls no longer threatened imminent collapse and the garden hedge was neatly clipped. The goats had new collars made of plaited baler twine, Doli's saddle was gleaming and supple and even her rope halter no longer came apart in the hand. Inside the cottage the stone floors were washed clean, carpets had been taken up and shaken properly, windows sparkled and shone and even the pots and pans had had a much-needed scouring. Meta's enthusiasm showed no sign of waning but eventually, with their own goats coming up to kidding time and Alan needing her at home, Meta had finally left, taking one of the pups with her.

The three months had bought me time in which to transfer to the farm all my editing machines, tape recorders, filing cabinets, typewriters and other paraphernalia of a broadcaster's life. Much of my work could be done from there, but I still had to be away for a few days at a time to collect interviews and finally to put programmes together or record scripts in the studio. This meant that I needed someone to feed the stock while I was absent and, above all, to sleep in and make sure that Mrs P was restrained from carrying in heavy buckets of coal or sneaking out to chop up wood.

At first I tried to find someone locally, but most of the farms around are small, family affairs and everyone is too busy; there are no big estates nearby which might have yielded a worker's wife happy to earn a bit of extra money. So I put an ad in *The Times*, a whimsical ad to which I had a lot of equally whimsical response. Other ads in other papers brought in more practical replies, but in spite of the fact that I'd stated there was accommodation for one person only, they were mostly from desperate families of six or more with a host of their own animals to house. However, from a combination of yet more ads and the earnest recommendations of friends, we did play host to quite a few starry-eyed volunteers.

After an initial period of enthusiasm, most of which was spent parked in front of a fire they'd done nothing towards lighting or feeding, expounding all their marvellous philosophies about ecology and conservation, the soul-destroying evils of the city and the wonders of the self-sufficient way of life – a life which none of them actually seemed prepared to help me get on and create – they left to return whence they came, still declaiming loudly about the beauty of it all.

In between, we found one or two enthusiastic youngsters who, if nothing else, would rush round and feed the animals and collect coal and wood for Mrs P, but they also had an astonishing variety of problems. When they weren't plucking mournful tunes from their guitars and making the dogs howl in sympathy, they ran us up frightful phone bills while they talked to distant boy friends and eyed us balefully until we crept out into the kitchen.

There was one otherwise delightful girl who drove all the local lads mad with lust, broke everything she touched, filled the entire kitchen with detergent bubbles on the one occasion Mrs P let her loose at the sink and received a great deal of mail, usually in the form of fat packages. It was at about the same time that Mrs P began to complain of the strange, pungent smell penetrating her room at night. Our feckless friend was equally concerned to help us trace the source of the smell and came up with all kinds of bright suggestions as to what it could be. And then suddenly, and with much regret on both sides, an urgent family matter required her immediate departure for home.

After I'd seen her off on the train, I came back to get her vacated room ready for a friend called Peter Jones who was coming to stay for a while. As I went in, the overpowering smell of strong, cheap perfume nearly knocked me out. It pervaded everything: the chest of drawers, the armchair and, most of all, the bed. When Peter arrived I was still frantically scrubbing woodwork and sponging the mattress but even so, he emerged from that room next morning smelling like a brothel.

'I'll swear she's spilled half of Woolworths in there!' he bellowed from the bathroom where he was taking the first of many baths in an attempt to get rid of 'that dam-ned stink' as he kept calling it. Poor man, he hardly dared go out of the gate all the time he was with us and even the dogs, who usually show a marked interest in any strange smell, avoided him carefully.

One morning he appeared with a packet of cigarette papers in his hand. 'Found 'em tucked into a cushion,' he explained. 'I didn't know you rolled your own, Jeanine.'

'I don't,' I said. Peter and I, struck with the same thought, looked at each other.

Some years before, a couple I knew well had spent a long weekend at the farm. For some reason or other I hadn't been there and it was only afterwards that I found out they'd passed most of the weekend smoking pot. Now I don't care whether people smoke pot – that's their own affair – but what worried me sick at the time was that I could be had up for allowing them to do it on my property. I could see the headlines in the local rag only too well: 'Broadcaster Holds Drug Orgies in Lonely Farmhouse'. I was so furious with these so-called friends for making such a headline possible that I was still muttering angrily years afterwards, and in fact I'd been telling the girl about it the very night before she announced her departure.

'And if ever I catch anyone doing it again,' I'd dramatically ended the story, 'so help me, I'll string them up by Doli's halter from the main beam in the barn.'

'You must have scared the living daylights out of the poor little thing,' hooted Peter. 'No wonder she left in such a hurry. I just wish she hadn't used such a clinging aroma to cover up the smell of the weed.' And he hurried off to have yet another bath so that we could bear to get downwind of him for the rest of the day.

When he left a week later, his expensive tweed jacket still smelled wonderfully, to his acute embarrassment on the long train journey back to Birmingham. I've often wondered what the other passengers thought of the reserved gentleman reading from his learned tome, only pausing to take a thoughtful pinch of snuff (for Peter, too, has his eccentricities) and all the while ponging to high heaven of cheap scent.

In the end, it was Mrs P who put her foot down by declaring she'd dish up arsenic to the next leadswinger masquerading as hired help and that if I could organise things so that she could feed the animals without actually having to go amongst them, she'd rather cope all by herself for the odd days I was away. Which was why the startled inhabitants of neighbouring farms were soon to hear the piercing note of a scout whistle echoing across the valley twice a day. It had taken me just a week to train all the outside stock, except the poultry, to go to their feeding stations as soon as they heard the whistle and to be ready and waiting for Mrs P to tip their feed into their troughs and buckets, which had been fixed just inside the gates, without being bowled over in the rush.

It was not just the possibility of her having an accident when she was alone which bothered me, though: I was also rather worried about the rest of the population. Mrs P, as anyone who knows her well will testify, is ferocious in defence of her young and their possessions. Once, some years before, on a hot July day when the animals panted in the shade of hedges and the mountain had lost its mystery and was just a stark cliff of baked earth and rock, I'd been alone in the cottage when a slick character in a cheap pin-striped suit had come knocking on the door demanding if I had 'any old furniture, brassware or feather beds' for sale. Nothing I could say would convince him I hadn't and he was only prevented from charging past me into the hall by Elke, the big golden lurcher, a most gentle dog but a wonderful actress when it came to seeing people off.

At about the same time there'd been quite a lot of scandal about these 'knockers' wresting valuable possessions from elderly people in particular, and indeed we'd covered the problem pretty thoroughly on the 'You and Yours' programme. Mrs P had obviously listened carefully both to my own story and to those she'd heard on the radio, and she never forgot to be on her guard.

Not long after Peter Jones had gone on his fragrant way, I was sitting peacefully on the bank behind the house, painting an old chicken run which I'd bought for a few shillings in a dilapidated state and which Peter had found time to repair for me in between baths. Beside me lay Merlin, flank to flank with two of the barn cats, Max and Muffin. It was one of those falsely balmy days which lull you into forgetting that the streaks of snow lingering on the hills are, as the farmers say, 'waiting for more to come down and join them'. A raven passed overhead and its husky call

made me look up and wonder idly if it was Croaky Joe, a tame raven which lived with Gerald and Imogen but spent his days flying free over the valley, when the sound of dogs screaming hysterically and a human voice raised in fury sent me and Merlin leaping to our feet and the two cats diving wildly for the hedge.

Rounding the side of the cottage, I was just in time to see a tweedy chap with bristling moustaches flying down the yard, desperately kicking away a pack of whippets snapping at him from all directions and glancing frantically over his shoulder at the terrifying sight of Mrs P, long grey plaits swinging while she brandished her walking stick. As she hobbled after him she was yelling, 'Get out of it, you stand-over merchant! Try to rob a helpless old woman, would you? When my son hears about it he'll come and break every bone in your smarmy body!'

Mrs P tends to forget in moments of stress that although my brother is indeed an expert at unarmed combat, he does live 12,000 miles away. Still, her unfortunate victim, whom I later found out to be a respectable antique dealer from a nearby town who'd just fancied a run out in the country and bethought himself to do a little business at the same time, was not to know that. He made a final, wild-eyed sprint for his car, scattering a shower of cards behind him, and took off with his coat still caught in the car door.

But if the mention of leadswingers and knockers are still apt to send Mrs P into a snarling rage and to bring forth some of the more explicit examples of a highly indecent vocabulary she picked up in her youth as a visiting midwife in the Woolloomoolloo district of Sydney, when Myrddin Parry invades her tiny, chaotic kitchen, she behaves like a perfect lady. It was the thought that Myrddin would keep a distant but careful watch on her that finally gave me the courage to leave my game little mother to cope alone.

I'd been aware of Myrddin in the background of our lives for some time, but his friendship had been with the Artist and he usually came to the farm when I was away. If our visits did coincide, he treated me with wary politeness. It seems odd now to think that I was just as nervous of him as he was of me, even though I'd heard that he was the kindest man in the district who took his neighbourly duty very seriously indeed. I'd also heard that he was a fervent Welsh Nationalist, that his own 142 acres

64

were run with clockwork efficiency and that he and his mother, with whom he lived, were staunch chapel-goers.

Tall and lean, his disciplined black hair always covered by a peaked cap, he never seemed to walk anywhere but always moved at a run, even when he was carrying a couple of bales of hay. He was not the sort of person I could see having any time at all for someone as unpractical or as prone to live in an atmosphere of high drama as I was. So, if the Bonneys' horrified reaction to my intention to sell up had been fairly predictable, Myrddin's quiet determination that I would finish what I had started was amazing.

I can't remember what errand it was that brought him to see us not long after the epic journey in the van, but I do remember telling him, 'Never mind, I won't be here long and when I've retired to an island in the Outer Hebrides' – which is something I'm always threatening to do – 'I'll invite you to come and visit us.'

Myrddin frowned and then he said, 'It'd be a lot easier if you stayed and invited me to visit you here. Now what did you say was wrong with that gate?' And since then he's mended a lot of gates, rescued us from a hundred urgent crises, seen that my sheep were dipped and wormed and vaccinated, made my hay, brought me straw, sawn up wood, driven me to the train through the snow when I needed to get to a studio on time, tried to teach my dogs Welsh when he gave up in despair on me, kept a firm eye on Mrs P and, above all, never let me give up hope.

There are only two things Myrddin will not do. One is to work on Sundays, apart from feeding his stock, even refusing to cart his hay when rain is predicted the next day. The other thing he simply will not countenance is to have anything to do with my goats.

# Chapter 8

I can't blame Myrddin for his prejudice against my goats. There are many times when I wish I didn't have to have anything to do with them either. After years of practice I've learned simply to go where I can neither see nor hear what they're up to and resolutely close my mind to the possibilities. The only place where I can do that successfully is in my office, the very same room which formed the odorous background of Peter Jones' ill- fated visit. It's a narrow room which was once the parlour, and has the great advantage of being reasonably insulated from the more active parts of the cottage.

It has its distractions, of course. The panes of the little window look out on three of the soaring hills which form the rim of the valley, hills that endlessly shift their perspective, with cloud shadows and sharp fingers of sun highlighting anonymous rocks and throwing hollows into relief. Distant specks of sheep drift across the slopes and men on ponies are silhouetted on the sharp crests.

66

More immediately in my vision is that section of the barn roof which in the gales throws its slates about like playing cards, and which causes me to stop my work at the desk and worry about it; and although at most times of the year I get a lift of the heart as the white wings of the doves glide home, in autumn I spend a lot of time rushing out to hunt their owners off the elderberry bushes. Usually, though, unless I've left a gate open and the chickens and ducks have come into the garden for a joyful maraud, the office is immune from the demands of the stock or the dogs and, more importantly, from Mrs P's latest Project.

All her life, Mrs P's Projects have had far-reaching and often devastating effects on much more than her immediate environment, but now she tends to confine them to more domestic things – excepting housework, of course, to which she remains steadfastly indifferent – and currently she's taking an interest in herbs. Apart from the fact that the animals are rather bored with having large wads of comfrey or other healants slapped on the slightest wound and I must suffer the administration of the wondrous concoctions Mrs P makes by experimenting wildly with the vast store of dried plants now stocking all our cupboards, I don't mind the herbs. Not much, anyway.

Mrs P's approach to the Project of the moment takes two forms. One is to advance on it, banners flying, and squash the opposition. The other is to worry quietly at the subject like a small terrier with a rat. It was the latter method she was employing on the matter of the eggs, or rather the preserving of them, as we entered our first spring together at the farm.

The hens and ducks had done us proud and, when the year picked up light and life again, eggs were stacked everywhere. As there were already more than enough purveyors of free-range eggs locally and I wasn't sure enough of either my wares or my marketing ability, I hesitated to take our surplus further afield. We curried favour by giving them to everyone who called. Some of the recipients returned the favour with pots of jam or small services. Gerald promptly tried to hatch some of the tiny bantam eggs under his pigeons and sent me as a present a huge pouter which immediately flew back. Still the eggs piled up and finally we ran out of people to give them to. Even the pigs and the dogs went off eggs for a bit so Mrs P came up with the bright idea of preserving them against the time when, unlikely as it seemed then, the hens stopped laying.

I was sent into town to buy the water-glass in which the eggs are preserved, and several of the big slipware crocks I'd bought at the original auction sale were dug out, thoroughly cleaned and pressed into service. Had I known then that the water-glass leaves a hard residue behind it and that the vessels were to be ruined forever, I'd have been less willing to give them up. At the time I was more concerned with avoiding them as they lurked in dark corners with their seething contents, and with Mrs P's swipes at the dogs when they went to investigate. When she began muttering about pickling the remaining eggs, I realised that we were in the middle of a full-scale Project and that for the foreseeable future our conversation would revolve solely around the matter of eggs and the preservation thereof.

There was no peace to be had outside either, for I was engaged simultaneously in a war of nerves with Daisy the goose on the subject of the Nest.

For most of the year the geese are not too much trouble. They spend their time yanking at the grass, shrieking at the ducks, applauding the gander when he makes threatening gestures at visitors, making an appalling mess in their pen at night and swearing at the dogs. Come the breeding season, though, and they're a pain in the neck. It's the Nest that causes all the trouble, and I'd made up my mind that this year it was going to be somewhere where I could go about my lawful concerns without the imminent amputation of my ankles, and where I didn't have to leap up like a hare every time I heard a movement in the yard at night, thundering to the rescue of goose, eggs and guardian gander with yells of 'Fox! Fox!' to the dogs and anyone else who was interested.

We'd got the geese from Cliff Griffiths, who'd offered us a pair if we'd like to come and catch them for ourselves. For the whole of one long, hot summer's afternoon, the Artist and I had careered madly around Cliff's fields in bewildered pursuit of a highly indignant gander and his large family of wives and offspring. Finally, after a few desperate encounters with irate cattle and clumps of malicious brambles, we'd lost sight of our quarry altogether.

We'd found them half an hour later, cooling off in the shelter of their own home and hissing at us reproachfully. 'The trouble is,' said Cliff, 'the wife's gone out and I can't tell which is which.'

'Don't worry,' smiled the Artist. 'I'll find one of each. No problem.' And he dived into the throbbing tide of geese.

I didn't see much of him for the next ten minutes, but finally he emerged triumphantly with a bundle of struggling white feathers and declared it to be the goose. Five more minutes and he came up for air once again with a grey and white striped bird, which was declaiming its innocence loudly to the world, and announced it to be the gander.

For the next six months Douglas strutted masterfully around the place with Daisy following meekly behind, but the following spring, the Artist's ability as a goose-sexer was cast in some doubt when 'Douglas' laid a clutch of eggs and began sitting on them right in the middle of the coal for the Rayburn.

From then on the geese had chosen the most inconvenient, most hazardous place they could find for their nest and the Artist had aided and abetted them. Now, with him gone to set up his own little nest elsewhere, I was having no more of it. I'd determined that with six geese and a gander to cope with, it was time for a firm stand. As soon as I noticed the rest of the flock pottering around outside the coal shelter and Douglas and Daisy conducting an earnest inspection inside, I shooed them all away and ruthlessly broke up the tell-tale circle Daisy had already started as her nest foundation.

Pandemonium broke out and all seven geese roared down the yard on the tips of their great feet, gathering speed for the take-off, and got airborne just near the gate where Doli and Mole were dreaming in the sun. I closed my eyes as the whole flock hit target, and opened them to see Doli pigrooting round in circles as if her life depended on it while Mole galloped hysterically down the field with two horrified geese balancing on his back and the rest of them hurtling along behind, screeching at them to jump.

An hour later, the flock was back and Daisy was trying out the stone wall around the pigsty. Douglas and the rest stood by in hushed silence, heads moving like tennis spectators, entranced as their mother pondered over the right spot. Finally, after much dithering, she eased herself down into a likely hollow, only to leap up like a fat lady having her bottom pinched as she made contact with a sharp edge of slate. Her indignant yelp set the whole lot off again and, as they hooted and whistled and flapped their wings and Douglas hissed in vain for order, Daisy got a desperate look in her eye, teetered over to the edge of the wall and let drop her first egg right on the unsuspecting head of Dolores the goat, who was quietly chewing her cud on the other side of the wall.

The Nest was no more of a problem that year because I caught Daisy and locked her up firmly in the renovated chicken house where she finally made a marvellous nest out of straw and moss and her own feathers. In the fullness of time she brought out fifteen healthy goslings which, had I but known it, were to be the subject of Mrs P's next Project.

Meanwhile, I took away all the other eggs from the rest of the geese and stored them in a tub of bran. I had some idea of selling them after seeing in the local paper that the going rate for fertile goose eggs was 25p each. But Mrs P commandeered a couple to try out, remembering the superb omelettes she'd once made out of emu's eggs when the hens on the sheep station where we were living at the time went on strike. She inspected the whites carefully and announced that she didn't think they were fertile, so I gave the others away without any guarantee that they'd produce any goslings.

'Perhaps you shouldn't have done that,' mused Mrs P afterwards. 'I wonder if you can preserve goose eggs.'

I looked at her for a long time. 'Why,' I suggested brightly, 'don't you go and ask Daisy?' And I whistled up Merlin and stomped out of the kitchen, for I too had a bit of a Project on hand. I was psychoanalysing the goats.

The goats have been responsible not only for putting a lot of strain on my friendship with Myrddin Parry but also, to a large degree, for the loss of my credibility as a professional person of integrity. Imagine the feelings of a young producer, fresh from university and burning with the importance of world events, told to ring me about some vitally significant programme. The phone rings for a long time and is answered at last by a breathless voice which interrupts abruptly the producer's quiet exposition of the facts: 'Sorry, love, you'll have to ring me back. I'm in the middle of giving a goat an enema!' The receiver crashes to the floor and is followed by the receding sounds of violent curses, flying furniture, screaming dogs and hysterical bleating. The young producer is not inclined to ring back – ever. Of course the older, more seasoned of my colleagues learned to take it in their stride over the years. I remember once telling Denis Lower, one of the editors at the BBC, that I now had an outside bell for the phone so that if he continued to ring, someone would answer it sooner or later.

'Even,' said Denis darkly, 'if it's only a goat!'

They haven't done my reputation as a serious smallholder much good either. If you're met at the gate by a goat attired in a bright purple cardigan, the sleeves rolled up elegantly above its hooves, and you observe another group sauntering along similarly arrayed, their long, aristocratic faces full of polite enquiry like county ladies at a point-to-point meeting, then it does make you wonder what kind of person runs the place. The fact that the person in question is hunting desperately through the woods for the invalids, who until a few minutes ago were lying at death's door in their shed, is of no immediate interest to the visitor and, by the time the frantic owner of the goats does appear, he or she has taken off in alarm and is unlikely to be seen in the valley again.

I now have only six goats, although at one time the number rose to eleven. But at the beginning of 1976 I had just the two. They were called Dolores and Nana and in order to tell you how they came to be there at all, I must go back in time a very long way.

# =====Chapter 9=====

Dolores is the third goat of that name I have known well. The first came into my life when I was five years old. It was during one of the few stationary periods in Mrs P's nomadic life and she was trying her hand as a businesswoman. It wasn't entirely her own idea to take on a small fruit and vegetable emporium in the unfashionable Sydney suburb of Clovelly: she'd been talked into it by Pop, my big, black-haired cavalier of a grandfather.

Pop's origins were a bit of a mystery. His father was a remittance man who came with his wife and young son to Australia, where he bred horses which were exported all over the world. With his sudden death both the remittance and the business collapsed, so the teenaged Pop was obliged to find work to help support his three younger brothers. The only thing he knew anything about was horses, and he spent the rest of his working life amongst the great beasts which carted everything from coal to beer all over Sydney.

He was an enormous man, wonderfully handsome and adored by every woman who set eyes on him. Pop adored them in return, but no woman ever meant as much to him as his horses, with the possible exception of his infant granddaughter. But then if Pop hadn't been around there probably would have been no granddaughter. I wasn't expected so soon and my mother was alone in the house except for Pop who, as usual on a Saturday afternoon, was listening to the races. It was he who had to dash for the midwife and do the honours with boiling water and cups of tea. And, when things went badly and the lady lost her nerve and tried to leave, it was Pop who hauled her back and stood guard outside the door while Mrs P talked her through the birth. Pop always told me afterwards that I arrived just in time to hear the favourite win the four o'clock race by a length and a half.

It was a propitious beginning to what was to be an unholy alliance against the rest of the world on behalf of all the animals Pop and I acquired between us to the great inconvenience of our relatives.

It was Ginger, though, who was mainly responsible for Mrs P taking up the profession of fruiterer. Ginger was a one-eyed racehorse who'd gone on a sad descent from his victories at the winning post (for he was a good horse in his day) to carting milk and then scrap and finally slow starvation at a livery stables because his owner hadn't paid his fodder bills. Pop found him there, a wretched skeleton, and, pausing only to knock the stable owner out cold, brought Ginger home and slowly back to health. It was to find a justification for buying and keeping him that Pop persuaded Mrs P to take on the shop. He suggested that he and Ginger would be invaluable to her in carting all the produce back from Paddy's Market and doing any deliveries when she'd built the business up.

Every other morning, then, Pop and Ginger and I met up with my beautifully groomed little mother amongst the burly porters and the hustling merchants, the profusion of colour and livestock that was Paddy's Market. She supervised the loading onto Ginger's cart of the produce she'd been buying and caught the next tram home, praying fervently that the driver either lacked a sporting nature or had a steady hand. By taking various short cuts, Pop was usually able to lie in wait for the tram as it got to the long, straight stretch near the racecourse. The sound of its rackety wheels clanking on the track was enough for Ginger's ears to prick, for Pop to start roaring 'She'll Be Comin' Round the Mountain' at the top of his voice and for me to go mad with excitement as we began to race the tram home. No tram driver ever resisted the challenge and passengers could be seen hanging on for their lives, the conductor yelling his encouragement to the driver. Only Mrs P sat primly as she desperately tried to ignore my shrill cries of recognition and the sight of assorted produce flying off the back of the cart as Ginger re-lived his past days of glory and Pop waved his bowler hat in the air.

It was on one of those momentous trips to Paddy's Market that Pop and I found the tiny white nanny kid whose asking price was two shillings. Dolores was tucked in amongst the crates of vegetables and the bunches of flowers on the cart, where her mournful bleats added to the early morning chaos along the tram-route. Once home, Mrs P philosophically allowed her to take up residence in the back shed along with the thirteen cats and a fat white duck called Magnolia who were currently on the strength.

Dolores' kidhood was, in conjunction with Ginger and Pop and myself, a highly eventful one, but the peak of her career and reputation came when Mrs P, fed up with cabbages and tram races, moved to Maroubra and a tuck shop opposite a school. Dolores had grown into a huge, horned animal by then and, apart from bailing up the traffic at the nearby road junction and earning the undying enmity of the local police, having the fire engine out at least once a week to get her down from every tree for miles around, invading the neighbours' outside loos and charging their bewildered owners in the dead of night, she inadvertently started a minor crime-wave when some of the boys at the school did a brief but brisk trade in her droppings, advertised as aniseed balls.

Dolores added another dimension to my five-year-old world and I nearly broke my heart when Mrs P finally persuaded a goat dairy many miles away to take her on. It was the first real bereavement of my life and one the years between have never blunted. Even so, I'd made up my mind that the one animal I would never have on the farm was a goat. I doubt if I would have done, either, if I hadn't gone to interview Thurlow Craig about his seven-toed cats.

Even now I can feel the damp fog seeping into my bones as we turned away from the lush country below and began the long

74

climb that led past desolate bogland and on and upwards till we found the rocky track leading to the Craigs' farm. Spring had come to the valleys below, but here winter still wrapped the bleached fields and the wind-stunted trees clinging for life to the rocks. A group of young horses galloped beside the wooden rails of the fence as the Artist and I drove cautiously towards the yard where barking dogs leapt around the tall, bow-legged man who waited to greet us.

Thurlow Craig was, like Gerald Summers, just as remarkable in person as anything he'd written in his books or in the weekly column he did for the *Sunday Express*. His voice was vibrant and husky and the first thing he did when we met him was to pop a monocle into his eye and peer closely at us before offering us a pinch of snuff and a strong drink. He moved with the unmistakable gait of a horseman and the smell of saddle leather and gun oil went with him. I often longed to bring him and Mrs P together for, like her, he claimed (with rather more justification) to be part gypsy and they shared a deep interest in the supernatural.

It was the supernatural which got in the way of the interview I'd come to do about the seven-toed cats, chubby-pawed little beasts which Thurlow Craig had been breeding for years. To do the interview, we went to stand in a patch of pale sun on a hillock near the house from where we could see the whole rise and layout of his farm. After doing the usual checks for voice levels and making sure that everything was in working order, I set the tape recorder in motion.

The strange story of how the ancestor of these extraordinary cats had appeared mysteriously out of a forest in Montgomeryshire, reared two litters of seven-toed kittens and disappeared again can be found in *The Up Country Year Book* of 1964, but it was all new to me then and so was the information thrown in for nothing that the holes bored into the stone gateposts were originally put there to keep away the Evil Eye. Mention of the Evil Eye and old country superstitions led naturally on to the ghost which frequented the Craigs' farmhouse and the lonely cries that could be heard from the bog we'd passed and into which, legend had it, the Saxons had once driven a whole village of Celts to drown. I was then treated to all the fearsome details of a murder which had taken place by the nearby bridge and the inevitable spectre it too had brought into being. I glanced down at the tape, which was running out by now, and quickly brought us back to the subject of the curious cats.

Before leaving, I played over the last few minutes of our conversation just to make quite sure everything was all right. It wasn't until we got home and I found time to listen through from the beginning that I realised anything was wrong.

The start of the tape and the story of the seven-toed cats was there, Thurlow Craig's confident voice and my own questioning one loud and clear. When we began to talk about the ghosts, the tape became nothing but a hideous gobbledygook of unidentifiable noises until the exact moment when I'd steered us back to the cats.

The Artist and I sat stunned, probably because it was just at that time that our own resident poltergeist had made a brief return. There could have been (and probably were) all kinds of reasonable technical explanations for the behaviour of the tape recorder, but we were in no mood to accept them. I was so impressed, in fact, that I persuaded a producer to let me go back and interview Thurlow Craig specifically about his ghosts.

We returned to that strange, lonely farm when summer had replaced the gleeful dancing of spring and even the sinister bog had lost its air of ancient tragedy as larks bounded joyfully above. Thurlow Craig was delighted to see us again but insisted on taking us to a small pub some miles distant where we could be sure there was no supernatural engineer in charge of my equipment and we could have a good lunch at the same time.

The stories I recorded that afternoon were weird indeed. I heard more about a friendly ghost with a suspect sense of humour (we agreed it was probably he who had messed up the last recording) and of an older, more elemental being who went in for terrorising the Craigs' guests. Lunch came and went and so did a lot of alcohol, and still the stories went on.

I have a faint recollection of leaving the pub and of driving back to the Craigs' farm. As I got out of the car there appeared, on a huge outcrop of rock above us, a creature which seemed the very essence of the arcane itself. The afternoon sun turned its great horns to ebony, made a golden nimbus of its shaggy coat and struck fire from its slanting eyes.

76

My companion immediately hailed it. 'Oliver, old chap,' he cried delightedly, 'come down and meet a friend!'

The goat glanced at us in disdain and resumed his contemplation of a small hill a field away. The hill, bare of life one moment, was abruptly occupied by a smaller goat, grazing unconcernedly as she topped its crest. Suddenly the whole hill burst into movement as a wild bacchanal of goats and kids joined her and leaped, cavorted, went round in circles, danced up in the air, kicked up their heels and generally rioted down into the yard, where they immediately began an earnest inspection of me and my belongings.

Mrs Craig appeared right on cue from the kitchen door. 'I don't suppose you'd like to buy a kid?' she enquired brightly.

Half an hour later we were driving homewards, a small brown and white kid lying at my feet, exhausted by her recent struggles to evade capture.

'But don't you see,' I was explaining to the Artist, who was muttering fearfully at me, 'it's Dolores all over again! I'm sure it's her come back.'

She might have come back, but Dolores didn't intend to stay long. We put the tiny, eight-week-old creature in the pigsty, a comfortable residence with a spacious windproof shelter, a concrete forecourt and beyond that a small, grassy yard surrounded by a high stone wall. It even has an ornamental wrought iron gate to add a touch of architectural style. Dolores took just five minutes to figure her way out of it and take off in a general southwesterly direction.

They say that when the god Pan was born, his human mother drowned herself in despair but his father Hermes took him up to Olympus to amuse the gods. That just about describes our whole relationship with Dolores: despair and laughter she dished out in equal quantities, but for the next eighteen months that scrubby little goat became the kingpin of our existence. She was in truth the embodiment of every prejudice against the goat and she committed every single crime that legend lays at its door. But she did it with such zest, with such glory in her own wickedness and with so much joy in the sheer wonder of being alive that it seemed impossible there had ever been a time when she hadn't been effectively wrecking our peace and property.

The rest of the animals detested her, especially the pigs, whose

77

unsuspecting behinds she used for target practice. Neither did the whippets appreciate her inclusion in their walks because when she wasn't bouncing off trees and rocks, she was bouncing off them. And even we took a dim view of her habit of leaping into the air in front of our faces and letting off a fusillade of explosions from her rear end in passing. I think it was the Artist who dubbed her 'The Genuine Fart-Propelled Goat'.

That Dolores might one day produce kids or milk occurred to us only vaguely. She was for us the very spirit of rebellion and anarchy – a spirit which in both of us was not very far from the surface and found its expression in our cossetting of that small but irrepressible goat.

She died, of course, the victim of our chronic ignorance. They say that one of the best teachers of animal husbandry is death. Today I doubt if Dolores would have died; today I would probably be able to diagnose her illness; today I would know the correct remedy or whether it was serious enough to call in the vet; today I would be prepared for her death if it was inevitable. Then I knew nothing and so I found her gasping in agony, watched the mad, bright eyes cloud over, saw the wild spirit stilled at last, and could find no barrier of hard experience to ward off my own desperate grief.

Left to myself, I think that would have been the end of my goat keeping, but the Artist, who had suffered the brunt of her behaviour, was anxious to replace Dolores. Our first idea was to get another kid from the same family, but by then the Craigs had moved to a smaller farm and Oliver and his wives had been sold. These days, when I'm always trying to sell goats, it seems incredible the amount of trouble we had in buying one. It was one of those years when nearly all the kids were males and even we weren't silly enough to opt for that. Our search for a replacement Dolores did teach us quite a lot, though.

Until that time we were totally unaware that there were actual breeds of goats. We found out over the next few weeks that there were white goats called Saanens and ones that came in assorted colours and had long floppy ears called Anglo-Nubians, while the brown and white ones like Dolores were Toggenbergs. We were not quite up to taking in the finer shades of difference even within those breeds, like what was a British Toggenberg and what was a plain Toggenberg.

78

During our mournful wanderings we also discovered that, breeding apart, there was a world of difference between their backgrounds, too. There were the High Church establishments where the goats lived in custom-built pens, had strictly controlled diets and routines, flaunted pedigrees as long as your arm and were privy to the mysterious rituals of the show-ring. They had massive udders but did nothing so vulgar as bringing up their own children, who lived in separate nurseries. There were hippy goats who existed, like their owners, in delirious chaos and were usually named after a character in Tolkien or, even more esoterically, simply 'Goat'. There were the single goats who were adored and spoilt by their owners and were more than likely called Heidi or, in rather more pretentious households, a French name like Hortense. There were the 'self-sufficiency' goats whose owners pretended to a degree of scientific knowledge about goat behaviour which the goats themselves dismissed contemptuously, and there were the gypsy goats who spent their lives amongst a clatter of tin sheds and dogs and old tyres and didn't give a damn.

Christine Palmer's goats came roughly into the category of High Church, but there was just enough lack of strict routine to make us feel less nervous about approaching her. Nonetheless, her goats were superb and when she did agree to sell us one of the kids, we found them bedded down in a large pen with fresh straw, playing amongst themselves. Next door, in a smaller pen, several newborn kids were curled up asleep under an infra-red lamp. The adults we had seen all quietly grazing out in the field behind an electric fence.

Christine pointed out the four older kids we could choose from and hurried off about her work. An hour later she came back to find us still agonising over our choice: would it be the mad little thing who kept leaping up the wall, or the one with the alluring habit of rubbing its head against us, or the smart black Anglo-Nubian with the floppy ears. The one we definitely didn't want was the creature which kept nibbling thoughtfully at the tails of the other kids and muttering quietly to herself all the while. We'd taken against her because she bore absolutely no resemblance to the chunky, solid Dolores, but was a delicate, finely drawn animal with a long neck, more like a fawn than a goat. Her coat was reddy-brown and, apart from the white

Toggenberg markings, there were tufts of bright orange hair around her ears and a saddle of the same colour on her shoulders. She was not, Christine Palmer had told us, full pedigree like the others.

Another hour passed and Christine, bored by now with the repetition of the stories about our lost goat, tried to speed things up by encouraging us to have the little goat with the friendly nature, but just as we were about to settle the matter finally, her daughter came in from school. 'Which would you have?' I asked her, and she pointed without hesitation to the technicolour goat, who repaid the compliment by calmly biting the bobble off her anorak. It was not the last bobble that Celtic Tri-Dolores was to consume in our long relationship.

She sat on the back seat of the car like a queen on progress, taking a polite interest in the passing traffic. At the end of our journey she emerged quite unruffled and proceeded calmly into the loosebox like a dowager being shown her room at Claridges. She acknowledged with a gracious nod the presence of Humble, a tiny white lamb which Myrddin had given us, and made a leisurely inspection of the premises. Overawed, we backed out and left her to settle down.

If only we had left matters there, my subsequent years as a goatkeeper might have been very much less fraught, but the Artist was not satisfied. After the roisterings and gaiety of the last Dolores, he felt that this one was frankly a bit of a bore. I wasn't so sure. I'd noticed a distinct gleam in those beautiful eyes and a decided air of play-acting behind the elegant progress, but I did think that she should have a companion of her own kind. So when we heard of another kid for sale, I agreed to go and look at it.

It was an idyllic setting for a smallholding. A bright stream chuckled through the little dell and daffodils rioted up the slopes to the buildings which someone was obviously engaged in restoring. But the middle-aged couple who had recently bought the place looked fraught and anxious, and they told us a dreadful story. They had arrived a few months earlier to find that the previous owner had left most of her livestock behind to fend for themselves in the six weeks before the new owners were able to take possession. The old white goat, though ill and half starved, had dragged herself up the road to be mated by a neighbouring

British Alpine. Little more than a bag of bones when they finally arrived, old Nana had impressed them enough, by her sheer guts, to put up a fight for her life and even to see her through the birth of her kid. They were now prepared to let her live out her days with them, but they had no intention of keeping any other goats and the kid would have to go. I glanced around the flock of brilliantly coloured, standard-bred poultry, in which not a mongrel was to be seen, and understood at once that if they ever changed their minds about goats, they would definitely have to be of the High Church variety.

I can't remember how we finally caught Little Nana, who was busily engaged in wrecking one of the poultry pens when we saw her, but I do know that we had to rope her person securely to every handle in the car and that she screamed at the top of her voice all the way home. When we tried to get her out of the car she flung herself on the ground, went completely rigid and began to sob. She sobbed for a whole week till I was in tears too, reminded of the black cloud of misery and homesickness that going back to school had wrapped me in for weeks after the holidays. I spent hours in the shed with her, Dolores and Humble the lamb were friendly to her, but nothing stopped that dreadful sobbing. We finally got her to drink from a bottle, but even when she was drinking she sobbed. It was awful.

Dolores and the lamb finally got through to Nana, but she never ever forgave us for taking her away from her game old mother. If goats can hate, then Nana hated us.

A year later, Dolores was just as charmingly interested in everything to do with the human race and Nana was still conducting a venomous but highly strategic war against it. Fortunately, Dolores' aristocratic nature was the stronger of the two, so when Nana waltzed up and down on the tin roof of the pigsty or tried to climb the higher branches of the ash tree, a quiet but meaningful glance from Dolores was all that was needed to get her down again.

Oddly enough, though, it was Dolores who turned Myrddin Parry against goats for life. She was, and still is, the most accomplished pickpocket in the business and, like all true professionals, leaves her victims blissfully unaware of their loss unless she happens to have difficulty in swallowing it.

That was how Myrddin managed to rescue the needle and

syringe she'd extracted soundlessly from his pocket. While he was still examining them for damage, she calmly plucked the sacred cap off his head and stood munching it benignly until Myrddin felt the draught around his ears and swung into outraged action again. The icy dignity of his retreat from the goat shed was somewhat marred by the haphazard state of his bootlaces, parts of which were seething around with his handkerchief in Dolores' first stomach.

So it was that with one goat totally unapproachable and the other rapidly alienating the neighbours, I decided to bring a little order into their lives.

At the time I was deeply under the influence of David McKenzie's book, *Goat Husbandry*. In particular the chapter on 'The Control of Goats' was proving a revelation. It should be called 'The Psychology of the Goat' and I can still recommend it to anyone who wants to understand what makes a goat tick. I learned, for instance, that the behaviour of the flock depends mainly on the personality of its leader. This, for all practical purposes, is the senior female, or queen. The male is only allowed to *think* he's the major decision maker. According to Mr McKenzie, properly managed goats can be organised into a routine and their owners can play a large part in establishing that routine if they appoint themselves as temporary flock leader.

My immediate problem was to convince Dolores and Nana that they would spend the day grazing peacefully on the brambles, gorse and other supposed goat delicacies which abounded down on the meadow by the river. They would then, as night fell, wend their way in an orderly fashion home again. With the exception of the bit about wending her way home, Nana took to the idea immediately, but Dolores remained unconvinced. She preferred the wending to anything else and she believed in doing it at once and as quickly as possible.

I referred again to David McKenzie who, obviously aware of the difficulties, had taken care to include a photograph of a cheerful flock of goats hurtling round a corner in frantic pursuit of their absent human leader. The next stage, it seemed, was to convince your flock to stay put while you went home and got on with your own affairs. I agreed, but had a few doubts about the efficacy of throwing small stones and sticks at them 'ceremonially'. The purpose of this was to 'insult' them and,

82

being creatures with a great sense of their own dignity and not slow to take a hint, the goats would then turn their backs on you and ignore your retreat.

When Nana saw me standing there sticking my tongue out and rudely chucking sticks and stones at her, it simply confirmed her worst suspicions about the sheer nastiness of the human beast and she took off up the nearest tree and spat at me.

Dolores merely looked at me sweetly, ate the sticks, sampled the stones and came looking for more. So we all wended together as usual, only Nana flying along in front in case I did it again.

The next day I sat quietly on a rock by the river until Dolores, satisfied that I wasn't going anywhere, disappeared behind a clump of brambles with Nana. Keeping my head well down, I crept to the shelter of the wood where the trees gave me cover for my silent flitting and I actually made it to the little gate at the top in safety. I couldn't see or hear a goat anywhere, but there was still time and the open field ahead presented a problem. Walking, it takes half a minute to cross that field. Crawling on your belly in the mud, it takes about a quarter of an hour.

I had just made it to the duck pond and paused to congratulate my aching limbs on the fact that we were nearly home safe, when I heard an amused bleat above my head. Dolores was gazing lovingly down at me and Nana was peering over her shoulder triumphantly, hoping no doubt that I'd never get up again.

When I came limping and cursing into the kitchen, I found the dogs smirking quietly and Mrs P clutching McKenzie's book as she rocked backwards and forwards and the tears streamed down her cheeks. 'They were following you,' she screamed at last, 'all the way! Every time you hopped behind a tree, they hopped behind one too! And that last bit! They tiptoed! They actually tiptoed, about three yards behind you! And you just kept on!' She collapsed across the table, still spluttering.

I spent a large part of that day locked up in my office, remote from Mrs P's intermittent cackling and the sight of Dolores and Nana sharpening up their invasion tactics. I drew a certain amount of solace from the view of the impersonal hills framed in the window, hills where the sheep knew their own walks and the men and women who owned them had long since banished the goat and all its works from their lives.

# Chapter 10

The two sheepdog pups quested joyfully over the polished lino on the surgery floor. Their owner regarded them with pride for a moment and then told them fiercely to sit down and behave themselves. He turned back to us and nodded towards the door through which the vet had just disappeared. 'And what would you be doing here with him, then?' he enquired.

My producer, Peter de Rosa, stopped smiling down at the pups. 'Actually, we're doing a Radio 4 feature programme with him about his work,' he replied.

The elderly farmer adjusted the shoulder of his old tweed jacket, glanced round conspiratorially and lowered his voice. 'Ah then,' he said, 'you've come to the right chap.' He nodded. 'He's quite intelligent, you know, this one is. Ah yes! Do you know, he's written a book or two? They're not too bad, either, I do believe.'

I felt that sick hopelessness which always comes when someone has just uttered pure gold and the wretched machine is switched off. Peter turned away and patted the pups and I could see that he was shaking with laughter. The door of the surgery swung open and the man known to the world as James Herriot came hurrying back in, apologising for keeping his client waiting.

For two days Peter and I had been travelling with him all round his practice in the Yorkshire Dales, watching him attend with equal concern to everything from a fabulously valuable Friesian bull to the almost invisible dew claws of a newborn Pomeranian puppy. We didn't see much of the scenery because we drove through thick wads of fog as we made our way between the big commercial farms, with their massive buildings of concrete and steel, and the little, traditional holdings crouching at the end of rutted tracks. At no time was there a hint of the internationally acclaimed author. He was just the vet doing his job.

It was an enchanted time, in spite of the fog and the piercing cold. Peter and I were in a glow on account of the wonderful radio material we were collecting almost effortlessly. Normally I don't like having a producer dancing around when I'm on a job: they tend to get in the way of that special chemistry you try to create between you and the person you're interviewing which, if it's successful, means the world of difference between a boring set of questions and answers and a real, live conversation open to all kinds of verbal possibilities. Everyone, no matter how seemingly ordinary on the surface, has a fascinating story to tell but to get it out of them often means building a very real bond between you. The presence of someone else makes this much more difficult.

Peter de Rosa was one of the exceptions, knowing exactly when to fade into the background and the precise moment to reappear and help. We worked on many successful programmes together and have remained friends. Had I known, therefore, that he was to be so inspired by his long conversations in the car with James Herriot that he would go on with writing his own best-selling book, *Bless Me Father*, and eventually leave the BBC, thus breaking up one of the best working relationships I've ever had with a producer, then I might not have been quite so euphoric.

Only complete fools could have made a mess of the programme we finally put together. Not only were the people and animals we met the kind that every interviewer dreams about, but Herriot himself was a joy to record with his soft Scottish burr, his marvellous way with words and his simple approach to life which kept him working hard as a vet in spite of all the money his books had made – books which in no way exaggerated the sense of fun and warmth emanating from that tall house in the Yorkshire market town where the legendary Siegfried Farnon still held sway.

Now I must confess that one of the reasons why my life has never run on smooth lines, but has been a jumbled chaos of half-baked ideas and wild dreams, is that I have a fatal tendency to exist in the fantasy worlds created by my favourite authors. I suppose a lot of people do this, but whereas most of them eventually leave the fantasy behind and get on with a normal, rational life, I keep trying to make it into reality. That is probably why I live on a totally unproductive smallholding in a remote Welsh valley. Absorbed as I became in the Herriot/Farnon world, I came back, turned a sour eye on the vets I knew and found them wanting.

Of course I was being totally unfair to Islwyn Thomas and the other highly competent men who had suffered my patronage for years. It wasn't their fault that my animals went down with diseases unknown to veterinary science, and it takes a person of much imagination and more patience to come rushing out because some hysterical woman has got a 'funny feeling' that one of her animals is not long for this world. Quite unfair because, when I did finally come upon a vet who was as witty, clever and eccentric as any I'd find in fiction and who would take unknown ailments and weird premonitions in his stride, I almost showed him the gate. By then Mrs P and I had settled ourselves down and I was facing for the first time the sharp reality of running the little farm alone. I was endeavouring to take a severely practical view of the world, but I can't have been succeeding too well because the first thing this particular vet did was to shatter an illusion, an illusion which I was sharing with Doli, the mare.

Spring that year came in fits and starts. One day there was a lazy air of well-being permeating the valley: the scent of narcissi in the garden mingled with a thousand other hidden perfumes as plants struggled their way back to life; chickens enjoyed ecstatic dust baths on the mole hills or carefully preened their feathers against the warm stones of the wall; sheep lazed, bellies to the sun, cudding slowly and luxuriantly. The next day we were plunged into winter again as icy winds and quick flurries of sleet and snow taught us not to take anything for granted.

86

There were five tiny black lambs hurtling about on the hay field, although I had missed the traumas of their birth. The odd bit of broadcasting work was still trickling in and, as a couple of complicated programmes were to coincide with lambing time, the three Black Welsh Mountain ewes I had bought eighteen months before had been sent over to the farm of some newly found friends, the Haffields. Humble, the pet white lamb, had grown into a fat, greedy yearling and remained at home with her old stable mates, Dolores and Nana. She instantly rejoined them in their battle against authority and fences, pinched their food and allowed them in return to chew the wool off her back. But when the three ewes returned home with four tups and one little female lamb in tow, Humble again switched her allegiance and became self-appointed lamb sitter. She took the opportunity to pass on, to the tups at least, much of the villainy she'd learnt from the goats, and all day long the air was rent with the frantic calls of their mothers, while the tups and Humble sniggered together behind the hedge.

The ewe lamb, who behaved impeccably at all times, I named Sarah, at the earnest request of a four-year-old friend of mine. Poor child, how was she to know that her boasting about the matter to the other children at her London nursery school was to have a shattering effect on her life: next Christmas, the teachers made her play a sheep in the Nativity scene. Having one named after her, they explained carefully, would give her a greater insight into the part; after all, anyone could play Mary.

If I had realised then how much of my time I was to spend that summer scouring the countryside for Humble's acolytes, I might have been a little less enchanted at the sight of my first lambs on my own fields, but for the moment at least, they gave me the warm feeling that at last I was getting down to the serious side of farming. I was so besotted by the lambs, in fact, that it took me a while to connect the gradual cessation of the egg bonanza with the furtive behaviour of the hens and the indignant squawks that erupted from clumps of nettles or the more inaccessible tangles in the hedge when I passed by. I should have been warned by the queues of pigeons waiting for me to open the barn doors and the frenetic arguments about ledge space going on in the dovecote. By the time I woke up to what was happening, searched out and confiscated all the addled eggs and earned the undying enmity of every bird on the place, who greeted me with cries of 'Herod!' every time I appeared, Daisy's brood had begun to chip and chirp their way into the world.

Now while it might be true that most animals are quite capable of bringing up their own young with the minimum of interference from us, I have never found this to be so with mine. The geese were a case in point. I have been told that it's the gander who actually does the rearing of the goslings, so Daisy's lot were a bit unfortunate in their father. Douglas spent a great deal of his time and energy on seeing off a perfectly inoffensive duck, while behind him assorted predators helped themselves to the goslings. He was absent-minded, too; he managed to squash several of his children and lost a couple more down a drain, so that by the end of their first week, out of fifteen healthy goslings only six remained.

Mrs P was delighted when I came into the kitchen with the bewildered and bedraggled survivors safely in a box, while Douglas and Daisy shrieked their fury at the back door. My mother has always been in love with young poultry and has been known to retire to her bed for a whole week to warm a clutch of chickens back into life. Friends have got used to being entertained at her bedside while a happy gang of chickens join in the conversation as they peep out between the bedclothes. This is all merely part of the family tradition: my great-grandmother was renowned for her ability to finish hatching out eggs down her cleavage.

Mrs P was just happily collecting a couple of hot water bottles, the Agatha Christie she was reading and a flask of tea, when I informed her that a box by the Rayburn would be quite sufficient to resuscitate the goslings. I reminded her at the same time that geese have rather more volatile digestive systems than chickens. Stoically hiding her disappointment, she put the hot water bottles under the straw in the box and prepared to devote herself exclusively to the care and attention of the orphans.

Our kitchen is a narrow one, converted from what was once a dark cave of a cold room and the place where they salted the pig on great slate slabs. When it's not swirling with dust from the rogue Rayburn or howling with draughts that penetrate the ceiling which the original builder I employed never got round to finishing properly, it's just about bearable as a kitchen.

Occupied by six noisy, rapidly growing goslings who live on disgusting messes of chopped-up egg, dandelion and lettuce, it's not a place to linger. Even the dogs gave up hanging around in hope and repaired to the living room. Oscar, her budgerigar, maintained an appalled silence, but Mrs P stayed at her post, clucking at her charges encouragingly or chatting amiably to them as she went about her work. My part in all this was to go hunting endlessly for the dandelions and then to spend a great deal of time staggering out to the muck heap with the last lot in processed form, hotly pursued by Douglas and Daisy, who hung around all day waiting for news of their children like relatives in an emergency ward.

I was thus engaged one bitterly cold afternoon at the back end of April when a battered red Mini, dragging its exhaust pipe noisily behind it, came to a halt at the gate. A face, adorned with round, granny glasses and a pair of luxuriant mutton-chop whiskers, appeared out of the window.

'I'm Ellis,' it announced. 'The Haffields said you wanted to see me.'

'Who did you say?' I queried.

'Ellis. Bertie. Can I bring the car in?'

I plonked my burden down, kicked Douglas and Daisy off and went slowly over to open the gate. My mind was reeling back in time and space to the plush comfort of an expensive restaurant in St James's where I'd been having lunch about a year before with a publisher's eager publicity lady. She'd enticed me there to talk about her firm's new list of books, but had made the mistake of walking me up Duke Street on our way to the restaurant. In Duke Street there is a pub called 'The Unicorn' which has a magnificent sign showing a spectacular unicorn rearing up against a dim background of mystic seas and crescent moon. She managed at last to drag me away from my ecstatic contemplation of the sign, but had to suffer a long dissertation on unicorns, why I'd had one for a weathervane at the farm, the farm itself, the way no ordinary vet seemed to understand the idiosyncratic diseases the animals went down with, and most of all Doli's current Problem. This last finally caught her attention, being a bit of a horsey person herself.

'What you need is a real horse specialist of a vet to look at her,' she mused. 'As a matter of fact, I know one who doesn't live all that far from you. His name's Bertie Ellis. Mad as a hatter, of course. He's got a sort of farm of his own which he mucks about with when he's not trying to stop the house collapsing or fooling around with clapped-out cars. But if you can get hold of him, he's the bloke to sort Doli out for you.' She scribbled an address on one of the paper napkins and pushed it over to me. 'Now, do you think we can talk about these books?'

I put the napkin away carefully. I've never seen it since and neither can I remember now which of Doli's Problems had me so exercised at the time. Doli, for as long as I've known her, has had some kind of Problem, whether physical or psychological, all of which have melted into an endless saga as contorted and improbable as an American soap opera. Her second foal to Dominic had again been born with the maximum of fuss and was as perfect as Moelwyn had been, but he had contracted pneumonia and had been one of the long list of casualties in that disastrous 1975.

Now I was once again waiting for her to foal, this time to a magnificent premium stallion. Islwyn Thomas had given Doli a blood test which proved positive, a relief in view of the large question mark hanging over the actual mating: Doli had made a very spirited attempt to kick her lover to death and needed three strong men to hold her while he mounted. Now, ten and a half months later, she was bulging beautifully and languishing about, gazing dreamily into the middle distance.

Mrs P was just as excited as I was about the coming birth. Although she'd delivered hundreds of human babies in her time, she'd never actually seen any other species give birth, with the exception of a cat who'd had a litter of kittens on her bed once when Mrs P was in it, immobilised by a broken leg. Now, she rejoiced with me over the swelling of Doli's udder and the few squirts of fluid it produced when I squeezed it.

The relationship between my mother and myself was not all sweetness and light, however. She developed an infuriating habit of prefacing all her responses to my remarks about Doli's pregnancy with 'Well now, if it was a *human*...' and would then go on to explain fully what the accepted procedure was in that case. Endlessly I reminded her that Doli was a horse and not likely to appreciate lying on her back doing relaxation exercises out in the mud; neither did I think that a post-natal diet of

90

peanuts to improve her milk supply would do much for her. I might have been one of the goslings chirping for all the good it did: as far as Mrs P was concerned, mothers were mothers and babies were babies, whatever shape they came in.

By the time Doli's full eleven months were up, the atmosphere in the house was growing tense, although the non-arrival of the foal didn't bother me too much as Doli's had always been a few days late. 'It's probably a boy,' said Mrs P. 'The girls are usually in a hurry and the boys take their time. That's what I've always found with *human* babies anyway.'

Instead of hitting her, I picked up the box of gosling mess and went out onto the yard just in time to see the red Mini arrive.

Whatever visions I'd formed of Bertie Ellis when his name had first been mentioned in the rich atmosphere of the restaurant in St James's, they were completely dispelled by the reality which emerged from the car. He was a short, perky figure with an ancient deerstalker pulled down over his dark hair; a tattered sheepskin jerkin covered a much-darned, polo-necked sweater, his feet were thrust into a pair of scuffed riding boots and the bowl of a pipe stuck out of the pocket of his faded jeans. I am not the first person to be taken aback by their first sight of Robert Ellis, PhD, BVSc, MRCVS, and to have serious doubts as to his professional ability on the strength of it.

As I watched him stretch himself so that the sweater rode up over his bare midriff, and then stand there calmly assessing the place, I sought reassurance from the fact that the Haffields had a very valuable stallion and surely they wouldn't let anyone incompetent near it. But then I remembered that they were the only people for miles around who'd even heard of the mysterious Bertie Ellis, whose address I'd long since lost. I was just about to laugh gaily and tell him that I'd simply wanted to meet him on the strength of a mutual acquaintance, when a tall girl with long blonde hair unwound herself from the front seat of the Mini and came to join him on the yard.

Bertie nodded in her direction. 'My wife, Sara,' he said briefly. 'Nice buildings you've got. Terrible place to live, though.'

'I think it's very beautiful,' said Sara. I turned to her in relief, thinking that if he had as pretty and normal a person as her for a wife, this curious-looking vet couldn't be too hopeless.

'The Haffields mentioned something about a mare in foal being a bit slow on the draw,' he said, sauntering over to the gate. He pointed to Doli, who was palely loitering by the fence. 'If it's that one there, I can tell you for nothing, she ain't!'

'What do you mean, "she ain't"?' I demanded.

'In foal. That's what you want to know, isn't it?'

'Oh yes she is in foal,' I said angrily. 'For a start the blood test was positive, she's as big as a house, her udder's filling up, and,' I concluded triumphantly, 'she's got milk!'

'I'll still bet you she's not in foal,' said Bertie casually. 'Want me to have a look and prove it?'

'How do you mean, "have a look"?'

'Stick my hand in and have a feel, of course. Go on. Get me a bucket of water, soap and towel.' He brought out the vet's litany with such authority that I was halfway up the yard before I remembered I didn't trust him. The thought that if he did start having 'a feel', Doli might kick a large hole in his ego kept me hurrying to the house.

As I slammed the bucket under the hot water tap, Mrs P paused in her conversation with the goslings. 'Who's that out there?' she enquired.

'That,' I informed her, 'is the famous horse vet, Bertie Ellis. He looks a complete maniac and he reckons Doli's not in foal.'

Mrs P looked up in alarm. 'How can he tell?' she asked.

'Just by looking, according to him. Now he wants to examine her to prove it to me. Stand by the first-aid kit, mother mine. I hope Doli murders him, the silly twit!'

'Well of course, if Doli was *human*, I could probably...'

'Oh, for God's sake,' I shrieked, 'for the last time, she's a bloody HORSE!'

As I thumped out of the kitchen I could hear Mrs P's aggrieved voice telling the goslings, 'She always was a rude girl. When I think how I starved myself to give her the best education money could buy!'

When I got back to the yard, I expected to see Bertie all togged up in plastic overalls and gauntlets, but he and Sara were still leaning over the gate, gazing at Doli. She eyed them apprehensively and gave one or two hopeful burps.

Bertie turned when he heard me approaching. 'She's good, mind you. That's a fair imitation of foaling colic she's doing.

92

Right then, let's have a look at this old malingerer and stop her little game. Sara, hop over and hold her steady, will you?' And he stripped off the jerkin and the old sweater and stood before us in the biting easterly wind, stark naked to the waist. He plunged his arms into the bucket of water and soaped them up to the elbow.

'What about your overalls and things?' I exclaimed.

'Never touch 'em. Not for mares. Scares hell out of them, coming up looking like something out of "2001".' He trotted round to Doli's rear.

'Don't you want bales of straw behind her?' I cried.

'Nope,' said a muffled voice. A hand came round and plonked a mass of steaming dung on the ground.

Sara smiled at me encouragingly. 'Don't worry,' she said. 'He's far more likely to get kicked by a pony than by a big girl like this.'

A few adventurous chickens came and pecked hopefully at the new pile of dung, the sharp fingers of the wind sniped spitefully at us and a couple of crows began fighting in the ash tree. Doli, apart from rolling her eye once or twice, never offered to move a muscle. I could have brained her.

At last Bertie emerged, his naked chest smeared with muck and his deerstalker sitting comically on the back of his head.

'Not in foal,' he announced cheerfully. 'She's been having you on, the old sod.'

'Don't be ridiculous,' I snarled. I reached under and squeezed Doli's udder. 'Look! She's even got milk.'

'Oh I know,' said Bertie. 'She knows this is about the time to have a foal, so she's convinced herself and you that that's what she's having. I'll bet you've been feeding her up like anything. That's why she's so fat. I liked the imitation foaling colic bit though. She's quite an artist, this one.' He slapped Doli's rump. 'Go on then, you old fraud, the game's up!'

Before I could rush once more to her defence, my beloved mare gave me a sheepish look, turned and trotted up the field, her tail in the air, did a skittish little dance to one side and settled down to graze. I didn't know who to hate most, her or Bertie.

# ===== *Chapter* II =====

Lightning, sharp and lethal, forked across the valley, throwing horizons into relief and making the little farms seem like lonely ships, sending flares for help. The brilliance went and the deep blue of a summer's night descended. Thunder, heartbeats distant, growled and worried at the hills which, lost in their primeval conversation with the storm, threw off the thin skin of human interference with its neat fields and tidy buildings and placid, tamed animals. So it seemed to me, anyway, standing at the window high up in the gable end of the house, praying as I always did that the lightning would ignore the great ash tree which stands between the house and the buildings.

A reasonable person would have had the tree cut down, not trusting to the pact I'd made with it years before: willing it to resist the southerly gales and the violent summer storms so that I could enjoy the sight of it framing the mountain, or lie at night listening to the owls calling from its branches. Once, in a fit of sanity and sick of the nerve-pulling tension of worrying about it, I'd asked a firm to come and cut it down. For a week I crept around, feeling like an executioner, as the tree suddenly sprouted reproachful eyes that followed me everywhere. At last, unable to imagine it gone, I'd rung and cancelled.

I paid for my weakness on nights like this, when the vulnerability of the vast branches and the defenceless roofs below them blanked out the beauty of the wild scene and caused me to stand, unable to sleep, staring into the centre of the tree, feeling with it every lash whipping from the sky and becoming almost part of its bruised, tormented being.

There was a moment of complete stillness before the rain came, bursting with long strokes out of a sky that had seemed cloudless and turning the dry yard into a river-bed. So absorbed was I in my concentration on the tree that I forgot the couple sleeping down on the meadow in their flimsy tent. Already that afternoon the sheep had invaded them like a bunch of old women at a jumble sale and made havoc of their neat piles of odds and ends so that they'd retreated to the river and the gnats. Somehow they'd managed to pitch their tent right in the path of the torrents pouring off the hill to join the river, which only moments before had been a quiet, lazy meander in its tunnel of cool, dark trees.

They came eventually, bearing the tattered remnants of their holiday, city minds already aghast at the malignancy of the gnats, now with nearly all their possessions washed away by the storm which had overtaken them unawares as they slept, unbelievably, through the noise.

Arthur and his wife spent the rest of their stay camped out in the old stone shed next to the cottage, already half converted from the foul smelling, rat infested poultry house it had been years before. The floor had been raised and damp proofed, a large window placed to look straight out across the valley to the Fans, and the walls rendered. At that point I'd run out of money, so it remained a shell for future plans, a handy place to store wood and junk and now a honeymoon flat. When Arthur had arranged to come from Birmingham to do some repairs on the hay barn and the roofs of the buildings, he had mentioned that a mate would be coming too. Instead he brought a fragile, newly-wed wife and the request to camp outside.

The buildings defeated him, of course. When you've spent your working life making square boxes for council tenants, barns which have been created out of river stones and uneven tree-trunks and added to haphazardly through the succeeding generations are likely to give you a bit of a culture shock. By the time he got round to adding a wall of corrugated iron sheeting to enclose the hay barn, Arthur had lost touch completely. That's why the barn, reprieved from my original intention of pulling it down, as its usefulness outweighed its ugliness, has a lopsided, drunken look about it to this day. Demoralised at last by the lost skill of building against the laws of gravity, Arthur left and I went back to propping up doors with rocks and tying gates together with baler twine.

The storm which had dealt so ruthlessly with Arthur's boyhood dreams of camping in the country was not the last that summer, but it was the only one to bring any rain with it. We might have known that there was a price to pay for a joyful, perfect haymaking, untroubled by the forecasts. Tractors whirred and the steady clunk of baling machines came almost immediately, collecting hay dried in record time.

My one field was the last to fall. Myrddin roared through the gate and dared all as he mowed the steep slope while swallows, accustomed to skimming over the tall, floating grass, sat indignantly on the electric wires and saw it laid low. He came back to turn the grass but I, not trusting the forecast and still unable to believe there was no rain for once, turned it by hand as well, going up and down the rows with my hay rake under the blistering sky, a lone peasant figure in a landscape where big, red machines went busily up and down the neighbouring fields and groups of people came out to throw the bales onto trailers, their voices clear in the hot, still air.

At last they came to me, too, a laughing gang, faces burnt brown, teasing and joking, enjoying briefly a return to the old days when neighbours needed each other more. Now only at haymaking time (and that fast disappearing as silage takes the place of hay) do a few of them come together in the annual dash against time and weather. That year they caught me up in their madness, counting out loud as the bales dropped from the big machine, amused but kind about my feeble harvest. They made a game of rolling the bales down the hill, some bales coming all the way to rest at the foot of the hay barn, others going off course and sticking by the hedge. There were ninety bales altogether from the small field: ninety bales of sweet meadow hay. As I struggled to lift them, muscles screaming in protest, other women flung them like pillows up onto the stacks and the gang finally left, still laughing, accepting nothing from me in return but the satisfaction of seeing another field in safe.

For a while I stood, lost in loneliness as the warmth of their kindness retreated with the sound of their voices, and then I took the hay rake and gleaned the last remaining precious wisps, working on under a moon that swung up flamboyantly between a cleft in the hills. It was already well on its journey before I finished and left the night to the owls and the whispering river.

Summer baked on relentlessly and no new grass came to cover the shorn fields. Only the bright, pernicious bracken thrived and even the docks, which might have been useful for once, fell to an invasion of tiny, red-gold beetles which left them delicate, lacy skeletons. The sheep, embarrassingly naked without their wool, chewed resignedly on burdock and nettles and the pigs made deep earth troughs under the trees. The stream running through the fields dried up and I carried bucket after bucket of water to the stock, pursued by a long line of dusty ducks.

The crisp dryness of the stubby grass, the cracking soil and the forestry, matchwood dry under the implacable sun, brought back the nightmare of Australian droughts and circling bush fires. The smell of smouldering peat on the other side of the mountain hung like a threat on the air, but on the meadow, patches of green lingered beneath the trees, the river continued to run on quietly and my spring, hidden under a bank of thorn and hazel high above the house, went on slowly but surely feeding the tank.

In spite of the blinding heat, heat which I'd travelled the world to escape from, my memories of that summer, filtered through time, are full of a strange, brooding magic, golden and benign. Perhaps it was because I spent the greater part of the day in the dim cool of the cottage, to emerge at dusk and work late into the night. Sometimes I worked by moonlight, often while silent lightning flicked across the sky; always under the stars, while the two horses, let out of their stable at night when the flies had gone, galloped about me or munched the dry grass companionably as I trundled back and forth with barrow loads of muck.

The shimmering silence of the lethargic days, after the

emotions and dramas of the year before, left me time to think at last about what I was doing in the valley at all and to try and justify my stubbornness in spite of the continued indifference of the BBC to my suggestions for a longer series of country programmes. I could see no way out of the mess I'd got myself into: landed with debts, no career to speak of and a place I was not only incompetent to run but which, even if I had been competent, was not likely ever to yield a living by itself.

'The best thing for being sad is to learn something,' says Merlyn to the young Arthur in *The Sword in the Stone*, and T. H. White, who wrote it (and followed the advice himself), has Merlyn teach his pupil to become a part of the natural world around him by turning him into different animals and birds. Years ago in Australia, another person, very like a Merlyn himself, at whose feet I'd sat when I was still young enough to believe everything, had told me, 'You only truly understand what you truly love' and had encouraged me, in quest of that understanding and love, to try and enter mentally the being of all kinds of beasts and at last to put on underwater gear, to walk out across the sharp reefs and even to dive down amongst the sharks of which I was mortally afraid. So now, terrified of the future, I set out to learn this tiny world for which I was responsible: the animals, the rocks, the soil, the trees and the legend which must have haunted my predecessors in that place as it was to haunt me, the legend of the Lady of the Lake.

Since that evening years before, when we had first heard from Rosemary Jenkins the story of the legendary Lady, I hadn't paid it a great deal of attention although I now lived only a short distance from the Lake and the farm where it had all begun. That I changed my attitude was almost entirely due to the radio playwright and critic, David Wade. He, on one brief visit to the Lake, had seen what I had failed to appreciate: that the legend was historically fascinating and composed of many layers of meaning. David had made of the story a beautifully sensitive radio play which brought it vividly to life.

David and his wife, Pan, had come to spend New Year with Mrs P and me at the beginning of 1976. I had asked David to bring a recording of the play with him and invited several people living in the valley to come and hear it. In spite of the furious weather, with the wind screaming up the yard so that earlier I was nearly blown backwards while trying to wheel several bags of feed along on the wheelbarrow, they came in small curious groups, shaking the rain from their clothes and crowding into the room where a huge fire leaped up the chimney and, in an effort to re-create the atmosphere of the legend, only candles lit the dim corners where Christmas tinsel still lingered and holly berries glowed dully against the stone walls.

David's play, set in the twelfth century, we heard through as once people must have listened to the story when it was first told, with only the background noise of the wind howling outside and the crackling of the fire. The atmosphere in the room was spell-like. Afterwards, over coffee and whisky, my guests continued to discuss the legend almost in a whisper, telling of odd little by-ways in the story as they'd heard it from grandparents long ago.

David Wade's interpretation of the people and events of the legend affected me deeply and, by the time of that summer of burning days and deep, blue nights lit by sharp stars and blazing moons, I'd begun to have my own theories about the story. Working outside in those cool evenings, or standing at my window gazing at the Fans framed darkly in the branches of the ash tree, I brooded on the Lady who seemed to grow into the very shape of the valley itself, laying a protective presence over the baking earth, for there was green in the valley when everywhere else was bleached or brown.

At last the trappings of the legend itself fell away and I wondered if once the valley had been a vast, sacred antechamber for the Lake and those 'plough marks' across the mountain could be the remains of an ancient trackway trodden by pilgrims visiting a goddess. There are places which have this feeling of deep magic, put down by the people who believed in it; look for it and you won't find it, but it will come upon you from one breath to the next, the air suddenly clear and shimmering with the sensation of voices just that moment ceasing into echoes.

Curiously, this obsession with the Lady stopped me from going to the Lake itself, I suppose because I was afraid of discovering there nothing but a sheet of water at the bottom of a cliff, a sheet of water moreover that had nothing more romantic to do with itself than to provide domestic water for the distant Llanelli district.

Still the summer burnt on with no rain, and the only thing the scorched earth produced in abundance was mushrooms, which surprised me because I'd always thought mushrooms and humidity went together and of humidity there was none. The spring had at last been reduced to a trickle of drops and the brick tank chose that moment to begin leaking its precious water into the surrounding earth. Blossom and Magnolia had discovered the trick of simply plugging their suction-pad noses against the brickwork and siphoning moisture through the ancient cement holding it together. It was nearly too late for the tank and our water supply before I caught them at it and got Bertie to come and ring them. It was a barbaric business, although most of the mind-blowing racket they made happened before he touched their noses and a bucket of feed helped them forget about it immediately.

Into the midst of all this worry over the drought and my strange infatuation with the legend dropped my brother-in-law from Australia. With him, everything swung back into normal focus again.

Byron, in spite of his name, is the least romantic of people. Not that he hasn't got his passions, but they're all of a scientific kind. The first time I was aware of him, he was a ghastly little bespectacled boy who was being kept in to write a very long essay. His crime had been nothing less than a plot (already well advanced) to blow up the sports field, so that he wouldn't have to play football. Being Byron, he would probably have succeeded in making some very nasty holes in the ground if the headmaster hadn't found him out thanks to a juvenile grass. At the time, I was a young teacher fresh out of college and busily uneducating the eight-year-olds while Byron was about to take off for the high school across the road, but the shock and scandal of the whole affair shook the school from end to end. For a long time the headmaster had his faith in himself seriously disturbed, not least by the effort to read the extremely complex and advanced essay on astronomy with which Byron had whiled away his long detentions.

When Byron did finally get to high school, he palled up with another rebel, my brother Peter. From then on our family got used to the sound of things going violently bump in the back yard as the two of them conducted unconventional experiments in our garden shed, having been banned from the school lab.

The last really vivid memory I had of Byron was mixed up with yelling hens and blue smoke, the sight of two blackened faces running for their lives with my stepfather on their trail and Mrs P trying to stop the cat going bananas up the kitchen wall. He and my brother went on causing havoc in their quest for scientific knowledge for years after I left home, and trailing along behind them was Byron's sister, Shelley, whom my brother married when they all grew up.

Now Byron had turned up quite unexpectedly and Mrs P and I quailed at the thought of the havoc his enquiring mind could cause in our lives. The quietly spoken, gentle-seeming man who got out of the hired car bore no resemblance to the wild-eyed boy I'd known. He wasn't interested, however, in doing the usual tourist things: Byron had come to Europe to see the great car rallies. Now it just so happens that Myrddin Parry is a rally fanatic too, and we'd no sooner introduced them than he and Byron disappeared up the mountain to see to Myrddin's sheep and talk rallying. They then progressed to the pub (which was odd, because Myrddin doesn't really like pubs too much) and that was the last we saw of Byron that night.

It was at about seven o'clock the next morning when a battered hire car and a sheepish Byron put in an appearance. Mrs P and I listened to a complicated story about Myrddin doing a spot of rally driving around the lanes to show Byron how they did it in Wales, and Byron then deciding at some awful hour to 'practise' alone. He had got himself horribly lost, driven the car into a ditch and spent the rest of the night wandering round in circles on the mountain till he had come upon a gang going off early to work and ended up with half the able-bodied men in the district helping to haul the car out. Byron may have changed outwardly, but chaos still followed him around like a faithful dog.

I think it was Mrs P who suggested that for the rest of his stay I keep Byron firmly under my own eye and why didn't I take him for a nice walk up to the Lake? He wasn't particularly interested in going for a nice walk, but my promise that he might find the Fans geologically interesting tempted him slightly, and when I told him of the peat beds around the Lake, he got that old gleam in his eye and muttered, 'Bones! There could be bones!'

Mrs P took me aside and reminded me that one of the ventures he and Peter had been engaged on between their various explosions had been the finding of bones of prehistoric animals. She shuddered as she recalled the various aftermaths of their finds.

'Just pray he doesn't have any luck,' she whispered, 'or he'll have Myrddin and everyone else organised into a full-scale dig.'

So it was to look for non-existent bones that we set out for the Lake. I did attempt on the way to tell Byron about the legend, but after listening distractedly for a few moments, he spent the rest of our climb describing some giant toads he'd once encountered.

By the time we got to the Lake I was well up on the life style of outsize toads and was despairing of any hope that the Lake would compete in interest. The sight of it was a shock. The drought had shrunk it away from the edges so that it looked like a diminishing African water hole. Where there had been water lapping, there was now a beach of stones and rocks, and the peat beds were standing high and dry.

Byron cast a clinical eye over the remains of the Lake and then turned an enchanted gaze on the peat beds. 'You know,' he said, 'it's just occurred to me that we could find some flints here. All that rubbish about the legend probably means people lived or hunted up here once. If we're really lucky we might find a proper arrowhead. You do know what I'm talking about, don't you?'

I knew what he was talking about all right. Something I'd always longed to find, and had spent hours searching for whenever I was in the kind of district where they were usually seen, was one of the little 'elf arrows' as people used to call them in the days before the anthropologists and archaeologists put us right as to their Stone Age origins. No matter how much I'd looked, I'd never found so much as a flint chipped by hand, and I was rather amused at Byron's optimism because this is not a flint area and, to my knowledge, nothing like that had ever been found on the mountain.

I tried to explain all this to Byron, but he was already on his knees, probing gently into the peat. I also tried to explain that we weren't supposed to walk so near the Lake anyway, in view of it being a water supply. I toyed with the idea of removing myself to a safe distance and pretending I'd never seen Byron in my life before if anyone came, but Mrs P's firm instructions not to let him out of my sight kept me havering like an anxious hen on the edge of the Lake.

Byron, disgusted that I hadn't joined him at the peat bed, called out that the least I could do was to have a look amongst the stones. Keeping one eye out for trouble, I did as I was told, quartering backwards and forwards over the ground and wishing something would turn up so that Byron would forget about his bones and flints and we could go home. Finally, seeing that he was too absorbed to notice what I was doing, I judged it safe to sit down and contemplate the Lake in peace.

Before I sat, I looked carefully at the stones at my feet, just in case I'd missed something, and then fell to gazing out across the shrinking surface of the Lake. For once it was quite still and those strange, fluttering eddies were absent. High above, on the rocks of the cliff, tiny distant sheep ventured out after the few bits of lichen and grass still clinging to them. The lonely mew of a buzzard came echoing down and somewhere a lark was shouting its head off. For the first time in months I felt free of all the nagging doubts and worries; in that timeless place they all seemed so trivial and unimportant.

What happened next was like an action replay in slow motion. The still surface of the Lake rippled from end to end as a current of air swept it; there was a soft, swishing noise as the water at my feet formed a tiny wave and, as it receded, there remained, glistening wet and balanced on top of one of the stones, the most perfect, white, flint arrowhead.

No matter what Byron said about coincidence and 'not looking properly in the first place', I still think of the tiny work of art as a gift, a gift from the past. No-one else had touched it in all those thousands of years, except the craftsman who had made it and repaired it and used it and finally lost it. He was a fact more wonderful than any legend, but perhaps he was also a clue to its origins. Had he come as part of a migratory band to hunt the red deer and the duck and the eels, or had he come there to worship his gods?

Perhaps one day someone will answer those questions. Meanwhile the finding of the arrowhead in so strange a way was like the toss of a coin for me. Sitting there by the Lake with my mind so clear, I'd been thinking that I simply had to make up my mind whether to struggle on with the farm or to go away forever. If I'd been looking for signs and symbols, here was one I could understand. To hell with the reasons; I'd stay anyway and learn, like that little hunter thousands of years ago, to live from day to day.

# Chapter 12

Looking back on it, that was a summer full of surprises, Byron's visit and the finding of prehistoric relics aside. For one thing the unicorn weathervane was unstuck at last by Robin Spedborough. He'd really come to scythe down the lawn which, before the drought took hold, had grown into a waist-high jungle because I still felt unable to cope with the Flymo, having a deep suspicion of any engine and in particular ones that have whirring blades run on petrol, which are liable to cut me to pieces or go bang.

As it happened, Robin didn't scythe the towering grass; he attacked it with a hand sickle and got the hedge and the nettles round the yard beaten into submission at the same time. For all of this he asked the ridiculous price of 50p an hour and, if it hadn't been for the fact that Robin had a dreadful disabling accident a year later, I doubt if I'd ever have faced up to the Flymo, which the Artist had persuaded me to buy and mercifully always used himself.

I've never been quite sure whether Mr Spedborough's real name is Robin, but that's what everyone calls him and it suits him very well: a small, chirpy man with a habit of cocking his head on one side just like the bird, and bright eyes always looking for something complicated to do. He was the only person I found in the district who remotely resembled that country archetype of the man who can turn his hand to anything. Although officially he earned his living as a peripatetic gardener, he always ended up by putting slates back on the roof, or unblocking the sink – or finally sorting out the unicorn.

The weathervane had been made with a light, hollow stem which in turn slotted over the fixed rod holding the arrow pointing north. The actual unicorn figure, weighted at its head, then swung round on the rod. Or it should have, but the Artist had neglected to grease the hollow stem before he put it in place and it had eventually rusted solid onto the rod, which was why the unicorn now resolutely pointed south.

Apart from the fact that it was no longer much use as a weathervane, I thought that the next time someone said, 'Oh look! Your unicorn's stuck', I'd brain them. Instead, if they looked fairly agile and had a head for heights, Mrs P pulled a sad face and got them to go up and see if they could unstick it. Most of them took up the challenge and, after a great deal of fussing with ladders and ropes and sharp instruments, mounted on high and bashed and pulled while Mrs P egged them on from ground level and looked suitably pained when they retired, defeated and mercifully silent.

Apart from a few near misses and the odd sprained wrist, we didn't have any casualties, but we did seem to lose a lot of regular visitors. This was no great sorrow, because at the time most of them were inspired by their armchair reading of various best-selling books on the simple life to come and tell us how to run the place and to express surprise and amazement at our lack of self-sufficiency as they departed back to their well appointed London homes. I was usually flattened physically and mentally by the time they left, having sat up most of the night listening to them and then whizzing around for an hour after they'd yawned and staggered off to bed, banking down fires, settling the dogs and generally clearing the decks so that all would be bright and cosy for the guests the next day. What hurt most was the patronising air with which they regarded me, still tired after getting up early and feeding the stock and carting in wood for

106

the fire and getting their breakfast – which they ate heartily
before going for a bracing ramble, while I spent the time
persuading the Rayburn to yield enough hot water for the baths
they'd want to sink into when they returned. Mrs P got her
revenge by waiting till I was out of the way and persuading them
to go up and sort the unicorn out.

In amongst all the 'freeloaders' as Mrs P called them, we did
however have a few friends we valued and it was getting more
and more difficult to keep them at ground level. We certainly
valued Robin Spedborough, but finally nothing could keep him
away from the unicorn. 'It needs a good paint,' he informed me,
squinting up at it against the sun.

'I know,' I said, squinting with him, 'but I'll have to get the
whole rod taken out and bring the lot down. There's no way to
get the unicorn off on its own.'

Robin gave a short, contemptuous snort and trotted off to get
the ladders. He clambered up them like a monkey and peered at
the obdurate weathervane. 'I was right,' he yelled down. 'It does
need a paint.'

'OK. Paint it if you must, but don't try to unstick it. You'll
never get it to move.' He did, though, after hours of struggling
with spanners and the bread knife and anything else we could
think of. That was when he nearly fell off, holding the released
unicorn aloft and trying to do a little jig on top of the ridge-
slates.

Later, when we'd all calmed down and Robin was a pint or two
of cider to the good, he announced that what the stem needed
was a plug of good old axle grease of which, to my knowledge,
I had none that wasn't actually in an axle. Robin disappeared,
frowning, to the barns and came back a while later with a
cobwebbed, dusty jar containing a truly loathsome mess which
he'd discovered lurking on a shelf in the old carriage shed,
hidden by a defunct birds' nest.

'They don't make it like this any more!' he cried
triumphantly.

'They must have had this grease before the war.' And he
yanked out a plug of the thick goo from the jar and filled the
stem with it. He then climbed back up the ladders and put the
unicorn, sparkling with gold paint once more, back on the rod
and spun it round and round.

I still have the jar of grease, and every year the unicorn comes down to be painted and have its stem topped up. And every year I think of Robin Spedborough dancing on the roof.

The goslings had by now quit the kitchen and Mrs P's loving care and, after a brief 'hardening off' period in an outdoor pen, had rejoined the rest of the flock. Mitzi, the mallard, disappeared for weeks and I'd long since given her up to the fox, but she came back with a violently active clutch of ducklings sired by the Khaki Campbell drake.

The lambs were growing fast and spent most of their time bashing each other up when they weren't pretending to be lost and causing me to wander frantically around the lanes, asking everyone if they'd seen them. They always reappeared innocently from somewhere in the wood to be reclaimed by desperate mothers with overloaded udders, just as I was about to go into overdrive and call out the cavalry – Myrddin and his dear old bitch, Collie – to mount a full-scale hunt on the mountain.

The only other young things on the place were about a dozen minute Barbu d'Anvers, or Belgian Bearded bantams, which emerged from their pigeon-sized eggs in glorious, iridescent colours, already equipped with an intelligence which convinced me once and for all that in the poultry world small is not only beautiful but very, very bright.

The parents of these exquisite chickens, Agatha and Poirot, had been given to me by a listener. It had been the year before and, as I was working in London, it had been arranged that she would bring the little hen and cock to Charing Cross station where I would collect them from her, rush across the city to Paddington and dispatch them by another train to Swansea where the Artist would take delivery. It was a drill we both knew fairly well by now; the men in the dispatch department at Paddington had got used to a frantic woman delivering squeaking boxes marked 'LIVESTOCK! URGENT! FRAGILE! THIS WAY UP!' and the porters at Swansea to the tall, thin man with a lurcher at his heels patiently meeting the London trains and going hopefully through the crates that had arrived.

Agatha and Poirot more than repaid all the trouble and expense we'd gone to and their tiny, alert faces, adorned with

108

tufts of feathers more like moustaches than beards, the little cock's silvery bell of a crow and the hen's cheerful cluck enchanted everyone who saw them. Now Agatha had laid thirteen eggs, sat on them, brought the whole lot out and didn't mind a bit when I borrowed each newly hatched chick to take and show to Mrs P who, in spite of all her poultry rearing, had never seen anything so exquisite.

If tomorrow I had to give up all but one breed of the many different types of chicken that wander about the place, I think it would be the little Barbs I'd keep. There might be a bit of trouble, though, deciding between them and the Pekins, who look like animated chrysanthemums. They too were a gift, this time from a gentleman who wrote and told me that he had to give up his flock but couldn't bear to sell them, and would I take them on? Although even then the place was getting crowded what with the Barbs, the Marans, the remains of our original stock of mixed bantams, some ancient Rhode Island Reds, a trio of Gold Laced Polands and some silkies, I couldn't resist the sad letter and agreed.

Somehow I'd expected the donor of this new batch of poultry to be a rather seedy, short person. It was a tall, elegant, world-weary man in cavalry twill trousers and a Shetland sweater who unwound himself from the smart new Datsun a few weeks later and unloaded boxes of irate little Pekins. Underneath their black  feathers their skin was yellow and, to complete the oriental image, as soon as they were released the cocks leapt up and down on their feathered feet like Japanese Samurai and fought everything, including the cats. The only one to stand up to them was Poirot, while Agatha and her brood dealt summarily with the Pekin hens, who'd already chased the big Marans out of the gate and sent the Polands screaming hysterically up the field.

Not that it's difficult to send the Polands into hysterics. Wonderful-looking creatures, each golden feather edged in black and their heads adorned with a great tuft of feathers which led a young friend of mine to call them 'hens with hats on', the Polands are completely brainless; so are the Araucanas I have now, which lay blue eggs but are as volatile and as emotional about everything as one might expect from their South American origins.

At the moment I can count eight different breeds of chickens if I look out of my window, all questing and picking and scratching their various ways over the fields, adding vivid splashes of colour to the bleached winter grass. It's a sight that causes more serious poultry owners to raise their hands in horror, but it gives me infinite delight. Except at night, none of them is ever locked up unless I want to breed from her, when she goes into a special pen with the relevant cockerel until she's laid enough eggs and Goldie the silkie or her mad, black daughter, Matilda, is set to bring them out. For the rest of the year, the hens are pretty good about laying their rent in the poultry shed and do an invaluable job of cleaning up all the bugs around the place. I have one old boy of uncertain ancestry called the Grenadier who breaks up any fights, even quelling the aggressiveness of the warlike little Pekes.

Apart from feeding them, worming them or giving them a good dusting every now and again with louse powder, creosoting their perches and nest boxes and making sure they have clean litter, I more or less let the poultry get on with it. For anyone wanting to go in for serious egg production or breeding it's all quite hopelessly inadequate, but I wouldn't be without that colourful crew sauntering around the place or greeting me in a happy clucking bunch every time they see me. I'll even put up with remarks like the one Bertie Ellis made sourly: 'This place is like a zoo where nobody pays to look.'

I'd got to know Bertie and his wife Sara fairly well since the fiasco with Doli: Sara because we shared an interest in hens and goats and Bertie because of many things like overdrafts and mediaeval history, books in general and the better thriller writers in particular, good whisky and the sillier side of politics. Mrs P and Sara also got their heads together over astrology and whether or not the Chinese Year of the current animal had started yet, much to Bertie's disgust, who hooted the place down because his wife was reading Kahlil Gibran and yet would himself compose poems in Tolkien Elvish if he was drunk enough. Apart from anything, though, Bertie was a brilliant vet and Sara a perfect, knowledgeable assistant.

In those days, because of his dalliance with farming, Bertie's practice was in its infancy and every call prized for its contribution towards reducing the Ellis overdraft. Still, he took it upon himself to give me a crash course in doing my own routine veterinary work so that only in the more serious cases would I need to get expensive professional help. Bertie showed me how to give injections, take temperatures and dose everything from the cats to the goats properly; he spent untold hours explaining basic anatomy and the various symptoms of common diseases and deficiencies, and above all he dispelled a great deal of the mystery of the veterinary world. He made sure I had an armoury of things like worming doses, a few essential drugs, needles and syringes, a proper first-aid cupboard and temperature charts for the various animals, and left me with the basic maxim: 'Prevention is better than a bloody great drama in the middle of the night!'

Not, as I was to find out, that he minded coming out in the middle of the night if you needed him, the battered red Mini rattling furiously across the wild stretches of the Epynt mountain in all kinds of weather, the full twenty-five miles from his farm. What he did seem to mind was being on time for some routine check or other less urgent appointment. After waiting in for him all day, unable to go out or get on with any proper work in case he turned up, I was often on the point of homicide by the time Bertie did casually saunter in. He never offered any excuses but coolly distracted my wrath with some vital piece of news about what he'd said to the current bank manager, or the latest cricket score, or how his dog, Odin, had pinched their last loaf of bread whole and Sara had half murdered him with the frying pan, or how Bert, his stallion, had sat on the fence again and let all the sheep into his neighbour's hay field.

Bert was a massive Cleveland bay which Bertie had bought as a foal after he'd won his class at the Royal Show. 'I was just standing there minding my own business when this woman brought young Bert back all tarted up in his rosette and I said as a joke, ''I'll give you a hundred quid for him'' and she said ''Done!''. So I mean, what could I do? I just borrowed the money from Sara and brought Bert home.' Since when, Bert had grown into an amiable giant, happily unaware of his own strength so that when he leaned on one of Bertie's precarious fences, they simply crumpled to the ground. By now he was standing at stud and several good thoroughbred mares had been brought to him in the hopes of producing hunter foals.

'The trouble with Bert, though,' declared his owner, 'is that

111

he's not really interested in sex. He has to think about it for a very long time, even when the mares are desperate, so I've usually got to have them to stay and to run out with him. Actually, Sara was leading him the other day when he made up his mind about a little filly we'd had here for ages, and before she knew where she was poor old Sara was in on the act too. Could have been very nasty if she hadn't let him go just in time!'

A few days after this conversation, a smart Land Rover and box drove into the yard and Bertie hailed me. 'Come to collect Doli! If you don't get her in foal soon it'll be too late, so I've borrowed this horse box and told Bert to stand by for action. You can come too, because Sara's expecting you for supper.'

She wasn't, of course, any more than I was expecting to drop everything and run, but when Bertie Ellis is in an organising mood you don't argue. Besides which, Doli was in season and I'd been unable to find a stud where they'd let her run out with the stallion. That was necessary with her because, like Bert, she took a while to make up her mind, as we'd discovered to our cost when the premium stallion came to cover her in hand and nearly got murdered.

I was still keeping the horses in out of the heat and away from the flies during the day, so while I rushed in to tell Mrs P what was happening and to change my jeans for a slightly less mucky pair, Bertie loaded Doli up and started the Land Rover again. 'Where's your tape recorder?' he bellowed over the engine as I was dealing with the gate. 'Go on, go back and get it. If Bert's in a virile mood, you might record the whole thing for the panting millions.'

I hesitated, because the last time I'd recorded a stallion serving a mare, I'd nearly got kicked to death. But as the intimate details of Doli's love life had been of absorbing interest to my listeners in the past and I had another country edition of 'You and Yours' coming up, I went back dutifully to get the equipment.

The single-track road that leads out of the valley is fraught with the kind of bends which nervous drivers like me negotiate in first gear, honking the horn like lunatics. Bertie charged them all remorselessly while I clung on to my precious equipment and my nerves. What Doli was doing in the box I couldn't bear to imagine, but Doli was passing the perilous miles in untying her headrope and turning her massive self round the other way, all

112

the better to admire the scenery and any stray stallions she might see.

When we stopped at last in answer to my frantic bleats of fright, she was standing with her great head dreamily propped up on the tailboard, quivering her big lips and gazing softly at the far horizon. We left her like that and continued on our way as the sun sank lower and lit the bleak moorland of the Epynt with rose and gold. The red flag was up, which is supposed to mean the army are carrying out dangerous exercises, but Bertie scoffed at it and kept on driving.

The Epynt was once occupied by many small farms and a whole community until, during the last war, the military took it over. Sometimes, if the wind is in the right direction, Mrs P and I can hear the dull thud of explosives, distant and menacing. I'd never been across the Epynt before and, in spite of Bertie's coolness and his assurance that they'd have closed the road completely if they'd really meant business, I was expecting any minute to be blown sky-high or arrested or something. Whether to stop me from leaping out, or whether the lonely, enigmatic landscape inspired him, I'm not certain, but Bertie spent the rest of the journey sketching out a thriller he was dreaming up, set on the Epynt.

'Can't you just see it?' he was explaining. 'There's you and me and half a ton of horse, driving along minding our own business, when this character staggers out of the grass and chokes, "Help me! I'm from MI5 and They're after me!" What would you do? Pretend to believe him and then shove him in the back with Doli and cart his mangled remains off to the nearest police? Or would you uncouple the Land Rover and help him dash across the country, get involved and end up shot? What would you do?'

I knew I'd die of fright and that's what I've done nearly every time I've driven that way alone at night, thanks to the memory of Bertie's story which got more and more sinister and gory as the miles went by. Myrddin hasn't helped much either, because on the several occasions I've been over the Epynt with him, he's pointed out all the places he's seen rally-drivers get into fearful smashes. But then you can drive almost anywhere in Wales with Myrddin and he'll do the same thing – I've often told him he ought to do a rally smash map.

As the Land Rover stormed onto the track leading to Bertie's farm, the sun was in its last throes and imparted a luminosity to the flat plain rimmed by hills half seen against the light. We stopped at the farmhouse to collect Sara and drove on down to a field where a tall stallion was calmly walking away from a fence which was slowly sinking to the ground while a small group of mares looked on admiringly.

'Now,' said Bertie, 'don't expect him to behave like those hot-blooded thoroughbreds who come and jump on straight-away. Come on, Bert! Got a really big woman for you this time.'

Bert regarded his owner sheepishly and then the lovelight glinted in his eye as he caught sight of Doli's massive flanks. Doli, who'd been unloaded with the greatest amount of drama, stood coolly observing Bert in return. She lifted her tail, peed and then swore at a delicate little mare who'd followed Bert up the field. The little mare retired and Bert continued to stare enchanted, while Doli tossed her head and waited for him to come closer so that she could aim a loving kick. Bert snorted and wandered off in the opposite direction. Doli, not used to having her men give up so easily, stood appalled.

'Saturday night at the Palais de Danse,' Bertie declared.

For the next fifteen minutes the stallion played it very cool indeed. He pottered back to see how his fence demolition was getting on, had a long and thoughtful investigation of a stranded bumble bee, munched a bit of grass, had a few words with one of his other mares, yawned, accepted a lump of sugar from Sara and ignored Doli completely.

'How much longer is this going on for?' I asked.

'I told you, it's like Saturday night at the local hop. One of 'em'll give in soon. And I'll bet you it's Doli. Hullo, here we go!'

Doli trotted up to Bert and nudged him hard. The stallion turned, gave her a calculating look and then, working the grass in his jaws to one side, lumbered up onto her back and served her with a loud, lingering snort.

'God!' crowed Bertie. 'She was desperate! The fee for that little bit of footwork, by the way, is twenty quid, but it's no foal, no fee and I think you ought to leave her here for a bit anyway, just in case she cycles again.'

No foal, no fee is a good way of getting your mare served. In some cases it means just what it says: no live, kicking foal and you

114

don't pay the stud fee. Sometimes you pay the fee and if there's no foal you get a return of service. In some cases you pay whatever the outcome, but that's usually at a stud where the stallion is very well-proven and where the mares accepted are carefully selected for quality and quantity so that he isn't unduly overworked. In fact Bert himself (known by his much grander, registered name) is standing at such a stud now and his fee is a great deal more than twenty pounds. That year, however, he was unproven as to both his fertility and the quality of his foals, and in any case I rather think Bertie was just letting him have a few mares to keep them both amused. To be honest, I suspected that Bertie's whole farming enterprise had been undertaken as a vast playground for him to try out his pet theories: like the possibility of indoor housing for sheep, an idea which was only just beginning to be considered here, or the trout lake he was setting up, to the great interest of all the local poachers.

As for the farmhouse and buildings, here Bertie was really letting his other side have full scope. Before he was a vet he had been an engineer, and he was employing those talents with his usual panache in making the old, tottering house habitable, while Sara had to run about with wheelbarrows of cement and later try to disguise Bertie's mistakes with vast quantities of plaster and emulsion paint. She also suffered the inconvenience of assorted odd-job men, shanghai'ed by Bertie from the dole queue, the impossibility of trying to make meals on a cooker even more evil minded than my own, and Odin.

Odin had ruled Bertie's recent bachelor household in style. He'd stolen his food, terrorised the few clients who braved the muddy entrance to the surgery and taken the passenger seat of the car as a right, until Sara came to wage war with frying pans and the stoutest of Bertie's veterinary reference books on the monstrously large English pointer.

The only other indoor member of the household was a big black cat called 'Working Class', who had knocked down all the tea towels from the front of the cooker and was reclining on them in state as we all came back from the Doli and Bert encounter for a hastily improvised meal of scrambled eggs and the eternal mushrooms. What with all Bertie's plans, the Ellis economy was more than reduced and Sara's invariable rejoinder to her husband's hearty demands as to what was for dinner was 'We *have* eggs' – a catchphrase which lingers to this day when my own larder is bare.

If Bertie's building eccentricities and her constant battles with his animals caused Sara to threaten to leave Bertie at least once a day, she got her own back with her goats. They effectively filled any gaps in normality left by Bert, Odin, Working Class and the gang of depraved sheep. Sara's goats ate the seats on Bertie's Mini, ruined what was left of the ancient cars he'd been restoring, invaded his surgery and, when bored with home amusements, took advantage of Bert's fence wrecking to go and pull somebody else's place apart, thus putting the very last strain on Bertie's relations with his neighbours. Which was why, if I mentioned my own goat problems, Bertie's first suggestion was to have them put down as soon as possible, offering with a longing look in his eye to come and do it for me free of charge. It always amuses me these days, when he is the object of much adulation by a large, far-flung clientele, to hear goat owners rave about Bertie as one of the few vets who really seems to take an interest in their goats and *understands*! He damned well ought to!

My own goats meanwhile had spent a fairly quiet summer. The heat sent them inside to laze around in the cool of their shed or to sit in the shade of the ash tree with little energy to do much except look at it. Goats, in spite of their reputation as animals of hot, dry climates, really don't like the direct sun too intense, and certainly the type of finely bred animals found in Britain today, with a large percentage of Swiss blood in them, are apt to get sunstroke.

The drought eventually broke on the very day that Robin Spedborough came to help me plug the pig-induced holes in the water tank properly. With the authorities muttering warnings about permanent damage to the national water levels and the appointment of a real live Minister of Drought, it seemed as if the obdurate sky would never have a cloud in it again, but Robin spotted one as we paused to see if the temporary plugs we'd made in the outside of the brick tank would hold.

'It's only a little cloud, Robin,' I said hopelessly as I went on counting the number of drops coming from the spring outlet – one every three seconds.

'Well then, it might have friends,' replied Robin cheerfully.

The cloud kept coming and, sure enough, behind it a few more tiny, dark puff-balls. Even so, when the first clap of thunder came only minutes later, it took us some time to understand. 'They're exploding over on the range. Sure to be,' said Robin, peering gloomily down into the tank again and catching a great drop of rain on his neck.

For the next few minutes we behaved as people everywhere must have done, leaping around like fools and holding up our faces to the glorious, wonderful stuff that was pouring out of the skies. Ungratefully, a few weeks later I was back to complaining again as I sloshed through the muddy yard and the rain we'd lacked for months all came down at once. The pond, which had dried and opened great cracks in its bed, was finally in business again and a party of gleeful ducks was fighting a rearguard action with the geese for its possession.

Doli came back from her extended honeymoon and bit and kicked Moelwyn who was pathetically glad to see her. Myrddin arrived to collect the ram lambs, who were so big that they were now lifting their mothers up into the air as they came to suckle.  The black ewes, he told me, were expected soon at a farm nearby to run with a new pedigree ram there, and Humble (or Fatty as he always called her) could run with his own Welsh ram.

That still left the goats' mating to be arranged. It was now almost eighteen months since I'd bought Dolores from Christine Palmer. During that time Christine had shown remarkable forbearance with my endless, trivial phone calls about goat management, so naturally I turned once more to her as the sharp autumn days drew in upon themselves and I knew that soon the goats would begin yelling their need for a mate.

Christine kept several stud males of various breeds including, on permanent loan, a magnificent British Toggenberg champion called Chessetts Concorde. I'd long since decided that my goats should go to Conky for mating, but the trouble was that Christine lived forty miles away and two return trips (I was sure I wouldn't be lucky enough for my perverse pair to come into season on the same day) did seem a bit excessive. Besides which, although the valley had rung with their deep, yodelling calls regularly every three weeks the year before when they were too young to go to stud, I still didn't feel confident enough to be sure when they were properly in season.

Some goats are very discreet about their cycling and actually come in for only a few hours, often in the middle of the night when everyone except the goat in question is asleep. Some goats are very obvious and yell hysterically, wag their tails seductively, try to entice the other females to jump on them and, if they won't, jump on them instead; others are very shy and don't make any fuss at all. Some goats get a very reddened vulva and a quite obvious discharge; others show barely any signs. Experienced, organised goatkeepers know to a second when and how their goats will be in season, but beginners often either miss them altogether or panic every time their goat bleats or wags its tail, and waste a great deal of their own and everyone else's time by rushing back and forth to the stud, only to have their goat calmly make fools of them.

As it happens, I needn't have worried about mine; every single one of them over the years has made the maximum amount of noise, fuss and tail wagging, and stays in season for the longest possible time. But I was not to know that then, so it was arranged that Dolores and Nana would stay over at the Palmers' place until they were both served.

Unable to countenance a forty mile journey with Nana and Dolores in the back of my decrepit Beetle, I persuaded a neighbour to take us in her equally decrepit but more spacious Land Rover. As it was, we had to tie all their moveable parts to something as the vehicle in question only had a canvas hood, which my two ladies would have found no trouble in demolishing if left free to do so. As always when I've given them a bad press, they travelled beautifully and, as we left them to settle down in their own special pen amidst Christine's calm, well organised goats, I was proud of their cool self-possession. Actually they were just casing the joint.

It was quite late that night when I got a frantic phone call from Christine Palmer who, along with the rest of the family, had just spent a terrifying hour endeavouring to recapture and restore her herd to sanity. It took me a while to get the gist of what she was saying.

'It was like a madhouse!' she cried. 'Somehow those two had got out of their own pen and over into the others and that started the whole lot off. There were goats jumping in and out of each other's pens, Dolores had chewed up all the hay nets and treed a couple of youngsters in a hay rack while she started on my best Anglo-Nubian's ears. Nana was flying along the top of the pens and jumping down on the backs of the rest and one of my Saanens has gone crazy! And' – she paused dramatically – 'as if that wasn't enough, while we were getting them all back to normal, Dolores ate my headscarf, right off my hair! Oh, and I had a visitor just after you left. She had a very smart new raincoat on and while she was talking to Dolores, the monster ate the belt of the coat. The poor woman was furious!'

I immediately offered to come and take my St Trinian's pair away, but Christine told me not to bother. 'It's all right,' she sighed wearily. 'I've put them in a shed away from the rest. It's got a wooden hay rack and a strong lock on the door. Besides which, I think Nana is coming into season, so with any luck, Dolores will too and then you can come and collect them in a day or so.'

Ten days later Dolores was still calmly virginal, although Nana had indeed come into season and been served by Conky on the morning after the punch-up in the goat house. My constant phone calls about Dolores began to get on Christine's nerves until at last she said she'd ring me if there was any news.

The bell of the phone shrilled loudly early one morning and this time Christine sounded past caring. 'You'll be delighted to know,' she said, carefully choosing her words, 'that Dolores has been served. Conky is exhausted, and so am I. The rest of the place is in an uproar, but Dolores is waltzing around asking for more and if you don't come and get her soon, I refuse to be responsible for her continued welfare.'

There was a long pause, and I waited apprehensively for the rest of the story. It was not a pretty one. Dolores, having been closely observed by the whole Palmer family for the past ten days, had chosen to come into season at some very early hour in the morning when everyone, including the rest of the goats, was asleep. Being Dolores, she wasn't going to wait till somebody got up, so she simply chewed through one of the wooden sides of the shed and found her way round to the pen of a very ancient Saanen. Now this old boy should have been retired a couple of years before, but he was such a good animal, and his offspring of such superb quality, that he was kept on and allowed to serve just a few select females each season. Because of his age it took him

119

a very long time to work up enough enthusiasm for his brides, and owners bringing their goats to him were resigned to having a long wait. By-passing several young and eager males, including Conky himself, it was this old patriarch whom Dolores had chosen to torment. How long she'd been dancing round in front of his pen and trying to get into him Christine didn't know, but by the time she emerged from the house, the poor old Saanen was in a terrible state.

'I thought he'd have a heart attack,' Christine concluded. 'I had a dreadful job to get Dolores away and leave her with Conky. Then, when I finally got back to them, Conky was stretched out exhausted on the floor and Dolores was trying to make him get up again!'

'What about the old Saanen?' I enquired anxiously. 'Was he all right?'

Christine giggled. 'Oh yes! It just so happened that one of his own females was due this morning. Her owners couldn't believe it – the old boy hopped up and did the job in record time. He's been sleeping ever since!'

It says much for Christine Palmer's fortitude that a couple of years later she had five of my goats to stay, but by then I'd learnt a lot more about goatkeeping and, more significantly, so had the goats. But that was all in the future and meanwhile a pair of extremely smug animals returned home. Even Mrs P admitted that things had been pretty dull without them.

# Chapter 13

Long shadowed autumn finally shook itself off in one almighty gale that sent dry leaves scratching down the chimney and twigs to rattle on the slates, while Mrs P and I retreated choking from the kitchen as smoke from the Rayburn flue blew straight back down and fine soot spread evilly over everything.

We'd both grown to hate that Rayburn over the past year, and only the return of the really cold weather induced me to light it again. During the summer we'd cooked on the very same Baby Belling I'd bought for £3 at that original auction sale. We relied for hot water on a little electric device over the kitchen sink and a similar one for the shower in the bathroom, glad for a few months to be free of the tyranny of coaxing the Rayburn to light.

Not that it was the fault of the Rayburn itself which, when the wind wasn't gusting at the back of the house, did supply us with a lot of scalding hot water, cooked the dinner, sent enough warmth up into the airing cupboard to dry our clothes and took the biting chill off the stone floors. The problem was that the only place to put the kitchen had been in the narrow lean-to which someone had added to the back of the house long, long ago. One end of this lean-to had served as a dairy and pig salting room, and that was where my kitchen was. Of course there was no fireplace to build the Rayburn into, so it just squatted there with a long, cast-iron pipe soaring straight up through the ceiling and the slates above. By rights it should have soared even higher and cleared the main roof, but the position of the lean-to made this impossible. So, when the roaring southwesterlies hit the back of the roof, they also sent the fumes from the Rayburn back down into the kitchen. The Artist and I had tried various pots to go on top of the flue, but then the wretched thing didn't draw at all. Finally we'd left it open to the skies and when those skies were full of rain, a large part of the kitchen was full of it too.

The only coal that this flue will tolerate for any length of time and allow the Rayburn to stay alight is the most expensive stuff on the market. It's made of pressed coal-dust mixed with some unspeakably foul-smelling stuff, and the soot from it is the finest of dust which creeps into every possible cranny, invades the cupboards and settles on the creeping tide of debris which I always seem to be running away from whether in kitchen, bedroom, living room or office.

Now, after years of trial and error and much expense, I've found that unless the wind is really bloody-minded, a simple 'Chinese hat' type of cap on the flue does work quite well and my continued war with the Rayburn is going through a period of relative truce. In those days, however, a great deal of my time was spent cleaning it, lighting it, cursing it, rushing outside to see if the smoke was actually going up instead of down and more often than not retreating from the malevolent fumes and sooty water.

If it hadn't been for the big open fire in the front room, there were times when life would have been very bleak. That hadn't been visible when we first moved in, hidden as it was by the red-tiled grate which was cheerful and colourful in itself but even more complex to deal with than the Rayburn. A few hefty blows from the builder's sledge-hammer and the laborious removal of a large quantity of red glazed bricks had revealed not only a vast oak beam and a great open fireplace, but also a neat bread oven, with its iron door intact, set into the stones of one wall. The chimney was enormous and I could sit on the stone seat at the side of the fire and gaze up at the stars and the thick encrustations of tar which generations of fire makers had left behind them. Sometimes the pigeons sat warming their behinds on the rim of the chimney, calling hopefully down to me if I was a bit late in feeding them.

With a touching faith in modern technology, the Artist arranged for a delightful gentleman from Carmarthen to come and sweep the chimney. He arrived, cheerfully hung a black curtain from the beam and then poked the nozzle of his electric sweeper up the chimney. Half an hour later he had collected a suspiciously small amount of soot and £5 for his trouble. The Artist spent the rest of the day hacking at the undisturbed crusts of tar and soot and I wheeled three barrow loads of it away to fill in a hole in the yard.

The next chimney sweep assured the public in his advert in the local paper that he would both brush and electrically sweep all sizes of chimneys – 'Distance No Object'. It took him a great deal of time and about four irate phone calls en route to find the farm, and he arrived in a tiny three-wheeler car in spite of his six foot of wandering blubber. He was still complaining about the mileage and time when he came into the room I'd cleared of furniture to make his work easier. He stood at the door aghast. 'You'll never be expecting me to sweep that!' he declared.

'No,' I snapped back, 'I don't think I'll ever expect anyone else but me to sweep it again.'

The sweep left in a storming rage which was a little less impressive when he nearly overturned the three-wheeler getting into it. I went back inside and donned a pair of sunglasses, an old artist's smock and a shower cap, climbed up the inside of the chimney on the loft ladder and attacked the tar with a hoe. And don't tell me that in the old days they did it with a holly bush or a goose. Not even the prickliest of holly bushes or the most violent of geese would have dislodged that tar.

Whoever built the fireplace was realist enough to know that the chances of there being no wind were fairly remote, and designed the chimney to operate in a high gale. So now the open fire smokes on those days when there is no wind – enough to turn the once sparkling white walls a dull cream and to ensure that the ceiling is as well kippered as any pub's.

The main troubles with the open fire are its appetite for large, preferably dry logs, and a tendency to cook one side of you while the other side freezes. With the aid of a strategically placed whippet, the frozen side can be attended to easily, but the problem of getting enough wood occupies almost as much of my attention as the vagaries of the Rayburn.

Like most people who are no good at hitting a ball or reversing a car, I'm quite useless at aiming a hammer or an axe in the right direction. Over the years the animals have learned to make themselves rapidly scarce if I emerge with any kind of implement in my hand, knowing from painful experience that if I'm endeavouring to hit a nail on the head, the chances are that the hammer will fly out of my hand and hit somebody else's instead. Mrs P is equally terrified if she sees me with an axe, sure in her mind that the thing I'm most likely to chop with it is my own foot. Even if I do manage to get the axe into the wood, it takes me a good half an hour to get it out again.

C. S. Lewis once said, 'Nature laid on me from birth the utter incapacity to make anything.... With a tool or a bat or a gun, a sleeve-link or a corkscrew, I have always been unteachable.' That just about describes my own case, except that I would go further and claim that inanimate objects bear me a real grudge and will writhe and twist in my hand and attack me back. After a lot of near misses with the axe, I have now acquiesced to my mother's nerves and leave wood chopping to my betters. This usually means paying for a load. Sometimes Myrddin has come along with his chain-saw and cut up fallen trees from the wood or the great piles of driftwood I've dragged out of the river after a storm; sometimes I find wood which is old enough to break in half when I jump up and down on it, but for the rest it's a question of paying up.

When my visitors sit admiring the blazing logs and declaiming about the evocative smell of wood-smoke, I try not to dispel their illusions, having spent a whole day before they arrived hunting for logs so that I can nonchalantly throw them onto the fire while they're dreaming in front of it. And sometimes, just sometimes, I sit in front of that same fire myself and dream of a miraculous supply of really dry logs spirited into the house by magic every day, and of a fire that doesn't need coaxing into flame through exhausting sessions with the bellows and never, but never, smokes.

As winter came in that year, I didn't have too much time for dreaming. The Bank Holiday editions of 'You and Yours' were about the only broadcasting work I still had left and even they were to end because the programme was being taken off that slot. However, there was one final edition to do for Boxing Day and I set off at the beginning of December to start collecting interviews for it.

By now Gwyneth Griffiths had come into our lives. It seems impossible to imagine a time when she wasn't steaming up to the gate on her little motor bike, blonde hair in damp ringlets round her beaming face which, no matter how tired she is, always has a cheerful grin on it as she enquires in her quiet, lilting voice, 'Ah then, and how are *you?*'

Gwyneth and her husband, Eddie, are the present owners of the farm in the legend, and they farm 150 acres of land almost to the Lake itself. The house is a fascinating historical relic in its own right, being one of the few gentry houses in Wales to remain practically unchanged since the sixteenth century. Its tall chimneys, thick, rounded walls, sloping floors, big, panelled rooms and curious, stone, spiralled staircase are almost as the first owners must have seen them.

The first time the Artist and I went to see the famous house, Eddie, who is as extrovert as his wife is quiet and softly spoken, took us on a tour to see if we could feel the 'Presence' in one of the rooms. 'I've never felt it myself, mind,' he said proudly, 'but this group came from one of those psychical research places and they all swore it was definitely there.'

We looked at each other in amazement. One of the most progressive farmers in the district, who flips over the Channel to the Paris Agricultural Show without a thought every year; a passionate Welsh Nationalist; usually to be seen streaking past in his latest Alfa Romeo; and already a legend in the district himself for his prodigious capacity for alcohol and the fact that he's the fastest silage maker for miles – Eddie was not the person you'd expect to take an interest in the occult. In fact he hates anything like that and it was simply pride in his house and its connections with Welsh history that inspired him to play unpaid host to the 'Presence'. But it is Gwyneth who really loves the house almost to the point of obsession. She never tires of looking at it and I suspect that one of the reasons she agreed to come and feed the stock for me when I was away is that from the hill above you get a perfect view of her whole farm, nestling against the hill that hides it from the Lake.

With a husband like Eddie, it was easy at first to overlook Gwyneth, who always stayed quietly in the background, only every now and again throwing in a remark which, for those who cared to listen, summed up in a few wry, witty words everything we'd been arguing about. I'd seen her mainly at haymaking time, flinging up the bales of hay in a way that left me marvelling, and then leaping onto the huge orange tractor and driving calmly off in it as if it were a Mini.

It was only on the night when David Wade had played his tape of the legend that I'd really noticed her as a person. She'd come alone and, while everyone else was chattering in groups afterwards, Gwyneth had said very little, sitting apart in her own world with only her shining eyes and gentle smile giving any indication of how much the play had affected her. Later she shyly asked David and Pan to come and see the house for themselves and it was after their visit that David pointed out what a very rare and special person she was; David is a poet and recognises another one.

How Gwyneth came to feed the stock I've no idea, but I can first remember her doing it during that hot summer of drought when I'd had to go away for a few days. By the time I got back, Mrs P could endorse David's assessment of Gwyneth who, apart from looking after her two children, keeping the house beautifully, walking the hill to check the sheep and seeing to the cattle, spent long, exhausting hours in the blinding heat, picking up rocks after Eddie had ploughed the silage fields, and then came in to cook enormous meals for him. Somehow she'd also found time and energy to come twice a day to see to my stock and give Mrs P a hand. Even more marvellously, from our experience, she did so without trying to reorganise us or even implying any criticism of the chaos I usually live in.

So, as I left in early December for Dorset and Devon to do recordings for the Boxing Day programme, I went confidently, knowing that Gwyneth would be there to keep everything ticking over. I wished I had as much confidence in my car.

Ever since I learned to drive on a 1928 Chevrolet which cost me £25 and was the pride of my life with its big, yellow, wooden-spoke wheels, I've never owned a new car. A 1936 Austin for £10 and a succession of extremely tatty VW Beetles have made my driving career slow of progress and fraught with anxiety. The

Chev and the Austin I had by chance and because they cost so little. If I'd kept them, they'd now be worth quite a bit, but at the time they'd missed the scrapyard by minutes. The Beetles all began when a student friend gave me his mashed-up old banger which even the scrapyard wasn't interested in. Nonetheless, it got me all over Britain and started a habit I can't seem to lose. My current, bright green Beetle is twelve years old and is known locally as the 'Dai Special' in tribute to the previous owner who spent a couple of years doing it up. Even if it's now beginning to look a little frayed around the edges, apart from the Chev, it's the smartest car I've ever owned.

The Beetle which was to convey me to the West Country was a pale aquamarine, dotted and dashed with rust. It had a number plate beginning FFU and a six-volt electrical system. The number plate got me blaring horns and rude gestures from fellow motorists, and the six-volt system meant driving along at night with little more than a pair of candles in front to see by. Apart from making night driving hazardous, the electrics were inclined to sulk and not work, or work when they weren't supposed to and run the battery down, or just plain blow up. In an attempt to tame it, I'd had the electrical system 'gone over' just before I left on my journey, but the person who'd done the repairs had also seen fit to add some 'improvements' of his own devising. So I was more than apprehensive, for if there's one thing a Beetle resents, it's being 'improved'.

The journey itself was awful, with brilliant, blinding sunshine one moment and torrential rain the next. It was made more difficult by the fact that every time I switched the windscreen wipers on, the horn blew and wouldn't stop until I switched them off again. Now, as most Beetle owners will verify, not a great number of garages like dealing with these back-to-front cars, and it took me ages to find one sympathetic enough to untangle the mess of wires so that I could see where I was going without being deafened or prosecuted. As I left the garage, I noticed fearfully the engine's ominous reluctance to start at all.

I went on my way through several flooded roads and finally got hopelessly lost when the police diverted traffic away from one that was totally impassable. Offering up prayers and rash promises to assorted divinities, I finally switched on the lights and drove round the dark country lanes, passing through one

127

festive-looking village at least four times as I obeyed lonely signposts that I thought led to somewhere quite different. The rain had been replaced by a rolling sea fog as I pulled up at last in front of a solitary roadside cottage.

It took me a while to make out what the old man who answered the door was mumbling through his toothless gums, and then I didn't believe him. 'Up by the church, you say, and there's a lane that leads to the farm?' I queried incredulously. 'But I've just been past there, and there's nothing but a graveyard.'

'Ah,' he nodded, 'you go through graveyard and you'll come to 'en.' And he shut the door firmly against the fog.

I hurried back to the car, which had sputtered into silence and only deigned to start again after several tries. Turning it round, I drove back up the hill and swung it onto the narrow track that led through the graveyard. The fog lifted for one brief moment and the feeble headlights showed the track dropping away down into a valley. I judged that the farm I was making for must be somewhere below me, but there was no friendly wink of light, just an awful, empty blackness.

Relying on my usual conviction that everywhere eventually leads somewhere, I kept nosing the car down the track and on into unremitting darkness. Eventually I arrived at a gate and could just make out the dim shape of buildings beyond it, but of life or light there was no sign at all. I sat waiting, hoping that the sound of the car would yield some response from somewhere but as it didn't, I got out and stumbled through the gate towards the most substantial-looking building. By the dim flicker of the torch I could just make out stately columns beside the solid door. I paused before knocking, regretting suddenly all those misspent hours reading ghost stories in which the characters are lost in a fog in some remote part of the countryside, apply for succour to the nearest likely mansion, are welcomed by a curiously dressed butler and are never seen alive again.

If I'd been there solely on my own account, I'd have braved the track back up the hill and through the graveyard and gone gibbering to the nearest pub, but the reporter in me lifted the big brass knocker and banged the door with it. Hesitant, shuffling footsteps finally sounded far off and at last the door opened slowly to reveal an apprehensive lady holding a candle in one hand. A candle? Shuffling footsteps? The scenario was hideously familiar.

'Charles Pinney?' I croaked.

The lady peered at me round the candle and smiled. When she spoke, her voice was wonderfully normal. 'It's my son you want,' she said. 'He lives in the cottage over there.' She pointed behind me into the blackness.

Cowardice takes many forms and I know them all well. Anxious to appear in command of the situation, it never occurred to me to ask exactly where in the vast gloom the cottage might be. As the lady shut the door, I turned and stumbled off to grope my way round a fence that had no recognisable opening in it.

I was still fumbling around hopelessly when a voice hailed me and a tall figure holding a hurricane lantern aloft swam towards me, seeming to advance and retreat as the fog eddied around it and its pool of light.

'Hullo! Is that the BBC? I'd given you up hours ago. Can't you see the gate? Hang on, I'll come and get you. Would you believe it, we've just had a bloody blackout!'

The voice kept coming towards me, a young voice where I'd expected something rather older. Charles Pinney was setting up courses in handling heavy horses and somehow I'd expected him to be an old, gnarled countryman, not the vigorous, trendy, leather jacketed young man who ushered me down the path and into the modern kitchen of the cottage.

The blackout was still on when we went back outside to do our interview in the stables. Charles had let the horses out, thinking I wasn't coming, but a low whistle brought a great Shire stallion and a fat Ardennes mare out of the fog to trot straight into their stalls and stand there quietly, munching hay. It was a scene straight from a Herring painting: the big, patient horses in the old, panelled stable and the gentle glow of the oil-lamp streaming across the golden straw spread on the cobbled floor.

Although he was only in his twenties at the time and had recently come back to the family farm after working as an artist in London, Charles was already making a name for himself by importing the massively built Ardennes from the Continent. The reviving interest in working horses in Britain had shown up a lack of animals strong and docile enough for agricultural work, so Charles was filling the gap with these horses, shorter in the leg, strong on muscle and more like the ones you'd have seen in Britain before the tractor replaced them on the land.

Standing there in the old stable, I listened entranced while Charles explained all this and much more about the working horse. I'd heard a lot of it before and I've heard it many times since, but never so vividly or so clearly as I heard it that night. We were still talking heavy horses hours later, before the fire in the cottage. The electricity had come back, so we'd been able to cook a meal for ourselves and Charles' wife, who was in bed with 'flu. Finally, after a stiff whisky to round things off, I said, 'You'll never believe it, but I was scared stupid when I went to knock on your parents' door. All that dark gloom and the fog and coming through that graveyard and everything had me thinking I was coming to the original haunted house or something.' And I settled back to my whisky with a laugh.

Charles gave me a speculative glance. 'Well, you could say you were coming to the original haunted house in a manner of speaking,' he said at last, gravely. 'Didn't you know that that was the House of the Screaming Skull?'

I looked at him aghast. 'Oh God!' I exclaimed. 'Not the skull left over from the Civil War that refuses to be buried with the rest of itself in the graveyard and goes berserk if anyone tries?'

'Nope, not that one!' grinned Charles. 'This chap was an African chieftain who'd got captured as a slave and taken to the West Indies. For some reason or other the family who owned him brought him back to England with them but before he died, he made them swear to send his body back to his own country. Well, in those days they didn't take much notice of promises to a slave, so they just popped him into the old long box and buried him in the graveyard out there. All hell broke loose! Yells and screams and gruesome things happening to the gentry, not to mention the cook, so they went and got his head back and kept it in the house. Whenever they try to bury it, it makes a nuisance of itself again. My parents keep it in an old hat-box. It's a bit late now, but next time you come I'll get 'em to show it to you. More whisky?'

Twenty-four hours later I was in North Devon, the tapes in my luggage replete with all the interviews I'd done on the way, and this time going to a farm I knew well.

130

Bunksland Farm lies in a hollow. To get there you wind and twist around the Devon lanes. If, when you finally arrive, the milking machine is still thumping away, it's advisable to stay in the car until it stops and the last of the herd of small black cows have melted away from the yards as they wend their way into the rotary parlour and back to their sheds or, if you're there in summer, are led out to the fields again by a tall, bespectacled woman in old trousers and a tattered coat. Not till then will the latter turn and acknowledge you, frowning until she recognises you. If she does, her face will light up in welcome, but even so, you'll go on waiting until the cows are properly settled or the calves have been fed or the bull is attended to. Then and only then will you be invited into the kitchen, the kettle put on and mugs of coffee produced.

In Beryl Rutherford's world, the cattle come first and people can wait their turn. It doesn't pay, either, to be too worried about cobwebs and dust or the fact that if you leave the kitchen you'll perish of cold or, in summer, do battle with the nettles trying to climb in through the windows. Sometimes, when guilt drives me to try and tame the garden or shift the mess in my house from one place to another, I think longingly of Beryl and her single-mindedness. 'I haven't got time for all that,' she'll say airily. 'Too much to do outside.'

She solves the problem of keeping her huge open fireplace fed by ignoring it, even in the depths of winter. The only warmth in the big old farmhouse comes from an oil-fired Aga in the kitchen, turned down as low as possible to conserve costs. Yet I've never been there without the place being full of friends and admirers who put up with the Spartan conditions without a murmur. Like me, they've come to see Beryl and the cows, and the rest is insignificant.

Beryl herself, when you've got past the frown, can be charming: passionately interested in what you've been doing and hiding her own problems to listen to yours. The cows are enchanting, for Beryl owns probably the largest commercial herd of Dexters in Britain.

Dexters are supposed to be the smallest cattle in the world. Like so many breeds of farm animal, their past is clouded in hearsay and speculation, but latterly they did come from Ireland. There, on heath and hills, they were a strictly practical beef and dairy animal, but their small size made them popular in England to grace the parks of stately homes. Like the stately homes, however, the little Dexters declined in numbers and, having been bred even smaller by their aristocratic owners, began to have problems in breeding. If it hadn't been for a few dedicated farmers like Beryl Rutherford, Dexters might have been little more than a memory by now.

Once again, I had seen my first Dexter at Joe Henson's Farm Park in the Cotswolds, in the days when the Rare Breeds Survival Trust was in its infancy. A few weeks later, to my amazement, I saw three heifers advertised for sale in a farming magazine.

It was a Saturday morning, very early, and I was almost hysterical with impatience as I dialled the number given for enquiries. Before the startled woman who answered had time to say much, I'd arranged to go and see them in Hampshire that very day. I was in the hall of my little flat in London and for some reason there was an electrician sitting up a ladder, doing things to the wiring. Excitement bubbling over, I explained to him where I was going and why. 'They're miniature cattle!' I cried. 'They're very, very rare, but I'm going off to buy three of them. Isn't it marvellous?'

The electrician gazed down at me cynically. 'Yeh? Miniature cattle, you say.' He turned back to his work and I heard him mutter, 'Christ, now I've 'eard the bloody lot!'

It wasn't until later, when I was sitting tense with expectation on the train rushing to Hampshire, that it struck me that I hadn't mentioned that the cattle were to go to the country and not, as he probably supposed, to be put out to graze on the tiny patch of lawn belonging to the flat.

The three little heifers, Polly, Puff and Mary, were duly bought and dispatched to Wales where the Artist reported their dramatic arrival, their wild rush out of the cattle truck and down the hill and the fact that it was only with Myrddin's help he'd been able to catch them again, ever. Trying to catch them was about the sum total of our relationship with those three and, as they defied all attempts to get them in calf by artificial insemination, they were finally loaded up again and sent to Devon to run with Beryl Rutherford's bull.

When the Artist left, I decided to sell Polly and Puff to Joe Henson, but asked Beryl to hang on to Mary for me. She'd not only agreed to make sure that Mary got in calf, but suggested that she should stay in Devon till she had actually had it. And that was why I was stopping off at Beryl's farm on that raw December day, for Mary was due to calve at any moment and, if everything went according to plan, I'd be there when she did.

Beryl was just as quiveringly anxious for Mary to calve on that one night I could spend with her, and the two of us lingered around until it was obvious that Mary had no intention of doing any such thing. As we left her stall and picked our way across the yard, I noticed blearily that the weather had got very much colder.

The next morning the whole of England was in the grip of freezing fog, the milk lorry had only just made it along Beryl's frozen lane and her ancient tractor had gone on the blink.

'The lorry driver said the roads are like glass,' warned Beryl as she desperately tried to thaw a tap to get water flowing for the cattle. 'Do you have to get back today? Why not wait and see if it's better tomorrow? You never know, Mary might have her calf before you leave.'

A quick phone call reassured me that Mrs P and Gwyneth were coping well at home and that the roads in Wales were reported to be very dangerous. My mother thought I should stay over another night.

I can never look at Beryl's vast, prairie-like cattle sheds without a shudder to this day. The old tractor was normally used to push the slurry out into the pit, but for the greater part of that day, while Beryl and another friend rushed around the cattle and calves and tried everything short of witchcraft to get the obdurate old machine working, I pushed that slurry out by hand. Everything else except the bitter cold, the cattle calmly munching their silage or hay, the tiny Dexter calves gambolling on their beds of deep straw and Mary literally shrugging her shoulders every time I dared to leave my Augean task to see what she was up to, is blurred from memory. I went to bed feeling more defunct than the tractor.

Any hopes that the weather would improve were dashed by the forecast. It seemed that if I didn't get home soon, I could be trapped by worse things than freezing fog. In spite of the non-appearance of the milk lorry, which almost turned over this time, I decided the next day to make a break for it. It took half an hour to get the car to stagger into life and I left Beryl and her friend to cope alone with gallons of uncollected milk and the new sea of slurry.

If the lanes of that part of North Devon are treacherous at the best of times, the main roads covered with solid sheets of ice were a nightmare. As I passed through dim, petrified villages and towns, shadowy policemen were out at the junctions advising us through loud-hailers to get our cars off the road unless our journeys were vital. Visibility was down to feet rather than yards and the fog smeared the windscreen with muck which the wipers only made worse. The water in the plastic washer bottle was frozen solid, so every now and again I had to stop, keep one foot on the accelerator in case the engine died, and clear the windscreen by hand.

I left North Devon at about eleven in the morning. By half past five that night, I was somewhere approaching Brecon, weary to death by now with peering and praying and coaxing the car along the icy, deserted roads. Then the snow started, replacing the fog I'd left behind somewhere in Gwent. It was only a few flurries at first, but enough to clog the windscreen completely. A lay-by loomed up out of the dark. I pulled in, forgot to disengage the gears and stalled the car. Nothing, but nothing would get it to start again.

'Duw, Duw! We'd better get her into our car and warm her up. She's looking a bit blue to me. Come on, dear', and the strong arm of the law pulled me from the driving seat of the Beetle and hustled me across the lay-by to the patrol car.

It was about three hours later and, as the heaters were turned full on and warmth seeped back into me, I tried to mumble my explanations, to describe the isolated phone-box with the bent five pence slot, how I'd made one frantic call to the AA with my sole two pence piece, how I'd finally flagged down a solicitor in a racy sports car and asked him to ring my mother and the AA, and how I'd declined his offer of a lift in case they turned up at last.

'And they didn't,' said the big, fatherly sergeant. 'Right, we'll soon fix that. Dai, get on the radio to Cardiff. God, woman, you could have frozen to death if you'd stayed here all night.' He paused for a while and peered at the derelict Beetle in front. 'That number-plate – how much did you pay for it? I'll

134

bet it's worth more than the car.' He didn't believe me either when I disclaimed all responsibility for that FFU.

In the end I just went to sleep. When I woke, the lay-by seemed to be full of police and AA men and flashing lights and radios crackling on and off. I got out of the patrol car to stand guard over my luggage and the tape recorders which were strewn on the ground, when yet another vehicle swung off the road, its door opened practically before it stopped and a tall, thin figure leapt out at a run.

'Causing trouble again, is she?' cried a familiar voice. It was Myrddin, who'd left his supper and driven off to find me when Mrs P had rung him in despair. There was a blizzard forecast but he hadn't even stopped to consider his own peril as he raced across the mountain.

'Just as well you came,' nodded the AA man. 'This is the flattest battery I've seen for ages. We'll get the car started, but if she'd stopped again, you'd never have got her going. Will you drive behind her?'

It was a race against time as we dashed the twenty-five miles home, the outrunners of the blizzard snapping and snarling at our heels. I drove the Beetle in front, while Myrddin followed behind. As I reached the top of the hill above the farm, his headlights had disappeared and I thought he must have simply turned off into his own drive, knowing I was on the home stretch. As I turned round the last bend there was a light flashing in front of me to wave me through the open gate. Myrddin had taken a short cut, got down the hill before me and opened the way so that I wouldn't have to stop the car.

'All safe, Mrs P,' he announced as he ushered me into the cottage. 'Right, I'll go back and finish my supper now.' And he dashed back to his car and was gone before we could thank him.

About a week later, when the snow had gone, a large, flowery greetings telegram was delivered. It read: 'Mary delivered safely of a daughter. 45 lbs weight. Both doing well. Love, Beryl'. God knows what they thought at the Post Office.

# ═══ *Chapter 14* ═══

Bright images of that winter crowd away the mud and the screaming winds that must have been there. Instead I see whitewashed barns streaked with the pale sun which lit the snow lingering on the Fans; the sepia silhouettes of trees blurring sharp horizons; frost snapping and sparkling in the torchlight; the Griffiths' huge orange tractor spearing through the quiet snowflakes as Eddie and Gwyneth in gay bobble hats bring me a load of logs for a present on Christmas Eve; Myrddin hurrying up the yard, the fur-trimmed hood of his anorak framing his face and his arms full of a small fir tree; the great gilt mirror in the front room reflecting polished brass and the deep blue-green tinsel glittering in the firelight; candles bursting into flame at midnight to welcome the Christ Child; Mrs P sitting in the big wing chair, whippets at her feet and two cats on her knee, while I push cloves into oranges as I always do on Christmas Eve so that the sharp, fresh smell of them will fill the house next day and, dried, the pomanders will remind us of that Christmas all year long.

Bertie and Sara and Imogen and Gerald came to share New

Year's Eve with us and to drop spoonfuls of molten lead into a pan of cold water to tell our futures. Mrs P read everyone's cup and gave us all fabulous fortunes. Gerald and Bertie were sent to stand out in the cold, clutching lumps of coal and pieces of silver so that we could welcome them in again, dark haired and luck bringing, to first-foot it over the doorstep as the New Year chimed in on the radio. Imogen nearly broke her teeth on the only dud in the jar of pickled walnuts while all the dogs sat round adoring her; Gerald and Bertie, glasses of whisky in hand, desperately strove to top each other's outrageous stories; Sara sat on the floor with her long blonde hair gleaming in the firelight and Mrs P and I just enjoyed them all.

At some extraordinary hour the next morning, the other Griffiths, Cliff and Kathleen and Terry, came singing at our window to wish us well and began a ritual which Cliff and Terry have kept up to this day, feeling, I sometimes suspect, that if they don't, their own luck will fade.

January left us, with drifts of snowdrops across the lawn and the tips of awakening crocuses, to face treacherous, snarling February, and I began to have nightmares about lambing and kidding which were only a month away. I took McKenzie's *Goat Husbandry* up to bed with me at night and fell asleep trying to memorise all the various forms of malpresentation and what you did when they happened.

The sheep, when they weren't blaaring at me for more food, pottered about picking at the withered grass and looking fairly normal, if a trifle stouter. The goats, however, bulged ominously, especially Dolores, who looked as if she might have at least a quartet of kids on board. Even Nana declared a truce and became, if not affectionate, at least mildly friendly. She took to falling into deep, deep slumber, lying with her head stretched out and snoring gently until I had to shout in her ear to wake her for her feed. I found this complete lowering of her defences somehow touching and for a short while began to have hopes that her whole character might change with motherhood.

Since I had been told that exercise was essential for pregnant goats and they showed no inclination to exercise themselves, the dogs and I escorted Dolores and Nana down to the river meadow when the weather was kind, for them to browse on gorse and brambles. With the whippets leaping ahead through the dead bracken, the goats carefully picking their way along behind me and the two young ginger cats, Max and Muffin, chasing each other up the trees, we'd progress gradually along the river bank, then back across the meadow where I'd sit at last on the big rock under the holly tree and wait for the goats to catch up. Finally the whole cavalcade would strike up through the wood to the badger sett above the great oak.

Long ago, when we first came, the Artist had seen one of the badgers ambling quietly along in the dusk, but I have never seen one in the wood. People often ask me why I don't go and spy on them at night, but somehow I never have. At night the wood and the meadow belong to the wild again and my reward is to see next day where the badgers have rolled in the long grass, or a fox has been feeding off blackberries, or an owl has dropped its mutes at the foot of a tree. It's a foolish notion of mine not to intrude on the wildlife at night, because I also see signs of the poacher: a hazel rod cut for a gaff, a cigarette packet on the bank, heavy boot-prints in the soft sand. Still, poachers on the river aside, I like to think that for a few hours the animals who belong in the wood can go about their business undisturbed, and I only go to the setts to see if they're still occupied and above all not dug out. There is a particularly horrible lot of people who dig badgers out to bait them, illegal though it is. Once, they almost got past my guard in full daylight with their spades and their terriers and a van parked in a nearby field to which they retreated when they saw me rushing towards them with a pitchfork I just happened to have in my hand at the time. I'm glad they ran. I've a feeling I might have used the pitchfork to protect the badgers.

The foxes have formed a strange truce with me. Once, they took ducks and chickens from the yard in broad daylight, almost casually. Now, unless some obstinate creature defies all attempts to lock it up for the night, they leave me in peace. They only come into the yard to die. Three times this happened: a young cub in agony from strychnine, one from a shotgun wound and one crippled and old.

March came bullying its way through the valley and soon, just faintly, the single cry of a lamb could be heard and, if it was still, the grunting of a ewe in labour. Torches began to flicker across the fields at night and the chorus of lambs and ewes grew louder till the hills rang and echoed with the sound.

138

My own tiny flock of Black Welsh Mountain ewes had begun a few years before with four six-month-old lambs I'd bought from Arwyn Davies' nearby farm. The lambs had been hustled into a pen and Arwyn's brother, Cynog, who was a closer neighbour of ours, observed the Artist and me with deep amusement. He took great delight in explaining to me that any I didn't buy would be going off to market the next day. His psychology was perfect because, if I'd had the money, I'd have bought the whole pen.

'So come on, girls,' Cynog exhorted them. 'The ones with the best smiles will be going to a nice cosy home. For the others it's...', and he brought his hand meaningfully across his throat, 'first thing tomorrow.'

'But surely not,' I said to his brother. 'These are pedigree ewe lambs.'

Arwyn shrugged his shoulders. 'I've got all the ones I need for replacements,' he said. 'Anyway, there's not much call for these. I keep the flock on because my father liked the black sheep. They're well bred, mind.'

They were, too. The Davies' flock had been in the Black Welsh Mountain flock book for a long time and the Davies family had been one of the few to go on breeding them. Of course, I'd seen the breed for the first time at the Cotswold Farm Park again, for at that time it was still on the Rare Breeds List. It must have been early spring, because the lambs were newborn and their tight little curls were coal-black, whereas their mothers' fleeces had a browny tinge to them. My reaction to them startled even Joe Henson, who'd got used to my cackles of amazement at each new breed I saw. This time, though, it was because they seemed so familiar.

The very first animal in my life was a black lamb and that was surprising in Australia, where every black lamb in those days was immediately marked down for slaughter and never kept for the breeding flock. This lamb was an orphan and fortunately fell into the hands of my Uncle Stewart, who'd retained his abiding love of animals even in the hustling, heartless shearing shed atmosphere of a large station about three hundred miles from Sydney. He was there as part of his training as a wool-classer but when he saw the black lamb, a late arrival, he begged it from the station owner, hitched a ride to Sydney with the lamb stuck down his jacket, presented it to my mother 'for the baby' and hitched another ride back again. 'The baby' was parked out in its playpen, two years old, able to talk the ears off everyone but showing no sign whatsoever of moving off its fat behind, even to crawl. The playpen was there solely to impress visitors, for its occupant was not likely to stray. But the lamb was, so Mrs P plonked it down in the pen beside me while the family went into conference over its future.

The family was rather large. There was my mother, who'd left my father again, my grandfather and grandmother who owned the house, six of their currently unmated sons and daughters, my father's mother who was temporarily homeless and my father, who was likewise without a roof and borrowing a room. It was that kind of family. And there was me, spoilt rotten by the lot of them.

The conference on the lamb's future was heated. My father's mother firmly vetoed having 'that goat' (on the paternal side they've always been hopeless about animals) which might eat her garden, for Granny Mac took charge of any patch of earth she alighted on, no matter who it belonged to, and started growing things on it. My father sided with her and so my mother's family were all immediately in favour of the lamb. My grandfather, Pop, busy poring over the racing results, dismissed his household by announcing firmly, 'If the bloody baby wants a bloody lamb, she can bloody well have one', and that was the end of that.

Actually the 'bloody baby' wanted the lamb so much that when it got fed up with the confines of the playpen, nudged the gate open and wandered out to have a go at Granny Mac's fuchsias, she hauled her fat, wobbly person up by the bars and took her first steps after it. From that moment the lamb was treated like royalty, especially as it achieved the other impossibility of getting rid of Granny Mac, who departed with her fuchsias and her dignity.

The lamb went on gardening for a long time. The neighbours for streets around borrowed it to mow their lawns and at last, when it grew up, it went to an aunt who bred greyhounds on a few acres of land outside Sydney, where it kept the encroaching bush at bay and terrorised the dogs.

I'd forgotten all about the unorthodox companion of my playpen till the day I saw those black ewes cavorting about Joe

140

Henson's fields. I silently saluted Uncle Stewart and Pop and Granny Mac's fuchsias and decided then and there that if I was going to have sheep at all they'd have to be black. Instead of one black lamb, now I could have as many as I wanted. Well, three to be precise, that being the limit of my funds and the number the Artist had agreed, tentatively, to look after.

'The grass,' I had declaimed, 'needs something to keep it grazed down and the land needs something besides horses and goats.' And there we were to pick them out from the Talsarn flock, with Cynog along to see the fun.

Cynog had the farm whose land borders the rest of the fields which once belonged to my place. He'd already observed with a cynical eye our hopeless inadequacies and had been summoned on various occasions to sort out our panic-stricken encounters with the affairs of our livestock and to bale up the meagre amount of hay we'd grown with more fretting and forecasts and anticipation than he expended on all his thousands of bales. Now, he hopped over the pen and began chasing the lambs who'd remained huddled together apprehensively. As they leapt past us in demented flight, his brother pointed out the three he thought I should have.

'Ah, but if she takes that one, what about it's poor little twin?' cried Cynog, shaking his head sorrowfully. 'It'll be lonely, you know', and he fell to guffawing loudly.

I endeavoured to look hard and knowing as I stared at the sheep desperately milling back and forth before Cynog's intermittent whoops and shouts. Half an hour later we loaded up the three Arwyn had advised and the 'poor little twin', which was half the size of its sister and was missing most of its tail.

'You'll know *her* again when you see her, won't you?' hooted Cynog, and he still hooted whenever he saw her again himself. Which was not so terribly clever of him, because Duchess has proved to be one of the best buys I ever made. She's produced twelve good lambs for me, survived every vicissitude to which a sheep's life is subject and, because of her greed, has been invaluable in leading the rest of the flock where I want them to go. Her big, strong twin succumbed a bare few months after I got her. I don't know if it's a common thing, but I've noticed amongst my own animals that of a pair of twins, one is usually docile and easy-going, whilst the other is wild, intractable and

afflicted with what Myrddin calls 'one eye over the fence'. So it was with Duchess and her sister, Dulcie. Unfortunately for Dulcie, her panic reaction to the arrival of the post-lady Eileen (who in those days tramped thirteen miles up and down the steep hills and tracks to deliver the post and the local news) ended in a desperate charge straight into the only gate on the place which wouldn't yield to pressure, and she broke her neck. That left me with Dorcas and Dinah and Duchess.

This spring, I didn't know the exact dates when the three were due to lamb as they'd been back at the Davies' farm at tupping time. I stalked them to distraction and snatched as little sleep as possible. Eventually, in their own good time after a hundred false alarms, they dropped their lambs without any fuss while I hovered about to take them down to the looseboxes where I could keep an eye on them for the first twenty-four hours. I did most of this hovering sitting on a bale of straw in the hay shed. From there I could watch the field in front of it and one mild afternoon splintered by rain and sun, Mrs P joined me.

'Look,' she whispered in delight, 'there's a rainbow with its end right in the field.'

'And if you look a bit closer,' I whispered back, 'you'll see Dorcas is in labour up there.' As I was still speaking, Dorcas gave one final heave and her lamb slid out, right into the rainbow. It was a ewe lamb, the only one the black sheep produced that year. I have Rainbow still.

Now there was only Humble to lamb and it was becoming obvious that if she didn't do it soon she wouldn't be able to waddle around. Over the last couple of weeks she had grown into a vast, ponderous mass and everyone predicted that she must have triplets. Humble ignored the various bets and remarks and spent her days grabbing all the concentrates or parked on a molehill, chewing her cud. When, at long, long last, she popped out one average sized pink and white ewe lamb, her bulk was scarcely diminished at all. She used it to flatten any of the black lambs who came near her young Rosie, who was strictly forbidden to play with them. If Rosie rebelled, her mother sat on her till I came and rescued the lamb, often in the last stages of asphyxiation. All the lambs sat on their mothers' backs sometimes, but only Humble was wide enough actually to walk about with Rosie still slumbering on top of her.

142

The sole exception to Humble's ban on fraternisation was the goats, and the lamb was allowed to curl up beside them when they emerged into the sun to sit like beached whales on the young grass.

If lambing had been a bit haphazard, I did at least know the due dates for the goats, Dolores and Nana. In principle anyway, because The Book warned that although the average gestation period is 150 days, it can vary from goat to goat and sometimes it's less and sometimes it's more. Just to be on the safe side, I began panicking about two weeks in advance. Over and over again, I read the chapter with the 'Imminent signs of kidding' bit in it. I drove the goats mad by feeling their swelling udders and their bulging sides and poking my fingers into the base of their spines to see if the pelvic ligaments had softened. Eventually Nana, fed up with being roused from her sleep, bit me hard and even Dolores started to avoid me. Bertie Ellis and Christine Palmer got tired of the sound of my voice ringing up to say that one or other of the goats was looking Different and was this IT? Mrs P went back to chorusing 'Well, if it was a *human...*', and this time I actually took notice of her.

One night, about three days before she was really due, I happened to see Nana arch her back and give a small pained cry as she produced a long stream of pellets. 'Pressure on the bowel,' nodded Mrs P when I mentioned it. I went back outside and put Nana on her own in the disinfected loosebox. She immediately settled down and fell into a profound sleep, showing no sign whatsoever of going into labour.

The alarm didn't go off next morning and I slept till six, worn out with a night of delivering malformed, mispresented and anything but normal kids in my dreams. Leaping frantically across the yard in dressing gown and wellies, I paused in dread before the closed door of the loosebox where I'd put Nana. There was a very odd noise going on behind it, a kind of whickering mutter answered by a clear infant voice. I opened the door very slowly and there, sitting on the straw, limp with adoration, was Nana. Cavorting unsteadily in front of her was a tiny fawn and white creature which had obviously been washed and fed. Behind her was another slimy, brown shape, struggling to free itself of the muck still clinging to it, which Nana was doing her best to ignore.

In the subsequent struggle to get Nana to accept full responsibility for the second kid, it was obvious that her bloody-minded character had not been changed by motherhood one bit. It had merely been endorsed. I was prepared to forgive her, though, because both of her kids were females and, as I'd already been brainwashed into believing by every goat owner I spoke to, that was the most incredible beginner's luck.

Sadly, unless their breeding is good and they show great promise as future stud males, or you intend to rear them for meat yourself, the kindest thing is to put the billy kids down at birth. To give them away or sell them as pets is often to condemn them to a far worse fate. As the pretty, affectionate little kids grow into smelly, bossy, frustrated adults of great strength, the horror stories of cruelty and starvation begin. Not trusting myself to rear them for meat, the idea of having the male kids put down had been another of my nightmares but now, bless her, Nana had lifted that problem off my mind. Besides which, to have two of Conky's daughters was wonderful at a time when the goat world was enjoying something of a boom and I'd have no trouble selling them well if I didn't want to keep them.

All in all I began to feel that at last, what with Humble's little Rosie and young Rainbow to swell the breeding sheep flock and Nana's kids being female, things were beginning to improve. A few weeks after Christmas I'd had a tragic call from Beryl to say that Mary's heifer calf had died, to her vet's total mystification, and I'd had a return of that old sense of horror, of nothing going right, of fate being firmly turned against me.

It was with a heart full of love, then, that a few days after she'd kidded, I prepared myself to milk Nana for the first time. Togged up in a clinically clean overall, with a brand-new bucket freshly scoured out in one hand and in the other a pail full of warm water and a mild disinfectant for washing her udder, I set off for the cowshed. The floor of her stall had been scrubbed down and Nana temporarily distracted with a bucket of feed. I was looking forward to the great moment of getting our first home-produced milk.

An hour later, with both buckets rolling around somewhere at the other end of the shed, Nana spitting and swearing and my curses ringing out across the valley, I came back to Mrs P, who was waiting excitedly in the kitchen, with about a cupful of dirty milk to give to the dogs. They wouldn't drink it.

For the next few days Nana and I went through mutual purgatory as I struggled to get her milk from her and she struggled just as hard to hang on to it. In the bosom of her family her behaviour was equally determined. With her firstborn, Whacky, she was neurotically possessive, whilst the other, Little Nana, would have starved if I hadn't been around to see she got her fair share.

By now I was back to panic stations again on Dolores' behalf. This time I was far more anxious about her than about the kids she would produce. Her pickpocketing and bizarre eating habits aside, she was a lovely animal. Beautiful to look at with her long, graceful neck and huge eyes alight with intelligence and humour, she was as affectionate and companionable as a favourite dog. Her superior breeding had become more obvious as she'd grown up and already her udder promised to be perfectly formed and productive, whereas Nana's hung down like a pair of bananas.

Forewarned by Nana's early delivery, I watched Dolores carefully and, on the morning she was due, had already spent most of the night in her box. Spring had been banished again by a later fall of snow which was still fluttering gently down as I sat on a bale of straw to watch her. This time I was sure I'd have to face up to the miserable business of having the billy kids dispatched. It was unthinkable that I could have the same luck twice.

'But I hope she has at least one female,' I told Mrs P. 'I wish it had been Nana who had the males and Dolores the females so we could have a duplicate of her.'

'You never know,' said Mrs P. 'Once things start going right, they have an odd habit of staying that way.' She's right: disaster will follow disaster and good things come together, particularly with animals. It's one of the reasons, I'm sure, why our rural ancestors believed so firmly in the Evil Eye and in talismans for luck, and why superstition has lingered longer in country districts.

All the same, I sat on my bale of straw that morning without too much hope for a repeat of Nana's lucky draw, while Dolores dug holes. Most goats will paw at their bedding when they're about to kid and make sure it's the way they want it, but Dolores just decided to get rid of it altogether. She was determined, it seemed, to kid straight onto the concrete. As goats often stand up just at the moment of birth, and not wanting the kids brained before I'd even had a chance to check on their sex, I had a hectic time for about an hour, with Dolores shovelling straw all over me while I shovelled it back under her. Eventually she took time off from excavating to sit down and strain, got up again, chewed some hay, did a bit more shovelling and sat down. So it went on and on, till my nerves were raw.

A few times I did attempt to go away and leave her because The Book assured me that goats really prefer to be alone at this time. Every time she saw me sneaking off, however, Dolores cried piteously and once, when I'd sat down again, she ambled over to me, put one hoof right up on my shoulder, rubbed her head against mine and whickered gently in my ear.

From then on she seemed to put her mind to what she was doing, her straining bouts became more frequent and she lay between them with her head turned on her flank, swan-like in her beauty even then. Mrs P came to join me, snowflakes in her hair, and we sat silently, dry towels and warm water at the ready.

'Look,' whispered Mrs P, 'the birth sac!' Sure enough, there it was emerging at last with two dark little feet just visible inside it. Another heave, and a tiny nose could be seen swimming in the fluid. Finally, with a great cry, Dolores made a convulsive effort and the kid fell to the ground as she got to her feet. I was right: it would have been brained if I'd let Dolores have the bare concrete she preferred. She, meanwhile, had swung round, and only by leaping across the box did I stop her from biting into the kid itself, so keen was she to devour the membrane clinging to it. This instinct that leads the animal mother to free its young and to clean it up is in Dolores a kind of fanaticism, and for a while her newborn kids are in danger of their lives. I was just trying to prevent her from munching through this one's leg when she began to strain once more and seconds later another kid slid out onto the straw.

What with protecting her offspring from Dolores and only allowing her access to their less vulnerable parts and clearing the mucus from their faces myself, it was a while before I got round to finding out their sex. Fearfully I examined the first one, which was a deep, bitter-chocolate brown.

'It's a girl!' I cried. 'She's had one girl!' Then I turned to the other, which was a replica of Dolores herself, reddy gold with a dark stripe down its back. I sighed.

'Go on, have a look,' said a voice from the door.

I glanced up to see Gwyneth, summoned by Mrs P when it looked as if Dolores' protracted labour might prove difficult, beaming at me happily.

'Oh Gwyneth,' I said. 'Isn't it a shame? This one's so like her, but it *can't* be another female.'

I picked the kid up and as I turned, speechless, to the door, Gwyneth said sagely, 'There you are, then. Now you've got six goats. Just like that!'

If she'd known what that was to mean, she might not have laughed so long and so merrily.

## ═══ *Chapter 15* ═══

'Peritonitis,' said Bertie, 'that's what she's got. How she got it I can't say, but I do know the poor devil must be in a hell of a lot of pain. What do you want me to do about it?'

We were standing on the field behind the house in a howling southerly gale with the rain driving horizontally into our faces. Magnolia, the smaller of the pigs, was lying at our feet in an improvised shelter of sacks and straw, groaning miserably. There was nothing of the usual indignant fury which pigs can produce fortissimo when they even imagine they're being hurt. The noise Magnolia was making had all the desperation of sheer agony in it. Every moan she made cut straight through me, and I was almost frantic with horror and the urgent need to stop that appalling suffering.

I knelt down in the mud beside her and tried to will her torment and mine to an end. If only we could have left the nightmare we were in and go back just a few hours into a day that had been clear and luminous, full of that languid warmth which somehow reminds you of every spring you've ever known.

Even before I woke properly, the haunting breath of new life stirring outside had seeped into my little room at the top of the house and, as the mist climbed out of the valley, I'd got up to stand at the window and watch the first shaft of the sun spear its

148

way over the Fans and pierce the dark hollows with light. Down in the garden, the daffodils were expanding in the growing warmth; a female thrush grabbed triumphantly at a worm while her mate began singing fervently from his perch in the plum tree on the lawn. A rush of white wings swept past the window as the doves started their early morning flight which takes them in a wide arc round the valley and then in ever decreasing circles till they land on the barn roof and wait to be fed.

Over on the hay field, a small posse of black lambs was galloping purposefully up the hill. One of the ewes lifted her head, yodelled a warning at them over her shoulder and went on muttering to herself as she grazed. The lambs flicked their tails, leapt onto the ridge at the top of the field, raced round and round the crab apple tree, banging at each other, before they charged down the hill again, bumping into the ewe who was still grumbling at them.

A couple of sleepy grunts announced that Blossom and Magnolia were abroad and a pair of black and white shapes began moving beyond the hedge. A minute later, two questing snouts appeared through the bars of the gate leading into their field and then turned, snout to snout in consultation. When I looked again, a couple of ponderous behinds were ambling up the slope to where the pigs had been digging a hole for the past week. They'd lost the rings in their noses about a fortnight before and until now I hadn't really felt up to going through the whole screaming match of having them put in again.

It had taken the pigs a while to realise they could root once more and they'd experimented tentatively on several likely places on their field. As their noses had toughened up, they'd found one place full of bracken roots and started work properly. Blossom was only interested in tearing the roots out and munching them ecstatically, but Magnolia became carried away with the whole glorious adventure of digging for digging's sake. By now there was a very deep hole which the pigs could fit into quite easily and it was a bit startling, as work progressed, to see nothing of the pair of them but their gently undulating behinds stuck up in the air.

Certainly Cliff Griffiths had found it startling when he came hopping over the fence to see what new and amazing project I had on hand. Cliff had long since given up expecting anything normal to be happening on his old farm and in fact was now collecting a fund of stories based on my feeble but often dramatic efforts. I'd got used to him appearing from nowhere, preceded by a couple of lean collies who peed over everything in the yard while Cliff stood there, feet apart, easing the belt around his formidable girth, his cap pushed back over his few remaining strands of hair, and enquiring, 'Well then, what's new in farming?'

He wasn't often disappointed. If it wasn't hens with hats or spotted pigs or miniature cattle or a new and remarkable breed of goat I was thinking of getting, there was always a bit of a highly unlikely building or excavating work going on. But the sight of a huge hole halfway up the pig field stopped him in his tracks and when the pigs themselves emerged to greet him, I saw him retreat hastily over the fence. The two collies slunk after him, snarling. Pigs, as far as Cliff is concerned, are things you keep in the sty, as generations of pigs had been kept in his day at the farm, and eventually they end up decorating the beams of the living room in the shape of fat hams. They do not spend all day digging enormous holes in the hillside.

Actually I couldn't figure out why they were digging that hole either. Left to themselves, pigs without a ring in their noses will root a field into soft plough, shifting huge rocks to get at a special morsel they fancy, but they don't usually put all their energies into one hole full of nothing but dirt and stones. Whatever the attraction, they were at work remarkably early for them that morning and, although they did come hurtling down when they heard the bucket being emptied into their trough, after a brief but decisive skirmish which Blossom won, they gulped their breakfast and pottered straight back to their hole.

I thought at the time that it was unusual for Blossom to win the fight at the trough. Magnolia was smaller, but tougher and faster. That morning she'd seemed less anxious to get the best of the feed and had actually given way to Blossom once or twice. It  was a small thing but, as most good stockmen will tell you, any unusual behaviour of an animal is worth taking notice of and I've learned since to investigate things like that. But in those days absolutely everything the animals did struck me as pretty strange anyway and, what with the extraordinary racist behaviour of Humble with her lamb and the ridiculous performances I had to go through with the goats at milking time, a pig losing a few mouthfuls at the trough somehow didn't seem particularly important.

Besides which, I was run off my feet that morning checking on broody hens, chasing nesting pigeons out of the barn and intervening in a battle to the death between Humble and one of the black ewes who was damned if she'd let her lamb be warned off playing with young Rosie, and of course that marvellous milking routine took up half the morning anyway.

By now Nana was beginning to look like Gulliver captured in Lilliput with a cat's-cradle of baler twine attaching her horizontally, vertically, diagonally and in circles to the milking stand. I could just about find her udder in amongst all that lot, but I still only managed to extract a couple of pints of milk from it. Someone had told me to observe the kids and imitate them when I was milking, hold the teats gently but firmly and, with a steady pushing, pulling movement, squeeze the milk out. I observed like anything, did a ludicrous impersonation of Whacky and Little Nana and gave their wretched mother a bucket of feed to keep her happy. She'd have that finished practically before I got the bucket into position and stand there rolling her eye at me, spitting furiously and hanging on like grim death to her blasted milk.

Part of the trouble (apart from the fact that Nana simply didn't like me and probably never would) was that she was keeping all her milk for Whacky. Little Nana she tolerated, but it was for Whacky that everything in Nana's black heart and bulging udder was exclusively reserved.

Whacky was identical to her mother at the same age. To look at she reminded me of those horrible little girls with sausage ringlets, frilly pants under flounced skirts, ankle socks and tap shoes, a thoroughly boring, precocious character and escorted by a deluded mother determined to put her offspring on the stage. What Nana had in mind for Whacky was a really spectacular rebellion against the human race and I often caught her, ignoring the elegant and affectionate Little Nana, in one corner of the goat shed with Whacky, encouraging the little wretch to leap up the wall. By the time she was a fortnight old, Whacky could go halfway up the ten foot wall as if she was running on a horizontal surface, do a double twist at the top and land bang on one of the other kids, knocking it flat. When she wasn't terrorising the other goats, Whacky was having most of Nana's milk and I was beginning to hate both of them.

Dolores, on the other hand, simply adored me pretending to be a kid and spent our milking session cudding happily, occasionally nudging me to make sure I was comfortable and letting down every last ounce she could scrape up for me. The only trouble was that she didn't like her kids, Minnie and Loveday, imitating *me*, and flatly refused to feed them for more than five seconds on the internal clock all goats seem to have about them. So if I wanted to make sure that her kids got enough milk, I had to tie her up in the approved Lilliput style and bring the kids to her. All of which Dolores resented deeply and even today, years afterwards, she's only got to see me with a kid or lamb in my arms to take off, Whacky-fashion, up the goat shed wall.

One way and another, I was going right off everything and everyone who was engaged in rearing young and the poor dogs were in wholehearted agreement with me, having had their behinds nipped, pecked, rammed and otherwise assaulted by resentful parents. Their pathetic looks encouraged me at last to give in to the beckoning glamour of that lovely day and escape to the water meadow to see if the primroses were out yet.

They weren't quite, but the wood was starred with celandines and wood anemones and, if I looked carefully, the first of the violets were just visible. For once I'd left the goats behind and the dogs had followed me quietly enough for us not to disturb the heron standing on the river bank. Further along, a dipper bobbed and danced on a rock in midstream. I sat there peacefully, glorying in the day and watching the buzzards who nest in the huge oak tree at the top of the wood, while the other dogs nosed about in the grass and pretended they could hear moles somewhere under there. Merlin sat beside me for a while and then disappeared into the wood where he had a rabbit hole he was keeping an eye on.

We didn't get back to the farmyard until lunchtime and I noticed, as I glanced up the hill, that there was only one pig's behind working away at the famous hole. I wondered about it in passing, but the assorted maternity units claimed my attention until late afternoon, when a deep roar in the chimney

152

announced the arrival of a bullying southerly and the fire hissed as the rain the wind brought with it spat a few drops onto the burning logs. Outside, lambs were rushing down the slope to the hay barn, hens were flapping their way to cover, goats and kids were galloping for home, the ash tree was twisting and whining and the bright glory of the day was lost in a battalion of heavy rain marching across the hills.

By the time I got round to feeding the pigs, it must have been after six. Head down against the wind and blinding rain, I didn't wait for them to emerge from their shelter but banged on the roof as I put their feed into the trough and rushed back to the rest of the stock. With everything finally done and everyone battened down for the night, I struggled out to the pig field to see that all was well. The food was gone from the trough and I peered inside the shelter to say good-night and put in some fresh straw. Ever hopeful, Blossom leapt up and emerged to see if I'd brought any more food. Magnolia lay completely still and then, when I put my hand down to touch her, struggled to lift her head, groaned piteously and lay still again.

Crouched against the increasing fury of the wind and avoiding the lashing thorns of the overgrown hedge smashing down onto the shelter, I tried to get Magnolia onto her feet and out into the open where I could see her properly.

Try as I might, I couldn't fit inside the pig shelter well enough to examine her, so I went back for a bucket and tried to tempt her to stand. Fending off Blossom with one foot, I succeeded in getting Magnolia to totter outside. My plan was to entice her down into the stable, but she took a few steps and then sank down onto the mud. As I dropped the bucket, Blossom immediately gobbled up the feed and went back to bed. For a while I tried to drag Magnolia along, but as soon as I began to heave at her she screamed in agony.

With the gale shrieking its taunts at me, I dashed through the gate and down to the house, opened the front door, yelled at Mrs P to ring Bertie quickly, rushed on to the barn to collect first a pile of sacks and the tarpaulin and then carried bales of straw painfully through the mud and onto the field. I was so absorbed with inching sacks under the suffering pig and rigging up some kind of protection against the weather for her that I didn't hear Bertie's car arrive.

'What's up, then?' said his voice behind me. 'Mrs P said it was a matter of life and death but she didn't say whose life or whose death. I gathered both were yours from the sound of her.'

I bent down and uncovered Magnolia, who was now groaning deeply with every breath.

'Oh,' said Bertie, 'it's one of the Flower Pigs, is it?' For the next ten minutes he probed gently, listened to the pig's chest, heart and stomach and took her temperature. I held the torch steady while Bertie read what the thermometer registered. He frowned and then inserted it again. After the second reading his frown deepened.

'It's bloody low,' he muttered. 'I'll just feel her stomach again. All right, old girl, steady now.' But Magnolia heaved in agony as he touched her.

I stood gazing down at the tableau in the torchlight and for one moment it seemed as if even the roaring of the gale stopped. Bertie stood up and shook his head at me. 'What is it?' I asked at last.

'Peritonitis,' said Bertie, 'that's what she's got. How she got it I can't say, but I do know the poor devil must be in a hell of a lot of pain. What do you want me to do about it?'

'What are her chances?'

'Practically nil, especially with that low temperature. The kindest thing would be to put her out of her misery, but I know you're very fond of her and we could try to put up a fight. It'll have to be some fight though. We could get someone with a tractor to cart her to the stable, rig up some form of heating and you could nurse her day and night. But she'll be in dreadful pain most of the time and her chances of surviving are pretty hopeless. If it was anyone else, I wouldn't even discuss the possibility, but I often find that sheer love of an animal will work a miracle. Whatever you decide, you'd better do it quickly.'

Only once before had I been forced to take a quick decision between life and death for a loved animal, when I had a dog with tetanus. That decision has haunted me ever since, with endless wonderings as to whether the vet's diagnosis had been right after all. I'd always sworn I'd get a second opinion if the occasion arose again, but now was no time for second opinions and I came face to face with another realisation at that moment. It wasn't a simple matter of having a suffering pig destroyed that was

154

making me hesitate: was I not even more reluctant to kill off part of a legend I'd been building up, already seeing in my mind the vision of myself nursing the pig back to health and adding to that legend? When Magnolia died, half the pig story would die with her, a story that had begun with so much hope. With her death another link with a happier, more optimistic past would go.

I looked at Bertie standing there patiently while the rain dripped off his hat and onto his sideburns as he waited for my decision, standing as he must have done so often while the owner of an animal wrestled with their own pain as well as the animal's.

'Have you got your humane killer with you?'

'No, I haven't. I rushed off without it like a fool. All I could do is give her a strong anaesthetic.'

By now Magnolia was making almost as much noise as the gale swirling around us and, as I nodded, Bertie turned and ran for his car. He came back, drawing liquid from a bottle into a syringe as he hurried across the mud. He bent over to find the large vein in Magnolia's ear and then he looked up again.

'There's one thing you should think about. This will have to be a massive dose to kill her,' he said. 'That means the Hunt won't want her and you're going to have a huge carcass on your hands. I could go back and get the humane killer.'

I looked at him, appalled. 'For God's sake, Bertie, get on with it. I'll worry about that later. Just stop that poor beast suffering now!'

Bertie shrugged and bent over Magnolia again. I turned my back and faced into the gale, welcoming the lashing rain on my face and marvelling again how so much loveliness could turn so quickly into horror.

A couple of minutes later, I heard Bertie say, 'She's gone, I think', and I turned round again to see Magnolia lying peacefully at last. There was no sign of the torture she'd suffered; she lay as I'd seen her basking out in the sun so often, completely relaxed. But already the heavy rain and the mud we were churning up with our boots were marring that peace and it struck me that I did indeed have a very big carcass on my hands.

'Well,' said Bertie at last, 'any idea how you're going to bury her? You'll need a hell of a big hole, you know, and that's not easy to dig on this hunk of rock. Bloody hell!' he yelped.

Unnoticed by either of us, Blossom had finally emerged into the storm to see what we were doing to Magnolia. She'd seen Bertie, summed up the situation immediately and charged him purposefully in the rear.

Poor old Blossom, she had been completely forgotten in all the drama of the past hour and, as Bertie fended her off and I tried to stop her nosing frantically at Magnolia, it struck me that I would also have a very large, unhappy, live pig on my hands. For all their fights and rivalry, the two pigs had been devoted to each other, but a moping Blossom was another problem I'd have to face up to later. Meanwhile I couldn't leave her on the field with Magnolia.

'I'll take her down into the stable,' I shouted at Bertie as he capered about, trying to avoid Blossom's massive snout. 'As for the body, it might fit into that enormous hole the pair of them have been digging. I'll sort it out tomorrow.'

'Where is this hole?' Bertie yelled back.

'At the top of the field,' I called over my shoulder as I collected the bucket I'd flung down earlier, picked up a few stones to make it rattle and ran on in front of Blossom. She hesitated for a moment, snuffled thoughtfully at Magnolia once more and then trotted after me, her great ears flapping as she pursued the tantalising rattle ahead.

I sat with her for a while in the stable and then left her snuffling into a fresh pile of hay while I returned to the field to make sure that no animals could get at Magnolia overnight. There was nothing to be seen except a pile of trampled straw and sacks soaking up the mud.

Above the screaming of the wind, I heard a faint shout from the hill above. Flashing the torch ahead, I stumbled upwards. There was no sign of Bertie or the pig, but from somewhere at my feet came the sound of vehement cursing. I shone the light downwards and there, at the bottom of the great pig excavation, was Bertie, struggling to arrange Magnolia in tasteful repose while the mud slopped down on him and his boots fought off a rising tide of water. He looked up at me, his rain-smeared glasses refracting the light and making him look like an eccentric mole.

'Always fancied myself as a grave-digger,' he called up. 'Shades of the old Shakespearian clown, don't you know.' He leapt up out of the hole and picked up the tattered remains of a sheep's jawbone. Holding it aloft, he intoned into the rushing wind, 'Alas poor Yum-Yum, I knew her well. 'Twas a valiant ewe I grant thee, even though she stank like a midden, poor old dear.' He flung down the jawbone and picked up a spade.

I stared at him in amazement. How he'd managed to drag that carcass up the slope and procure a spade in the short time I'd been away, I couldn't imagine. 'I'll do that,' I said, making a move to take the spade from him.

'Go on, get away,' he said. 'Go and feel all miserable about your Flower Pig. You might sort a cup of tea out while you're about it and you could ring Sara and tell her I'm still here. Go on, I can't stand blubbering clients.' He dug the spade into the soft earth the pigs had rooted up from the hole and began throwing it down onto Magnolia.

I turned and picked my way through the mud and as I went I heard, borne on the wind, Bertie's voice once more:

> 'A pick-axe, and a spade, a spade,
> For and a shrouding sheet;
> O! a pit of clay for to be made
> For such a guest is meet.'

In spite of everything, I burst out laughing.

About an hour later, Bertie was sitting completely at his ease in front of the fire. On his feet were an old pair of carpet slippers, around his shoulders one of Mrs P's technicolour shawls was draped, and there was a pipe stuck in his mouth. Beside him was a glass of whisky and on his lap were two cats, a whippet and a book of mediaeval romances he'd grabbed from the shelf in passing. He looked up as Mrs P came in from the kitchen with his coat, socks and shoes, still faintly steaming but no longer dripping water.

'Bloody marvellous, isn't it?' he said, pointing at me. 'She's got a bad back and I end up burying her pig in a force nine gale!' Bertie was already getting his story ready for the public.

Mrs P looked at him quietly. 'You've been very kind, Bertie,' she said.

He cleared his throat and looked embarrassed for a moment, and then from behind his glasses his eyes gleamed maliciously. 'Mind you, I don't know anyone else who'd have a pig that was thoughtful enough to dig its own grave. If only we could have got her to stand beside it and fall in. Ah well, too late now. She's dead and buried, good and deep.'

But that was where he was wrong. Neither he nor I had seen the last of Magnolia – not by a long way we hadn't.

# Chapter 16

As I crawled sorrowfully to bed that night, the rain still hammered on the roof only a few feet above my head and a couple of loose slates castanetted aggressively in the wind, but by morning the storm had worn itself out. The valley, new washed, sang into life and the sheep shook the rain from their fleeces and dried out in the sun. Still comparatively new to the fact of sudden death, I looked sourly at the bright world, so oblivious of the pain and tragedy of the night before, and went to release Blossom from the stable and console her for the loss of the sister from whom she'd never been parted before.

As I carried rocks up the hill to put on Magnolia's grave (not out of sentiment, but to stop anything digging her up again) I wondered how Blossom would cope. I looked down at her blissfully stretched out in the sun and began to suspect that if anything, the dear old girl was quite happy to have the place to herself at last. In fact, that was when Blossom began her career as a Character.

Released from the necessity of fighting with Magnolia for space and food, Blossom could now allow her benign personality full expansion. The lambs were quick to take advantage and the tin shelter began to resemble one of those competitions to see how many people can fit into a phone-box. Every morning, lamb after lamb erupted from it and, when I was sure that not so much as a flea could still be inside, Blossom herself would emerge, stretching and grunting happily. Breakfast over, she then pottered up the hill to graze, but one cry of 'Pig!' brought her thundering down again, big ears flapping, to see what I wanted.

The field behind the house where Blossom resided most of the time rises very steeply, so steeply in fact that if you walk up the slope and then turn round in a hurry you can get vertigo. You also get a superb view of the whole valley and I love sitting there, feeling as if I was in a giant amphitheatre with hills soaring all around me while below, everything seems small and compact and busy. Blossom came in very handy in these idle moments of contemplation for, seeing that I was thus inclined, she took to rolling over on her side so that I could scratch her belly while I perched on her big, soft flanks. Sometimes I took the opportunity to clean her ears or see to her feet or give her a good wash.

We had a few arguments of course, mainly on the subject of the feed bags in the barn. Enormously strong, Blossom had no trouble in lifting the gate off its hinges until I fortified it with wire. Once she was in the yard, the barn door was no problem, but in order to find the feed she liked best, Blossom simply ripped up all the bags till she discovered what she was looking for or leaned against the bins till they rolled over. Luckily, I always found her before she'd had time to eat enough to kill herself with bloat, but it was small consolation at the time for the ruined feed.

In winter she kept her shelter beautifully. Of course I always gave her armfuls of straw for bedding, but Blossom spent a busy autumn each year collecting dried bracken, which was still growing unabated, and carried it down in her mouth. Anything she didn't want she placed in a neat pile outside the shelter and

160

I would often see her picking carefully through it in case there was something useful to her comfort she had missed. When the lambs were not around to get her up early, she stayed in bed, buried under a mound of straw and bracken, till a bang on her roof sent her yipping outside to her trough.

If everyone else found Blossom endearing, it was Mrs P who championed her and loved her in a way I found remarkable. Patiently enduring my worries and panics and the animals I seemed to be accumulating to bother me even more, my mother hoped, I think, that one day I'd come to my senses and give it all up. Until I did, she was prepared to stick with me, but she tolerated rather than liked the animals. The exception was Blossom, with whom she held long, sympathetic conversations over the fence while she presented her with the tasty messes she'd saved. I was always being slapped off 'Specials for Blossom' when I tried to steal them for the poultry or the goats. It was Mrs P who put her foot down when I made a last effort to get Blossom in pig by sending her away to a boar before it was finally too late for her to breed at all.

'Something awful might happen to her,' she declared. 'And don't you tell me, my girl, that you'd sell the piglets! You'd find some excuse to keep the lot and then where would we be? You leave Blossom alone, she's quite happy as she is.'

This wasn't strictly true because Blossom, like Doli, was a randy devil and came into season noisily and regularly. Inspired by lust, at these times she serenaded the world under our windows at night or trotted after an irritable Doli all day. Mrs P lovingly said she was just like the fat girl at the party who attaches herself hopefully to the girl with all the boy friends. But then Mrs P's vision of all the animals does tend to be more like a Disney cartoon than real life.

It was this attitude, along with my mother's instinct to feed anything with a mouth, that caused a bit of family friction not long after Magnolia died. 'Has Gerald's eagle gone missing again?' she enquired thoughtfully one day.

'No, I don't think so,' I replied. 'We'd have heard something about it if it had.'

Gerald's golden eagle, Random, had been lost the year before and the local radio news bulletins had kept everyone fully informed.

At last, Gerald had been told by a farmer some miles distant that Random was sitting on a post at the end of his garden, that all attempts to entice her with a sausage had failed, that the farmer's wife and children were now too terrified to come out of the house, and would Gerald come and remove his property. Since when, Mrs P has been convinced that all large, unidentified birds belong to Gerald and should be pacified with sausages until he can come and get them.

'Well, there's a big bird with goldy-brown wings hanging about and I threw it a sausage just in case,' she now informed me. 'One of those horrible crows got the sausage, though, and the big bird went and sat in the ash tree.'

A careful inspection of the ash tree declared it to be empty of all save an energetic treecreeper, and I imagined that Mrs P's bird must be one of the buzzards who nest down in the wood, getting a little bolder in view of all the largesse at the kitchen door. Further reports of her visitor from Mrs P only irritated me because it was never around when I was, although I often saw the buzzards wheeling slowly above the field or sitting on the fence posts, and I watched them coming and going from the oak tree when I was down on the meadow. So I wasn't very impressed when Mrs P emerged reproachfully from the front door one day when I was attending to the goats and called out, 'There it is, flying towards the hay field. It doesn't look like one of those buzzard things to me.'

Sighing, I put down the bucket and looked up. No, it wasn't a buzzard. No buzzard is capable of that regal drift of flight. Neither do buzzards have the sharply forked tail I was gazing up at against the sun. Mrs P's 'big, goldy-brown bird' was a kite.

I've got more or less used to seeing the kites now. There was even one breathless time when Myrddin (who's a great bird-watcher) and I thought they might be planning to nest in the wood and prepared to keep them safe. We planned our campaign of watches, even speaking in whispers on the telephone, but the buzzards hold the wood against all comers and never again did the kite come to see my mother at the back door or sit in the ash tree while she chatted to it. But sometimes I look up and see a kite drifting over the valley while the crows and buzzards argue irritably with it and at last it floats away across the mountain, leaving me to curse and rail at those lesser scavengers, now busily dogfighting amongst themselves, who with their mob violence have driven away the rare and beautiful.

At about the same time as I was exulting in that first view of the kite, I was trying to say farewell to another much loved and far more familiar animal. Doli's son, Moelwyn, was now getting on for three years old and it was becoming obvious that he would soon need a stronger minded, more experienced person to handle him. Like his mother, Moelwyn had a firm, quirky will of his own and although there had been a time when I suppose I could have handled him better, I was also conscious of the fact that somewhere along the line I'd lost my nerve with horses. Part of this had been sparked off by Moelwyn himself when, through no fault of his own, he'd brought both his massive front hooves smashing down on my skull with a sound that someone half a field away said they thought was a pistol-shot. Although it was entirely my own mistake and I didn't at the time take much notice, I'd found myself growing more and more jumpy about being kicked and remembering suddenly all those other, far more drastic falls and kicks I'd had when I'd racketed about recklessly on the tough, hardmouthed horses of the Australian Outback.

It's funny how the past can come back to terrorise you. I remember once being in a motorway accident that could have been fatal but miraculously ended up with nothing more than a deep dent in the side of the sports car a friend was driving. Both of us were so angry at the idiot who'd simply swung out without any kind of signal that we hunted him up the motorway till we forced him to stop. It wasn't until about six months later, when I was driving past the same spot as I'd done many times since, that I began shaking and shivering and finally had to get off the motorway altogether. This was pretty much the same stupid state I was in over Moelwyn although it had been a good eighteen months since he'd nearly brained me.

One way and another, I battened down my nervousness pretty well and led him around and mucked his stable out and groomed him and picked his feet out, but horses are quick to sense insecurity and although I knew that given time I would overcome it, I also felt that for his own sake, Moelwyn should go to someone who would handle him calmly, break him in properly and, at this early stage in his career, set him on the right track.

163

There were a couple of other considerations, too. Bertie had examined Doli and declared her to be definitely in foal to Bert. She was already becoming more and more irritable with Moelwyn, to his great bewilderment, and, if her next foal was to be the 'tank on hooves' which Bertie predicted, my few rocky acres would be hard put to support them all. Already Doli's great hooves had done dreadful damage to the pasture and Moelwyn's habit of sliding his way down the slopes didn't help. Then again, big horses mean big feed bills if you're short on grass, and that overdraft was still growing steadily.

Thinking I should sell him and doing anything about it were two different things, though. Moelwyn reminded me of all those bright, foolish hopes the Artist and I had discussed endlessly while waiting for him to be born; of the sturdy little foal he'd been, trotting confidently beside his mother; of the whole wonder and joy of him as he explored his new world; of his snort of amazement as a chicken burst out from a clump of grass under his nose; and of the mad teasing games he played with the goats. I even thought fondly of his trick of holding water in his mouth and, on a cold morning when I was off my guard, tipping it down my neck. I simply couldn't imagine the place without him.

I was still dithering about it when Sedley and Diana Sweeney came to visit me. I'd met Sedley some years before when the Tibetan Farm School was closing down. The idea of the school had been to train a group of young Tibetan exiles in all those special farming skills which are needed to cultivate the mountain fields of their homeland where things like tractors are pretty useless. It was a project based on hope: the hope that one day they could return to their land and be ready to take up the traditional Tibetan way of life. So there in the Welsh mountains they cultivated crops, raised livestock, made butter and cheese, spun their wool and made their own implements under the direction of Sedley Sweeney, who also saw to it that they could strip down a tractor and handle other modern machinery as well. Above all, they were to be as self-sufficient from the outside world as possible.

The story of how this was achieved and of why, in spite of its success, the school had to close is not mine to tell, but there are reminders of it all around me. I was lucky enough to buy some of the Tibetans' homemade hay rakes and duck arks and the pig shelter which Blossom regarded as home. On that first visit, as Sedley showed us around the deserted buildings, he had been understandably rather distracted. With more people arriving to pick over the bones of his dream, he had curtly left the Artist and me to pack up our purchases and be gone.

Some time later I heard of Sedley's new project. This time, on his own ten acres, he'd set up the Smallholder's Training Centre where students of any nationality could learn how to run a small acreage as productively as possible. Again, the story behind that centre belongs to Sedley, and my only concern with it at that time was to do a series of six short programmes on how he organised his land and his time. Frankly, I wasn't looking forward to it. My one brief meeting with this tall, lean, sandy haired man had left me with an impression of driving efficiency and split-second organisation, the complete opposite to my own indecisive, muddleheaded incompetence. Diana, his wife, had endorsed that impression and I could tell at a glance that here was a lady who did not take serious contributions from idiots kindly.

I was quite right about both of them, but the curious thing was that I found those two days of recording not only inspirational and exciting, but comforting as well. Here was how it could be done, I thought. Here were the neat crops and the tidy barns full of sweet, green hay, the sleek, contented cows and the fat, healthy sheep. Here was a vegetable garden, well composted and free of weeds, surrounded by another plot bursting with roses, a newly planted orchard with beehives humming gently in one corner and, by the house, old gnarled apple and plum trees carefully pruned and yielding new life. Here were the fat poultry pottering in and out of their spotless shed and the promising sound of others cackling in the nest boxes. Here were the old implements like chaff cutters and horse drawn ploughs all carefully greased and newly painted. Here were workshops where cheese presses and gate stops were made for sale, and up there was a loft where sheepskins covered with salt were waiting to be cured. Here was a dairy full of shining pails and bowls of big, brown eggs and curds dripping quietly through muslin. Here was a cool storeroom where round yellow cheeses matured in the gloom. Here was the house, solidly comfortable yet bright with colour and smelling faintly of wood-smoke and beeswax and drying herbs. Here in fact was the ideal, desired by so many and achieved by so few.

That was the excitement and inspiration. The comfort came from the Sweeneys' understanding and interest in my own feeble attempts to hold my place together, inexperienced and fumbling as I was. They were quite different from that other group of self-sufficers who'd come through my gate uninvited one day, crying children at their heels, the women's long skirts trailing cumbrously through the mud and the men's faces ferociously disapproving as they subjected me to a lecture on why I should be growing cabbages (which give me wind) instead of pruning roses.

When the Sweeneys finally came, they brought pots of yoghurt and honey, homemade bread, newly churned butter, their own cheese and vegetables and strawberries from their garden. Sedley brought me a gate stop and put it in straightaway. Instead of the disapproving criticism I'd expected when I showed them around, Diana and Sedley expressed themselves delighted with everything, mourned the fact that they didn't have a wild wood and a river meadow like mine and made me an offer for Moelwyn. It was a good offer and it meant that he'd be living only thirty miles away at a place where I could go and see him often and where I knew he'd get the best of attention. It was the perfect solution to my dilemma.

It would have been easier, of course, if Sedley had been able to load Moelwyn up and take him then and there. As it was, I had a whole fortnight in which to get myself thoroughly miserable about his going. When it came to it, Moelwyn didn't help matters by flatly refusing to be boxed, Doli meanwhile screaming encouragement to him in a complete volte face after spending the previous week trying to kick him to death if he came near her.

As the horse box, with Moelwyn finally loaded up, snaked its way out of the gate, I knew again that heart-rending moment when an animal leaves which you've raised, fed and cared for, its face bewildered at this complete change of routine and looking dreadfully vulnerable as you stay behind and watch it go.

Sedley rang me later that evening to say that Moelwyn had only consented to leave the horse box for Diana but was now

166

settled down in the stable with a good feed, and he was very pleased with him. Sedley then made me another offer. It was one I simply didn't want to hear.

'She's not for sale!' I cried dramatically. 'Not Doli! You can't have Doli!'

'I thought that's what you might say,' Sedley replied gently, 'but Jeanine, you should think about it. It's a pity for her not to be doing any work. She's not a cheap horse to keep and really this idea of having her as a brood mare isn't very practical. Even if you sell her foals at weaning, it hardly covers the cost of producing them. I need another horse for pulling. I'll tell you what I'll do: I'll give you £500 for her and you can have the foal back at weaning if you want it.'

It was a wonderful offer and even though I stoutly refused it, I knew it was one I should accept. Sedley was right about Doli needing work and proper handling, and if my bank manager had known I was refusing the £500, he would not have been pleased. That night, what with the traumas of Moelwyn's departure and the knowledge that I really had no excuse apart from sentiment for keeping Doli, I howled myself to sleep.

Sedley rang up several times after that and always I put him off without actually saying 'No!' again. At last one evening he issued an ultimatum. 'I really must know what you're going to do,' he said. 'I've had an offer of another mare like Doli and I have to give them an answer fairly quickly.'

'Give me another couple of days,' I pleaded. 'I promise then I'll let you have a firm answer one way or the other.'

'Right,' agreed Sedley, 'but make it soon.'

I don't know why I asked for the extra time. I'd already made up my mind that even though I was quite happy to let Doli go on in idleness and longed to see her have Bert's foal (which I was convinced would be a filly), I really did need that £500 badly.

After I'd put the phone down, I wandered disconsolately out to the field where Doli was standing by the gate in the moonlight. I'd formed a silly habit over the years of going to stand with her when I felt miserable. Often, with my head against her broad neck, I would tell her what was bothering me and get some kind of comfort from the warmth and smell of her. Doli, who could be so uncooperative when she wanted, always stood quite still when I was in this mood, her eyes half closed, mumbling softly through her nose at me.

I stood there for a long time that night and finally I said, 'Doli, me old devil, I simply need the money. I'll have to ring up tomorrow and say yes.' The mare shifted her weight and snorted gently. 'I tell you what, though,' I continued. 'I won't do it till after the post comes. You never know what might turn up then.' Which was stupid of me, because there was no hope of anything but more bills turning up in that post.

The next day was one of those miserable, halfhearted affairs that echoed my own state of mind perfectly. I was busy at something or other when the postman arrived and I took the three brown envelopes from him and shoved them in my pocket. It was lunchtime before I remembered them. One was a circular, another was a mercifully small bill and the other had come from Newmarket. Newmarket?

'I don't know anyone in Newmarket,' I told Mrs P.

'Probably one of the bills got re-routed,' she replied.

Still wondering, I opened the envelope slowly and drew out of it a cheque for £300. It was a present, with no strings attached, from a friend I hadn't seen for years, a friend whose compassion for the weak and lonely and great love of animals had been a beacon in my life for a very long time. He knew nothing of my deadline over Doli, but he did know that the little farm was only coasting along on hope. Now, with his help, Doli could go on coasting with it a bit longer.

# Chapter 17

'Get it away! Get it away! Oh, how dreadful!' Mrs P's horrified scream caused me to drop the log I was carrying onto the fire in a blaze of sparks and rush out to find her leaning weakly against the back door. 'It's a rat,' she moaned, pointing outside to the path.

My mother is afraid of practically nothing on this earth. All my life, while I've been cowering behind the nearest large object, I've watched her march into battle without giving a thought to the size or ferocity of her adversary. If immediate words or actions fail, she falls back on her prayers, in which she has such an unshakeable faith that only the most hard-bitten cynic can be with her for long without believing, if not in prayer in general, at least in Mrs P's own personal hot line to God.

The one time both her courage and her power of prayer desert her is when she comes upon a rat, dead or alive. She doesn't much fancy mice or bats either, but as both of them inhabit the loft and occasionally penetrate into her bedroom by mistake, she's more or less learned to tolerate them. But just mention that you've seen a rat recently and, when she stops yelling and shuddering, she starts packing her bags again. Perhaps it's not quite so bad now that she's got her chihuahua, Winston, constantly at her heels and in her bed and generally about her person. Even a rat would think twice before it stood up to Winston, who's not your average sized chihuahua but ten pounds of solid muscle and fight. The only thing that scares the hell out of Winston is a chihuahua bitch in season.

On the morning I found Mrs P wilting against the back door, Winston was not yet born and she'd come unprotected upon her foe. 'I think it must be dead,' she confessed, 'but I don't care. You'll have to take it away. I can't go out there. Oh God! What are you doing?'

I was holding the 'rat' on my hand. 'It's not a rat,' I said sternly, 'it's a mole. A perfectly harmless, very dead mole. Now you've scared Tinka away.'

I needn't have worried. Tinka the cat knew his rights and was sitting on a nearby fence post, gazing at us reproachfully. Finally, seeing Mrs P's panic subside, he leapt down and picked his way carefully through the grass to the doorstep, where he sat down and waited for the extra bowl of food he expected as his fee for mole catching.

Tinka doesn't look the kind of cat who would be fast or clever enough to catch a mole. A big, languorous, ginger Persian, he seems far more suited to a silk-lined basket and the adoration of two spinster ladies in the best part of Kensington – which is exactly how he spent the first seven years of his life. When his owners departed for Australia, they decided against taking Tinka to fret in quarantine and so he arrived in Wales complete with basket, toys, brushes and combs and an exhaustive list of his fads and fancies. Tinka took one look at the wide open spaces and remembered that for a cat, Paradise was really rat hunting and mole catching. This was handy because, I sometimes believed, every mole in the valley had set up house on my land. Kicking down molehills had become a way of life, a practice which I don't advise after a heavy frost when the mounds of earth are frozen solid – I've nursed a lot of very painful toes to prove it. The thought of using poison or those dreadful spiked traps never entered my mind, but the moles were doing a great deal of damage to the pasture. Until Tinka came along. I think he must have caught the first one by accident, found it unpalatable and brought it to the house to be explained. We made such a fuss of him that he went back and got another one.

Tinka's moles were always quite unmarked and it seemed much the kindest way of getting rid of them, but it was the Artist who had the bright idea of bribing Tinka for every mole he brought in. It became a very definite transaction between them because the Artist wanted a real moleskin jerkin of all things, and soon lots of pathetic little skins were pegged out, drying on a board. Although I entertained no such ambitions, when the Artist left, I kept up the business arrangement with Tinka simply to encourage him to go on keeping the moles down. We usually did our trading before Mrs P got up and by the time she emerged, the moles were decently interred, but that morning Tinka had been a bit late and had plonked his catch at her feet.

'I don't care,' my mother was saying now. 'It could have been a rat.'

'No, it couldn't,' I said firmly. 'The Rat Squad always eat rats. It's just that they don't like moles, so if you see any bodies about, that's what they are. Anyway, I haven't seen a rat hole for ages.'

It was true, and a great relief, because when we first moved in, the rats were a real menace. They not only killed baby chicks, took eggs from under the geese and broke into the feed bags, but they sat up in the loft at night gnawing at the plaster under the slates and even, the Artist swore, peering at him through the knotholes in the wooden ceiling. He got terribly neurotic about it and actually stood up on a chair with his head through the loft hatch, informing them that he intended to shoot them if they didn't cut it out. To my utter embarrassment, he told Derek Jones about this when Derek came to do a programme called 'Two Pigs in a Poke' at the farm. Not that I can blame the Artist: it was Mrs P who told him to tell the rats to go away, having heard that it worked with ants, and I've done the same thing myself when the bats are making more noise than usual as they come roistering home in the early hours. Happily, the bats have so far ignored me, but according to the Artist, the rats left immediately.

They may have deserted the loft, but the rats continued to swagger around the rest of the buildings till the day Kate came

171

crawling into the stable to die. It was difficult at first to see the little tortoiseshell cat under the mass of blood and wounds. What had happened to her or where she came from we never quite discovered, but she had lost a back leg and most of her tail and was covered with great ugly gashes. The Artist rushed her to Islwyn, the vet, and nursed her carefully until, by the time I got back from London, she was beginning to recover.

As soon as she could hobble around, Kate repaid us for our help by waging war on the rats. The loss of her leg hardly reduced her speed and we got used to the sound of her yowling triumphantly over each catch. Soon the rats retreated before the onslaughts of this tiny, elderly cat who was wise in their ways and far more ferocious. We had her spayed before we realised what a brilliant ratter she was, so the Artist bought two ginger kittens, Max and Muffin. Kate, who'd obviously had the handling of pupils before, taught them how to hunt. Together they formed such an efficient team that I called them the Rat Squad and would have backed them against any 'rodent officer' in the country.

'So you see,' I told Mrs P that morning, 'all this nonsense about rats is plain silly!'

She gave me a sour look and, as is her way when she's getting the worst of an argument, quickly switched the subject: 'How much longer,' she demanded, 'are you going to go on bringing that goat into the house?' And she pointed vindictively to a small fawn face gazing at her complacently from the middle of the whippets' beds.

Most of the new kids had settled down perfectly. They bonked each other and bounced off the walls and fought for possession of the straw bales I'd given them to lie on up out of the draught. Often I sat on the bales myself, though, watching the mad games the kids played or letting them crawl all over me. Little Nana and Loveday would curl up in my arms and go to sleep, but Minnie was slightly less inclined to use me as a bed, preferring like her mother to chew the bobbles off my anorak or just generally racket about.

I wasn't the only one to find the kids irresistible. Gwyneth Griffiths and her two children, Dafydd and Siân, often came over to join me in kid-gazing and even Eddie himself succumbed. I'd expected him to be contemptuous of anything so

172

commercially unviable as a goat kid, but instead he was more besotted than any of us, chuckling to them and picking them up and finally even asking if he could buy one. He wanted Loveday, the chocolate-brown kid who was as affectionate and loving as Whacky was rebellious. The trouble was that I couldn't bear to part with her and in any case, all my resolutions to sell at least three of the kids had long since been forgotten. They were my first success and, as usual, I'd already begun to think of myself as the owner of a real goat herd who at some time in the future would be selling milk and making cheese and possibly even entering the ranks of those High Church goatkeepers I admired so much.

So, in spite of Eddie's extraordinary request, I refused and offered him instead some of the milk from Loveday's mother to try. Eddie, to whom by now the goats could do no wrong, declared that the milk was far superior to cow's milk and suggested to his long-suffering wife that she should arrange to buy our milk for the house. Thrilled with my first convert, I likewise refused to sell them the milk. Instead they could have as much as we could spare; I felt privileged that they should want it at all. So every afternoon, the school car stopped at my gate and Dafydd and Siân hopped out to collect the ice-cold bottles of milk I'd left for them. I was incredibly pleased with myself.

Actually, we did have quite a bit of milk to spare. Dolores was giving a good gallon and Nana had finally let her milk down for me and was yielding about six pints. To Mrs P's delight, we were getting quite a lot of cream from the fresh milk, simply by skimming off the thick crust which formed on the bowls in the fridge overnight.

I left all that sort of thing to my mother, who began to pore over books on cheese and yoghurt making and refused to leave the kitchen in case Suyin and Pip, the Burmese cats, took a fancy to the blobs of oozing muslin she had hanging up to make soft cheese. I escaped from all this mad activity, taking the kids out to play under the crab apple tree at the top of the hay field or to romp up and down on the banks of the stream which ran along one side of it, investigating twigs or nibbling at the grass and soil. Sometimes Rosie and Humble joined us, Rosie to get the worst of her attempts to take part in their games, and Humble to settle down and cud while they all jumped off her broad back or picked at her wool. Occasionally we all went up to sit on Blossom, who was as enchanted with the kids as I was. I wish now I'd had the foresight to take a photograph of that huge black and white body stretched out in the sun with a line-up of three kids, ranging in colour from coffee-fawn through deep bitter-chocolate to red-gold, sitting on her back, their little jaws working as they made their first baby attempts at cudding.

Heaven only knows where I found all the time to sit around watching kids and lambs and the comings and goings and skirmishings between the chickens, ducks and geese, while the garden grew choked with weeds, the housework waited to be done and there were gates to be painted and barns to be whitewashed.

All I know is that the warm smell of that late springtime has always lingered and that I got myself a crash course in animal behaviour.

By sitting and staring so much, I began slowly to develop that sixth sense which more or less knows what an animal is about to do before it does it. In day to day terms this helps simply to avoid disaster, but when the time came at last for me to bring my microphone out of mothballs again, it meant that I had more chance than before of being able to record the sounds of a farm. Domestic animals are if anything even more perverse than wildlife about doing what you want them to do when you want them to do it, and they have a habit of staying quite dumb if they sense that you are urging them to bleat or baa or moo or neigh or cluck or whatever. If I'm more successful now at bamboozling them into performing, it's all because of the hours I've wasted watching my own.

The goat to whose presence in the house Mrs P had objected was quite different from the other kids. It lay on the whippets' bed while Bea carefully washed its face. It was Whacky, Nana's kid, and I was very proud of the calm, friendly character I'd finally hewn out of the wild, stubborn little beast she'd been only a couple of weeks before. It was then, fed up with trying to get Nana to let me have her milk and fighting equally hard with Dolores to let her kids have any, that I finally left them in the cowshed and set up a kid crèche in the larger of the two looseboxes. Their mothers yelled blue murder, the kids screamed back and, although Little Nana, Minnie and Loveday did finally

174

give in and accept an ersatz teat and milk out of a bottle, Whacky went on hunger strike.

By now I was so sick of Nana's little pet that I didn't care all that much, but Whacky was living off her fat and continued to cause total chaos. Every time I opened the door of the loosebox, Whacky did a standing take-off and panicked the others into flying around like a troupe of performing fleas so that I had to field them off the walls, one by one, before I could feed them. At last, with bleeding knuckles, a bruised chin and an eye full of milk that Whacky had spat back at me, I did a quick flying tackle across the floor of the shed, caught her with a yell and bore her off, screaming and struggling, to the old stable. It seemed amazing that anything so small could fight so long and so hard.

As I closed the stable door, I caught a glimpse of Whacky taking a flying leap up in the air and landing in the wooden manger that runs the length of the wall. 'Sod you!' I bellowed through the door and went, grinding with rage, back to the house.

'You'll have a heart attack one of these days if you go on like this,' said my mother, observing my red, furious face. 'I should sell that kid if I were you.'

'Nobody, but nobody, would be fool enough to buy her,' I said through clenched teeth. 'If I gave her away, somebody would brain her within five minutes. Anyway, she's probably strangled herself up in the hay rack by now. Oh God! I'll bet she has, too!' And I flew out of the door and back down the yard.

All my temper had drained out of me by the time I got to the stable and, terrified of what I might see, peered through the little window. Whacky was lying on some hay in the feeding trough sound asleep, a small baby goat worn out with all her fighting. Her defences were gone so completely that pity and admiration moved me at the same time. She must have been very hungry by now, but she was determined to resist with the last ounce of her strength the brutal human who had separated her from the mother she adored. She was that mother all over again and in fact, the pair of them reminded me a little of my own, I thought as I tiptoed away from the stable and went to lean over the gate and look across at the Fans, sharply outlined against a brilliant sky.

If she had been seemingly defenceless as I crept away from the window of the stable, Whacky was booted and spurred for action by the time I returned, full of optimism, with a bottle of milk. When I finally caught her, the milk was stone cold and Whacky had her jaws shut like a trap anyway. When I tried to open them she screamed so loudly and so long that Mrs P came hurrying down to see if I was at last murdering her.

The mad look in Whacky's eye and her furious, tight-mouthed determination to accept no nourishment from my hands began to remind me of something. She made a violent effort and struggled free. Making a wild grab, I inadvertently caught her by the back legs and she hung, for one brief moment, upside down. The words that had been lingering on the edge of my mind came to me at last:

'For an instant he stared upon me with a mad, marigold eye, all his plumage flat to the body and his head crouched like a snake's in fear or hatred, then bated wildly from the fist. Bated – it meant the headlong dive of rage and terror, by which a leashed hawk leaps from the fist in a wild bid for freedom and hangs upside down by his jesses in a flurry of pinions like a chicken being decapitated, revolving, struggling, in danger of damaging his primaries.'

'That,' I said to Whacky, 'is what you remind me of – a constantly bating hawk!'

T. H. White's description of his first encounter with his goshawk could almost have applied to my struggles with this tiny goat. I sat on in the dark stable as she glared at me defiantly from her perch back on the manger, and wondered. A couple of pigeons alighted outside on the wide sill of the window, the male bobbing up and down with one thing on his mind, while the more foresighted hen peered through the window, searching for a nest site. She'd been born herself on one of the ledges high up in the rafters and, in spite of the fact that I had banned all pigeon nests inside the barn because of the mess they made, she and her mother constantly came back to see if there was a way in.

The sound of the pigeons and the cool shadows of the stable took me back to another room and a Christmas many years before when another white pigeon and a small brown Burmese cat had kept me company. The pigeon I'd rescued from, of all unlikely places, a graveyard in Birmingham. On its first flight, a

176

cat had attacked it just as I was passing by on my way to do an interview. A quick dash to a nearby paper shop to procure a box and a packet of Kleenex which I shredded to make a soft nest, and I went on my way with the injured bird, did my interview while the receptionist minded the box, and took the bird back with me to London to recuperate in my bed-sit.

It was a rather special bed-sit: a long basement room with French windows opening straight onto the garden of a tall, beautifully maintained Victorian house near Holland Park. I remember fondly all the bed-sits in which I've lived, from Sydney to Barcelona to a village in Surrey to London, all of them with long-suffering landladies who've borne nobly with the assorted livestock I've kept, but the one near Holland Park outshines the rest. I'd shared it for a couple of years already with Suyin, small, brown and very vocal, who, when she first met Bonkers the pigeon, thought to finish off what the Birmingham cat had begun. A few sharp pecks on her head for her pains, and she suffered the pigeon to share her window ledge and her dinner and learned to move quickly when he dive-bombed her off the top of the cupboard. As his injured wing grew better, he lived for the most part high up in a tree in the garden, only coming back through the window at night or if the weather was wet and cold.

It was not only cold but snowing gently on that Christmas when the three of us were left alone in the house. Everyone else had gone to the country and I had only stayed behind to meet up with an American friend who then found himself stranded by the snow in deepest Norfolk. So there I was, with nowhere to go and nothing to do and only a pigeon and a cat in a state of armed neutrality to keep me company. I shared some chicken with Suyin and a mince pie with Bonkers and shuffled about looking for something to read. Lying on a shelf was a tattered paperback. I picked it up and sighed. It had been lent to me by another friend who had been nagging at me for months to read it.

'You'll love it,' she'd urged. 'They based the musical, Camelot, on it. I mean, you must have heard of T. H. White! You're so mad on Arthurian legends and things.'

'Mad enough,' I'd said, 'not to like people messing about with them. I can't imagine anything nastier than an American musical based on King Arthur.'

177

'But this isn't like that,' my friend had pleaded. 'Just read it and you'll see. Look, I'll leave this here. Just read it. Please!'

I hadn't, though, and the book had gathered dust until, bored on that lonely Christmas, I thought to look at it so that at least I'd be able to give it back with an assurance that I'd loathed it. I began to read.

I can't remember much else about the next twenty-four hours except lying on my stomach on a rug in front of the electric fire with Suyin curled up asleep in the small of my back and Bonkers nodding off on top of the cupboard, while outside the snow drifted down into the silent garden.

By the time everyone came home and the American had got through from Norfolk and borne me off to celebrate, I'd read *The Once And Future King* through twice and could talk of nothing else. When the libraries and bookshops opened again I stormed them, looking for more T. H. White. All they could come up with immediately was *The Goshawk* and it has taken me since then to find the rest of his out-of-print books; the last of them is on its way to me as I write this. If ever I am foolish enough to try and analyse what it was that made me pause on the hill above, look down and decide to buy this place on the spur of the moment, I get lost in all the many strands of experience and influences which brought me to that place at that point in time and made up my mind for me, but one of the thickest strands is the one which began on that strange Christmas day.

And here I was, years later, sitting in the stable with a small goat with a will as indomitable as White's unmanned hawk, a whole dovecote of white pigeons like Bonkers outside and Suyin still chittering at them from her window.

I glanced up at Whacky, who was glaring defiantly at me and ready for instant take-off if I moved. 'Perhaps,' I told her, 'I should try to "man" you just like a hawk. Of course, not quite the same as White did it, misguidedly, to poor old Gos, but I shall stay here till you're tired enough to sleep while I watch you and you learn that I am the bringer of food and comfort.'

I spent all that night in the stable, leaning against the wall in the corner with a captured Whacky in my arms. For a long while I had but to relax my hold a little for her to start struggling free again, but at last she began to nod off to sleep and I could pick up the book I'd brought with me and, very gently, get some coffee from the flask. Once or twice the kid awoke and I kept up the delicate stroking of her ears until she slept again. And so we sat, the two of us, a circle of light in the blackness, only the distant bark of a fox sometimes breaking the silence. At some time I must have slept too, and I awoke with the kid still slumbering in my arms, the book fallen to the ground and a faint light from outside taking away the intensity of the artificial one inside. Carefully I unscrewed the top of the other thermos, into which I had put warm milk the evening before, and dipped my finger into it. I placed my finger cautiously into Whacky's mouth and she began to suck on it in her sleep. Gradually she started to wake and I dipped my finger once more in the milk and back into her mouth. This time Whacky began to suck on the finger quite consciously and so it went on, one drop of milk at a time till she was looking for more and I replaced the finger with the rubber teat dipped in milk. Inch by inch, talking to her in a monotone all the while, I filled the bottle with one hand from the thermos, manoeuvred the teat onto it and gave it to her.

That was not the end of our struggles. It took several days more and a great part of the nights, sitting on the straw in the stable, talking to her and bringing her little delicacies like dandelion shoots, before Whacky came to me of her own accord, but any sudden movement from me and she was flying up into the manger again. It was becoming more and more difficult to spend so much time with her, and every hour I was away from her we went back a few steps. I decided at last to take her to the house for Mrs P to keep her company while I was busy outside.

It was Bea who completed Whacky's 'manning'. The little whippet bitch immediately inspected the small defiant goat and, discovering a patch of her coat that was not quite as it should be, rasped her tongue over it. What communication went on between them I've no idea, but before long, Whacky was parked on the dogs' bed or curled up with them in front of the fire, even ousting Bea off my lap sometimes, and demanding her bottles of milk by standing with her sharp little hooves against the fridge door. Only Mrs P's pointed remarks about 'things on the floor' induced me to return her to her stable at night. There she happily returned to her nest up in the manger, only bleating sleepily at me as I left her, her eyes shining like sapphires in the torchlight as she watched me go.

One day, as a kind of final test, I took her with me in the car to see Mrs Parry. Small and brown as a nut after working for hours in her vegetable garden, Myrddin's mother was someone for whom I had a lot of respect, not least because she told me she had once cleared a three-acre field of bracken alone, with nothing but a hand sickle. Her greatest joy in retirement seemed to be that she was no longer expected to carry bales of straw and hay about, but being in her late seventies and crippled with arthritis didn't stop her helping Myrddin with the cattle and sheep or climbing up the tallest ladders, still in her wellington boots, to keep her windows sparkling. I always felt that there was nothing I could ever surprise her with, so I took Whacky to see her, both of us sitting in Mrs Parry's spotless kitchen while she stroked the little goat's ears and smiled.

There is nothing so beguiling, so flattering to the human ego, as an animal once wilder than the wind, now tamed and submissive. I had become absolutely besotted with Whacky, but I had enough sense left to realise that she'd have to be re-introduced to life with the other kids. I put it off for a while, fearful that, having lost her place in the pecking order and being the smallest, Whacky would find herself beaten up by them.

No mother taking her child to kindergarten for the first time could have been more nervous than I was as I led Whacky into the loosebox, no mother more furious when the other kids ganged up on her and charged from all directions till she was spinning around dizzily, trying to keep on her feet. Only the arrival of a vast lorry with a load of feed on it, and the usual disruption as the driver tried to turn it and reverse on the steep yard, stopped me from whisking her away and back to the unnatural comforts she'd been used to.

I suppose I was away for no more than half an hour. When I got back, Whacky was standing in undisputed possession of the straw bales while the other kids staggered about looking bemused and apprehensive. As she saw me, Whacky flung herself up the wall, knocked me flying as she descended, shot over the open half-door of the box and was squeezing under the gate of the field as I raced after her, the rest of the kids scattering frantically behind. Nana, who hadn't seen her kid for three weeks, spotted her immediately from the bottom of the field where she and Dolores had been grazing peacefully and galloped up to join Whacky. The last I saw of them was two white behinds bobbing down into the wood where, on those slippery, almost vertical slopes interlaced with brambles, they would have no trouble at all in evading capture.

If it hadn't been for Dolores they'd probably still be there, a pair of feral goats defying the world, but Dolores wasn't having part of her herd disappear without permission. She'd always had a hypnotic power over the larger, more aggressive Nana, and she followed the fugitives rapidly while I got on with rounding up the rest of the kids who by now were flying hysterically about the yard. About a quarter of an hour later I saw Dolores butting a subdued Nana in front of her right up into the cowshed. Behind them at a distance followed Whacky, bleating querulously. Nothing, but nothing would induce her to follow her mother into the cowshed.

It was some time around midnight when finally cold, loneliness and hunger brought her to the door where I lurked in wait. As she came in, one hesitant footstep at a time, I shut the door quickly. The cowshed is about thirty feet long, with the old cow-ties forming a barrier between it and the feeding channel. A small, active kid has no trouble in slipping through the barrier; a large, tired human takes a while to scramble painfully over it and, while she is doing so, the kid has no trouble in slipping back the other way. I can't remember how I finally caught Whacky, but the only reason I didn't brain her with a blunt instrument was that I didn't have one handy.

Back in solitary state in her stable, Whacky switched character as if the day's traumas had never been. That was to be the pattern of her life from then on: with the other goats she was wild, intractable and infuriating; on her own she was gentle, loving and biddable. She was to provide me with more near heart attacks than even her mother had been able to achieve, but she was also to prove a wonderfully easy, prolific milker and of all the goats I've helped to be born, anguished over, raised and loved, Whacky remains unique and unforgotten.

Later that summer, I sold Nana on trial to a couple who were desperate for a goat in milk. The kids then rejoined Dolores in the cowshed, from whence she led them out to graze, brought them home and nipped in the bud any rebellion offered to her or to me. She still rules them and me to this day and never again have I tried to 'man' a goat. That, as she is fond of reminding me with a firm look, is Dolores' sole responsibility.

# *Chapter 18*

Harsh and tuneless as an old cow gong, the hollow note of the bell pleaded forlornly to the empty hills. I started guiltily and dropped the whitewash brush. Could it be Sunday again already? Had another week begun, leaving the work of the previous one hardly touched, so that once more I was dashing to catch up and unprepared to answer the summons to the old fourteenth century church at the top of the hill? Soon Mr Hughes would be regarding the almost deserted pews and his beautiful voice would be echoing off the thick white walls.

I've belonged to too many religions, too many sects, too many philosophies, to feel any longer that going to a church is necessary for salvation (whatever that may be), but I did feel regret that it seemed impossible to organise my time so as to leave room for something that was not so much an act of worship as a moment of peace in a church which, in its age, its solitary setting, its very plainness and austerity, has a great feeling of spirituality. Sprung from the very stones of the place of which it is part, the hopes and prayers and labour of the people who built it linger like the songs they have sung within its walls.

The Church of St Simon and St Jude stands alone except for a vicarage which is now in private hands, a youth hostel which was once a pub and an old, grey stone hall. There is nothing else except the panorama of the valley and the Fans. It has no need of great spires or fussy architecture, for its setting is more inspiring than any cathedral.

In the days when I was searching for reasons and justifications for coming to live at the farm not far from the church, I used to joke that St Jude had organised it; St Jude, patron saint of hopeless causes, had also given his name to the church where I was baptised, which somehow I'd always found rather comforting. In fact, St Jude and his partner were imported saints to the church which in Welsh gives its name to the whole district. According to the scholars, the original two saints were probably Notolius and Potolius. It's unfortunate that they sound so ridiculous, these Romano-Celtic saints, less happy in their names than their brother, Paulinus, who first built his monastery on that site when he came to settle amongst the tough, suspicious people of the Black Mountain (reputed to be remnants of the original inhabitants of Britain). Whether or not he was the very same Paulinus who later went via Cornwall to Brittany and became their St Pol is not certain, but he did go away and left his brothers to look after his foundation.

Whoever Paulinus was or became, he had the soul of a poet to build his church where it overlooked so much splendour; and so must the spiritual or temporal agency which later foiled attempts to rebuild the church two miles away, down in the village. It's the old familiar story of foundations being mysteriously thrown down again and again by some superhuman agency until finally the church was restarted on the old site. Who knows what intense village passions were roused to give birth to that story, but I really do like to believe the other one about the stones to build the church coming from the river and being passed, hand over hand, up the hill to the masons.

Today there is no longer enough of a congregation answering the forlorn sound of the bell to give the church, built in legend and love, a full-time vicar. Neither is there any chance for the casual visitor to go in and meditate alone in a place unravaged by Cromwell or the horrors of Victorian church decoration, for now the church is locked against more modern vandals. Sometimes, though, I wander up to stand amongst the worn gravestones and seek out those of my predecessors; linked with them by the name of the farm, faint but still visible on the lichened stone, I feel curiously apologetic for all those neglected walls and hedges and the softness of my life compared to their hard, peasant grind. I find myself talking out loud to them, explaining away my lack of stewardship while the sorrowing trees murmur behind me. There are times when the world of Paulinus and his brothers, passionate with prayer and self-denial, is there superimposed on the old stones, and I glimpse for a moment wooden huts and tilled earth and the adventure of a new way of life, for Paulinus was the son of a rich nobleman and used to different things.

At certain times of the year, the little church warms itself with the press of people between its walls: at Harvest Festival, when the hymns are joyful and the late afternoon sun streams over the massive windowsills onto the bright flowers and vegetables; at the Carol Service, when candlelight flickers over the uneven stones and the red faces and gay mufflers of the bright Christmas crowd; more starkly at a funeral service conducted against the sound of a screaming gale, when the congregation overflows into the porch and later, clergymen stand in the graveyard with their black robes whipping around them in the wind and the coffin is lowered, while a group of grey-suited men stand on a hillock and sing in unison a great sorrowing lament to the soaring hills.

A neighbour's car changed gear by the gate and ground up the hill, bringing me back to my work. They, of course, had had their barns whitewashed weeks before, when the spring sun was soft and warm and not liable to dry the lime too quickly so that it flaked off at the first touch of frost, as mine was probably going to do.

All the stone buildings, walls and gateposts have been covered over for years by layers of whitewash, in places like the thick icing on a wedding cake. Sometimes, when frost and wind have combined to weaken the heavy crust and pulled it away in places, you can see those layers clearly: chapters telling the work of generations. On other walls, more exposed to the full force of the wind and rain, the brush is laid almost on the bare stone.

There is something so deeply satisfying about the sight of newly limed buildings that even if it wasn't necessary, I would try to get it done each year. But after the first rapturous sploshing of the thin liquid, it is not a job I enjoy. The temptation is to apply the lime as thickly as possible to get the immediate pleasure of seeing it solid and white on the shadowed contours of the stones. It's a momentary pleasure, however, and all the work is liable to amount to little more than a yard full of brittle white flakes at the very first sign of rain and wind.

The trick, as I've discovered (although recipes for the perfect mixture vary bewilderingly), is to lay the whitewash on quite thinly, to add a few lumps of lard to the lime and water when it is still heating and, if possible, to choose a day of fine mistiness to be followed by a gentle sun. The longer it takes to dry, the longer the whitewash seems to stay. The only trouble is that this thinner stuff affords no instant sense of satisfaction and I've spent a whole day laying on whitewash I couldn't even see, consoling my aching arms and cricked neck with the thought that the next morning I would see a dazzling transformation of brilliant walls against the black doors and the blue slate of the roofs. Still, I always manage to find plenty of excuses for not doing the whitewashing until at last my neighbours' buildings across the valley spring into vivid relief against the rich green of their heavily fertilised fields and my own seem suddenly shabby and neglected.

That year, what with all the Whacky watching and the dramas of milking sessions and another trip I had to make to Devon, I was later than usual getting the buckets and brushes out, and already the summer was getting into its stride as the silent Sunday echoed to the sound of the church bell and my neighbours hastened up the hill to answer its summons. Once, that other family which lay together in the graveyard would have been going up the hill too and not desecrating the Sabbath by whitewashing. A swallow zipped busily out of the cowshed, not giving a damn about Sunday, or history, or anything except the urgency of breeding.

The swallows had only come back to the farm that year. Although twittering congregations of them sat on the electricity wires behind the house and skimmed in relays over the pond or the waving grass on the hayfield, the previous year not one of them had nested in the buildings. True, some had quested around the old carriage shed but, as the beams in there are only head-high and well within cat range, I'd discouraged them. In spite of many other perfectly safe sites for their nests, the swallows had flipped their wings at me and gone elsewhere with their patronage. I felt absurdly rejected, as if the farm's three-star rating had been taken away, but if the swallows did not regard it as 'The House of the Perfect Eaves', the martins were perfectly satisfied with it. Soon, the gable end of the cottage was plastered with their mud nests and their debris littered the window-sills and the little herb garden below. The ash tree a few yards away seemed to become a meeting place for martins all over the district and at eleven o'clock every morning, shoals of them circled around it and spun through its great branches for about half an hour until at last the wild chirruping ended and only the resident colony was left. As the martin broods hatched out, I went to bed at night to the sound of their sleepy murmurings under my window and was consoled for the absence of the swallows.

This year, to my joy, I'd seen a pair of swallows flying in and out of the cowshed, sizing it up for possibilities. A few days later, looking up from milking, I saw them bringing in beakfuls of mud and flying high up into the rafters, safe from even the most ambitious cat. There was some inconvenience to me in their choice, because I had to avoid the odd spurt into the milk bucket as they shot over my head, but it proved to be an ideal swallow nursery and, as the nestlings grew, their parents diligently trained them to fly up and down the long shed until their flight was strong enough to lead them out of doors. Once all the chicks fell out of the nest, miraculously unhurt, and Myrddin climbed the full height of the big extension ladder to put them back and tack a safety net of wire underneath for them. The descendants of that first pair come back every year to the cowshed and I know them by their air of confidence as they arrive from the long journey and go straight in without hesitation to the old nest site, safety net and all.

To me, the sound of summer will always be the swishing of the whitewash brush, the rich, satisfying sound of milk spurting into the froth of a nearly full bucket, the shrill cries of baby swallows, the irritable chittering of their parents if I get in their way, and the lamentations of the sheep coming down from the mountain for shearing and dipping.

My own sheep took kindly to neither experience although, after a few wild bids to escape our clutches, they did resign themselves to being sat on their behinds and deprived of their fleeces by Gwyneth and her noisy, smelly machine. Gwyneth, who's won several shearing competitions, treated them as if their skins were made of fine silk but I still stood by with a pot of Pettifer's Green Ointment in case she inadvertently nicked them. Not that the sheep noticed too much, but my neurosis about maggots couldn't allow even a minute cut to remain untended, so I added more foreign smell to the shorn bodies and created even greater confusion when the ewes were turned out, naked not only of their wool but of their own individual smell. Their lambs drew back in alarm from these shrunken effigies of their mothers and cried urgently for help from elsewhere. The ewes, puzzled by the mass breakdown in family communication, bellowed at them to stop being fools or pottered anxiously around like passengers just off a plane looking for their luggage, investigating lambs and then rejecting them with a stamp of their hoof and a quick bang.

A few days later Myrddin appeared and demanded the whole flock for dipping. I was glad to see him, waiting for the day when the sheep would smell potent enough to ward off the flies while the summer menace waxed strong and persistent. It's the same every year: I long for them to be dipped and yet, as they are herded into the trailer and bumped, bewildered and protesting, up the hill and down Myrddin's perilous track, I am indignant on their behalf. After all, would you like someone to chuck you from a great height into a bath of foul smelling disinfectant and then, every time you came up for air, shove your head under again and again and sometimes even throw another large body in on top of you?

There's the difference between a real farmer and someone like me. I've been watching sheep being dipped since I was a child and I've never been able to divorce myself from what it must feel like. When the sheep are my own, I can hardly bear it. It's not so bad when Myrddin and I are alone and I can make a plea for each individual sheep so that it doesn't get thrown in quite so summarily, and I'm in charge of the dipping stick and can make sure that the heads are pushed under fairly gently. But when one of the other men is around and I'm torn between wanting to appear hard and nonchalant and the urge to try and help my poor animals, then it gets difficult. I know, too, that when you've got to do something unpleasant to animals, it's far better to be quick and decisive about it; emotive bumblers like me cause far more distress in the long run. Even so, when Cynog

Davies is standing there, roaring with laughter at my clucking, and cheering when each of my poor old girls hits the water, I can't stop myself commiserating with them as later they stand, shocked and shivering, in the pens.

Although my original reason for having the little black sheep was purely sentimental, I couldn't have chosen better for my kind of place. They are tough and hardy, usually produce twins and, being small, are ideal sheep for someone with muscles as feeble as mine to handle. Their qualities have been appreciated by a lot more people these days and their numbers have increased enough for them to be taken off the Rare Breeds List. For this advancement in the breed my own tiny flock could claim no credit and even Cynog, putting aside levity for once, admitted that I'd had bad luck in the gene lottery. With the death of Dulcie, one of the original four I'd bought from Cynog's brother, Arwyn, and only two ewe lambs being born since then, I'd effectively increased my breeding flock of Black Welsh Mountain sheep by only one. Humble and Rosie, of course, were ordinary white Welsh Mountain sheep with a dash of North Country Cheviot.

'Maybe the old farmers were right,' I said to Gwyneth one hot day not long after all the dramas of shearing and dipping were over. 'They reckoned black sheep were unlucky. Ah well, they've produced plenty of tups between them and a right lot of little sods they are too. They're on the field below the house and when you come over, I'd be glad if you'd count them. They have a habit of disappearing down into the wood and pretending they can't get back again. I don't want to come back and spend half the night hunting them.'

Gwyneth chuckled. 'The way Mrs P stands out the back counting them, I won't have to worry much,' she said. 'Anyway, you go off and we'll sort it', and she went to open the gate for me.

As I drove across the mountain, the sun shimmered off the peaks of the Fans, larks rose from the tufts of wiry grass on the open moorland and a group of ponies with their chunky little foals like creatures off a merry-go-round trotted across the road in front of me. All across the slopes, newly shorn sheep with gay splotches of red and blue marking paint on their flanks sauntered about grazing calmly and I felt a marvellous sense of

release. All my pandering and worrying, confined within my insular little world, seemed suddenly ridiculous with this great concourse of life going on.

I realised, as I always do when I leave them, how much my animals and my fussing on their behalf bind me tighter than chains. Even after all these years, to force myself into the car and drive out of the gate requires an almighty effort of self-control, arrogantly supposing as I do that only my presence will avert tragedy and disaster. I never leave without looking back as if seeing the farm for the last time. Once on the open road, however, everything swings back into perspective and the image of that tiny cosmos of scratching hens and demanding sheep and barking dogs is thrust to the back of my mind, encapsulated in time as if everything would stand still and wait for my return to move forward again.

On that bright, clear day, therefore, I drove on happily towards Brecon where I was to meet a Bee Master, Arthur Pavord, and record a half-hour programme on bees. I'd had quite a lot of trouble setting the interviews up, mostly because the phone had been out of order on and off for over a month, but at last we'd arranged to meet at Brecon College where he gave evening classes and the College hives contained very docile bees.

As I drove down the gravelled path to the annexe where the classes are held, a thin, elderly man greeted me excitedly. 'We've got a swarm in the orchard,' he told me. 'We left it until you came so that you could record us taking it.'

One of the great disappointments of my life is that I don't keep bees. Apart from the fact that I'm a honey freak, the sight of a group of beehives sitting snugly at one end of a garden conjures up to me the perfect vision of rural content: of hollyhocks blazing in the sun, of the lazy, bee-haunted days of summer and of the cottager with his cow for his milk and his pig for his bacon, his vegetable plot carefully worked and weeded and his bees, with whom he's on extremely familiar terms, for his honey.

The reality of swarms and stings and foul brood and vandalised hives I carefully leave out of this charming picture, but I do acknowledge two things: one is that I am far too fidgety and impatient to have the handling of bees which need calm, methodical masters; the other is that I am dreadfully allergic to

190

stings of any kind, so that even a gnat-bite makes me swell up like a balloon and, as is usually the way, if there are six people in a group and I am one of them, every stinging thing for miles around will home in on me and me alone.

So when I was invited by Arthur Pavord to put on veil and gauntlets and come and help him catch a swarm, I was absolutely terrified. It was the good old reporter who took charge and actually had me and the microphone right up by the swarm, anxious only that I would capture the sound of it on tape. I needn't have worried, for Arthur Pavord is a true Bee Master. He approached the glistening mass hanging in the fork of an apple tree and held his ungloved hands over them 'to get their scent on me'. Then he gave the branch a quick shake, and the swarm fell into the straw skep he had waiting below for them.

It was a magical piece of work and even a misguided and decidedly aggressive bee questing up the inside of the veil I was wearing couldn't make me decide otherwise. For the rest of that hot day I was made privy to the inner secrets of the hives themselves, to the intricate codes which bees dance to let their sisters know where the food source is, to the marvellous mating flights of the virgin queen and the drones waiting for her like squadrons of fighter-planes on high; to the whole amazing world of the honey bee. Finally, we sat in Arthur Pavord's superb garden at Abergavenny and drank delicate, honey flavoured wine. I was still spellbound as I drove home, pots of honey and a couple of bottles of the enchanted wine tucked up on the back seat, and longing only to get back and share my bounty of experience with my mother.

The sun was still lingering above the fretted outline of the forestry as I opened the gate and saw Gwyneth and Mrs P, surrounded by a circle of patiently waiting whippets, standing on the grass bank behind the house. They were both looking soberly in the direction of the home field and were oblivious of the racket the Beetle made as I drove into the yard.

Puzzled at what could be absorbing their attention so deeply, ignoring even the delirious barking of the dogs as they saw me, I hailed them. 'God, I've had a marvellous day!' I shouted, and then faltered as two faces creased with dismay turned and confronted me.

'One of the black ewes is dead,' my mother announced

bluntly, 'just within the last hour.'

'And stinking already,' Gwyneth chimed in. 'Blown up she is, too.'

All the glory of the day left me. 'Bloat?' I asked.

'Well, I can't see how,' replied Gwyneth. 'They aren't on rich grass and the others are all right. Duw, she stinks, though!'

She did too, and already clouds of flies were homing in on the carcass with its huge, distended belly. It was Dinah, who had been as healthy as the rest of the flock when I left that morning.

What happened next I can only blame on ignorance, on the fact that I had brainwashed myself with any number of books and pamphlets (all of them full of the most dreadful warnings about Notifiable Diseases) and on lightheadedness from too much sun and that honey wine.

'It must be something really awful,' I declared dramatically. 'She was fully vaccinated. I must get her over to Bertie's.'

'What for?' asked Gwyneth. 'She's dead. He can't do anything. Best bury her quick.' She drew back from the appalling stench.

Old Goody Two-Shoes, that's me. 'You are supposed,' I informed her severely, 'to have unexplained deaths investigated immediately.'

Gwyneth looked at me wonderingly. 'There we are then,' she said at last. 'You do what you think, but if you change your mind I'll come and help you bury her.' She turned to go and then came back. 'How are you going to get her there in the back of the Beetle?'

That of course was the question. As usual, it was answered by the long-suffering Myrddin. Actually he agreed with Gwyneth that the ewe had choked to death, but by then I was so hysterically convinced that the whole flock was about to drop dead that, more to calm me than anything, he came over and hoisted that dreadful carcass into his Land Rover. It became apparent by the time we'd gone a few yards up the hill that we'd be asphyxiated with the stench long before we got to Bertie's place. Myrddin turned the Land Rover into the drive of his own farm.

'What are you going to do?' I asked tearfully.

'Put it in the boot of the Alfa,' he replied grimly. He did too, although we both had to sit on the lid to close it over that swollen

192

belly. I've often thought that the Alfa Romeo people should use Myrddin as an example of how the boot of one of their cars can be used to carry anything from a dead, stinking sheep to a wildly alive, fully grown goat in season sitting padded with straw and hay, and still remain afterwards as immaculate as the day it came off the production line, for Myrddin is as meticulously tidy with his car as he is generous in offering it to carry bizarre loads.

We had to wait a long while for Bertie, who was out on a life and death case which left him looking drawn and haggard as he came back to be confronted by that hideous corpse I'd brought to his doorstep. To his eternal credit he sent us into the kitchen to wait with Sara and tackled the awful task straight away. By now Myrddin's resigned air, Bertie's ribald jokes and Sara's quiet reassurance had put a lid on my panic and I was beginning to feel a complete fool. We sat and drank coffee and talked bees and tried to forget what was going on out in the surgery. Time went by and Myrddin began to look surreptitiously at his watch.

At last we heard the door of the surgery slam and Bertie came into the kitchen. All of us turned to face him, expecting another joke. I waited for a diatribe on the evils of bringing foul smelling animals to be disembowelled by exhausted vets on a hot summer's evening. But Bertie's face was serious for once. He paused wearily in the doorway and signalled with his eyes to Sara as if warning her to expect trouble.

'I don't want you to panic,' he said to me at last. 'I won't know till I get the lab report back, but the purple rods I saw under the microscope could be one of two things – enterotoxaemia or anthrax. You say she's been vaccinated against enterotoxaemia, so until I know otherwise we have to recognise the possibility that that ewe died of anthrax.'

For a long time I didn't believe him. I vaguely remember Myrddin's shocked stare, Sara's horrified gasp and finally Bertie cracking his inevitable black joke. 'If it is anthrax, it'll mean you and Mrs P and the budgerigar and everything going up in one bloody great Viking funeral pyre.'

As Myrddin drove me back across the Epynt, I had only one dreadful thought. Thanks to my panic we had brought the infected sheep to his own farm and thence across the county border and into Bertie's own flock. I'd not only behaved like a fool, I'd been a dangerous one.

The next twenty-four hours passed very slowly. Mrs P was in a perfect paroxysm of prayer, Myrddin maintained that it was all ridiculous and couldn't be anthrax, and I wandered forlornly round the stock which grazed unconcernedly while their fate was decided by a man in a laboratory. When the outside bell of the phone finally split the air, it sounded like the crack of doom.

'Right,' said Bertie's voice on the other end of the line. 'As you were! All clear! It was enterotoxaemia. Obviously the vaccination didn't take on her. I had to be sure, though, because until the full lab test is done, the purple rods look pretty much the same as anthrax.'

I sat there holding the phone, amazed that the name of a disease like enterotoxaemia could sound so marvellous. Actually it's a horrible disease. The bugs that cause it are present pretty much all the time either in the ground or in the stomach of the grazing animals themselves, but given a certain set of circumstances they can multiply very rapidly and kill off a sheep or goat so quickly that some people say that the first sign of it is a dead animal. That's not strictly true, but it takes a very observant and lucky person to spot the beginning of such a rapid killer. The safest thing to do is to vaccinate against it, but sometimes even that doesn't work.

'Are you still there?' asked Bertie.

'Just about,' I said weakly.

'Good. I thought you'd keeled over for a bit. Well, now you can go off and do your star turn without a worry in your head. If that's possible,' he added darkly as he rang off.

My 'star turn' had almost been forgotten in the horror of the past twenty-four hours. I was due to go to Bristol to take part in the TV series 'The Country Game', later to be known as 'In the Country'. The only reason I was asked at all was because of my supposed country knowledge after doing all those years of the 'You and Yours' country programmes. The year before, Peter Crawford, the producer of 'The Country Game' had brought along a crew and made a small film of the mountains, the goats, the ducks and Blossom and Magnolia, ending up with a fetching sequence of me, togged up in suspiciously clean gear, taking a stroll along the river with Merlin and the rest of the dogs.

The film of the farm was very pretty and idyllic, but my own appearance in the studio was not such a success and I'd looked

194

like the walking dead plastered with make-up. Added to which, it soon became apparent that as an expert on smallholding life I was a complete loss. However, for some reason they'd asked me back again to see how the past year had gone and to pay lip service to the simple life. Frankly, if I hadn't needed the money, I doubt if I'd have gone, but the fee was good and a day out in Bristol, being made to feel important, was very tempting.

A bare few hours after the anthrax nightmare had been lifted, I was in the Beetle once more, hot, ungroomed and desperately late. Knowing the parlous state of my transport, Peter had arranged for me to come the night before and stay overnight at a good hotel near the Clifton Suspension Bridge where he and Julian Pettifer, the presenter, and the rest of the people taking part in the programme would be waiting for me to go out to dinner so that we could discuss things in a civilised way. I had planned to arrive cool, calm and arrayed in my best black. Instead I was flying out of the gate with my hair yanked back into an untidy pony-tail, the best black scrunched into my case unironed, and praying that the car would make it at all.

I was recklessly dashing down towards the old ruined mill which lies in a hollow by a vicious bend leading to a steep hill and hidden by a thick hedge as you approach. Usually I take the bend slowly in case something is coming unseen down the hill, but that day I tore round it and came face to face with a massive cattle truck. Both of us stood on our brakes and I began to back slowly down the hill – straight into the ditch, where the Beetle settled with a nasty scrunch and stopped. It was too much. I crawled out of the left side and swore at the men in the cab of the truck. They emerged, two enormous beefy sets of muscle, and grinned at me cheerfully. Without a word, they walked over to the Beetle, took one end each and lifted it back onto the road.

Unless I'm going straight to the BBC, I always get lost in Bristol. I got lost that day. By the time I had found the hotel, spent an hour trying to park the car and staggered dishevelled and wild-eyed into the plush grandeur of the reception area, I was past caring about the look of withering contempt from the clerk as he cast an eye over my dusty suitcase and my red face. The rest of the party were already having drinks as I joined them breathlessly in my crumpled black dress.

Dinner in the elegant, softly lit French restaurant was lovely, but what I really needed was a good night's sleep. One way and another, by the time we were ready to film the next day, I was too tired to give a damn. The hot lights of the studio did nothing to rouse me from my stupor and I know that at one point while we were waiting, I actually nodded off to sleep. Julian Pettifer prodded me with his toe and cued me in by asking how I was still liking life on the smallholding.

It was then that a curious thing happened. Whereas the previous year I had been desperately nervous of the cameras and sycophantically eager to please and to play the game of declaring that all was lovely in the country, this time the carefully prepared answers deserted me. I found myself talking about how many things could go wrong, how I'd chosen the wrong place, that it was far better, unless you felt you *had* to live on a farm, to stay in the town and go to the country for holidays so that you could keep your illusions intact. I ended, though, by saying that I wouldn't change my life as it was just then, not for anything. And I meant it. I suddenly knew that no matter what happened, my city days were over for good.

Bertie's reaction, when the programme was transmitted some weeks later, was to ask, 'Why didn't you tell them you'd got suspected anthrax on the farm and clear the studio? Now that *would* have been something worth watching!'

# Chapter 19

'Ah then, Doli, when are you going to pop, eh, girl?'

'Pop's what she'll do, if she's not careful,' I growled.

Gwyneth and I were leaning over the gate, gazing at Doli who mooched around, irritably flicking her tail at the flies trying to find standing room on her growing udder. Sometimes a shadow of movement across her distended side proclaimed that her foal was alive and getting impatient.

'When's she really due, then?' asked Gwyneth.

'Ha, you may well ask,' I said grimly. 'Bertie reckons the old devil didn't take till her third cycle. She was over there with the stallion a full six weeks from the time the stallion served her, but we think she didn't take till just before she came home. It's either due in a few days time or not for another three weeks, for heaven's sake!'

'It'll be a pretty late foal then,' said Gwyneth, shaking her head. Her own little cob mare had already produced a colt foal back in the spring and, being a normal sort of horse, had since been back to the stallion once to be covered in hand. Now she was in foal again.

'Yes, and the nuisance is that it'll be too late to have her covered again this year. Otherwise next year's foal will be born some time in late autumn at the rate she goes.'

Gwyneth grinned. 'I wonder what she'll have,' she said.

'A tank on hooves, according to Bertie,' I replied. 'I just hope it's a filly this time.'

We stood silently for a while. 'He's busy over there,' said Gwyneth, nodding across the valley to where a tractor crawled up and down a long bare slope, followed by a drift of seagulls.

Once that slope had been an intricate pattern of little green fields sewn round with hedges and graced here and there by massive, sheltering oaks. Bulldozers and JCB's had come one day like a blight and turned it all into desolation. At last only one vast oak had been left in the midst of the ruin and it seemed for a while that it, at least, would be spared, but finally that too was plucked away to join the rest of the carnage at the bottom of the valley. Since then great drainage scars had seared the red earth and now the endless work of ploughing and re-seeding went on across the empty slope.

Behind the tractors came the gulls, not a common sight in the valley unless there is a storm out at sea, when I look up and see them flying high above, their wild cries bringing the sound and smell of the distant crashing waves. When they go, they take a part of me with them, for I love the sea and sometimes, to be away from it is a kind of death. If ever I leave here of my own accord it will be because the sea dreams won't be quietened. There was a time when they almost won: an island for sale; weeks of planning how it could be done; the grey day when reality took over and I turned sorrowfully away, for I had lost the courage to do and dare the impossible. Only now, when the gulls come inland, does the old dream shake its tatters and make me restless. Then the only place where I can find relief is in the white room at the top of the house where the words of other sea lovers are stacked on the bookshelves and a little sea unicorn rears on its panel of carved wood and the ash tree sighs at the window like the waves.

'Ah well.' Gwyneth stretched her arms out in the sun. 'I'd better get back. Eddie'll be wanting his dinner, I suppose. You'll let me know when she has it, won't you?'

'You and the rest of the world! The phone's never stopped ringing to see if she's had that foal yet. All I'm sure of is that she'll have it at the most difficult, inconvenient time she can manage.'

'The old sod,' said Gwyneth affectionately and, with a wave of

198

her hand, she went off down the lane and I could hear her singing till the noise of the river drowned the light note of her voice.

After she'd left, I stood for a while watching the growing kids hurtling around the crab apple tree, showing off to Little Nana who was hobbling after them uncertainly. It was her first day out after weeks incarcerated in the stable with a broken leg. When eventually I'd allowed Whacky back with the others full-time, I'd put them all into the old stable where the big wooden slabs holding up the manger gave them protection from the draughts at night and they could fling themselves against the solid door without breaking it. Already the newer, flimsier doors of the looseboxes were beginning to show signs of strain. Besides which, I'd soon want the looseboxes with their easily cleaned concrete floors and smooth, rendered walls which I could disinfect properly in case Doli needed to be brought inside to foal.

The old stable with its rough stone walls, cobbled floor and long wooden manger may have been ideal for the kids in principle, but Little Nana had got stuck up in the feeding rack and broken her back leg in the slats trying to get down. The first time I'd thought of it as a freak accident, wired the manger to stop it happening again and got Bertie to set the leg, which had broken cleanly and mended perfectly. Then, within a day of Little Nana's return to the boisterous company of the other kids, she got straight up over the wire and did it again, this time to her front leg.

Considering the way the rest of them flung themselves up and down the walls and galloped along behind the slats and hurtled out again unscathed, it was a clear case of Sod's Law. Again, the break was clean and this time I applied the splints myself and took her to Bertie to have the plaster put on when the swelling had subsided. Fortunately it didn't seem to bother Little Nana in the slightest except that it kept her at ground level for a while. What it did for me, after my first sickened reaction, was to inure me to broken bones so that I could cope with them without passing out. For me that was a big step forward because I'd been lugged out of every first-aid class I'd ever attended: as soon as they got to the bit about fractures, I went out like a light.

The old farmer who said to me that the best teachers of animal husbandry are death and disaster was quite right. No matter how much you look and listen and read, it's having to cope with one of your own animals that drives the lesson right down deep. Only going through the nightmare of Marek's disease in the poultry finally taught me to recognise and, more importantly, to try and prevent it; the death of the first Dolores I bought from Thurlow Craig has probably saved the lives of the goats I have now; it took an outburst of twin lamb disease one year finally to make me really aware of the need for the sheep to have a proper winter diet. I could go on endlessly but more important, I think, is the way a real brush with disease and accident can make you face up to it in future.

I always lived in almost hysterical dread of maggot-strike until the day not so long ago when I found a wounded sheep covered with them from the tip of her nose to the middle of her back: a horrible, obscene, white, seething blanket. Myrddin showed me how to get most of the ghastly things to leave their living feast by pouring diluted maggot oil over them, but there were a lot left that I had to pick out myself by hand. That I also saved the ewe by day and night nursing amazed everyone and gave me a great feeling of confidence. Now, instead of having useless hysterics, I can attack that particular horror with some hope of defeating it.

One other thing I've learned is that no matter how much you prepare for and defend against disaster, when it strikes it will be in the very place you've overlooked. For instance, in looking after Little Nana and watching Doli for signs of that long-awaited foal, my attention was turned away from the one animal which, with Suyin and Pip, the Burmese cats, was the most precious of all.

On the morning after Gwyneth's visit, I was up early, long before the sun had swung itself clear of the Fans. As I blearily opened the back door, a stream of dogs poured out and the two cats began wailing for their breakfast. I turned to go back into the kitchen and realised that Merlin was still lying on the dogs' bed. I bent over him to whistle in his ear and get him moving, but he lay there, horribly still. I shook him with a laugh but he was stone cold and, as far as I could see, quite dead.

I picked up the beautiful, silver-blue body, still limp, and cradled it in my arms, too numb even to cry or to believe fully that that perfection of shape and speed and intelligence could be

200

still forever. The faintest flutter of a heartbeat stirred under my hand. Merlin wasn't dead, but he was in so deep a coma that it was only a matter of time before his great heart followed his brain into that awful silence.

After eight hours, he was full of injections but still alive, warmed by blankets and hot water bottles and my own body. Vets had been and gone, Gwyneth had come silently to see to the stock, Mrs P had kept the other dogs quiet and made me cups of tea. They had all been like wraiths, seen dimly at the edge of consciousness. I make no apology for grieving so deeply for my dog; I was grieving as much for myself and for all the joy he'd given and was now taking out of my life. Most bitter of all, his death would be my fault for not attending properly to that mound where Magnolia was buried, for not making sure that it had been undisturbed by foxes, for not actually digging the whole thing out and pouring lime over the corpse and burying it deeper. It was yet another example of not wanting to face what I could hardly bear to see. Now my cowardice and laziness would kill Merlin, who had finished what the foxes had begun by digging up and eating the very part of the pig's body where the massive dose of anaesthetic had lodged, its potency undisturbed by time.

Few vets like operating on whippets. As a breed they have a low tolerance of anaesthetic and it takes them a lot longer to come out of it than most dogs. With part of a dose large enough to kill a fully grown pig inside him, Merlin stood little chance of surviving. That he was still alive at all was something of a miracle. There was nothing further I could do now but keep him warm and somehow give him my strength and will him to live. And so I sat there, holding the years of his life in my mind.

As I waited for him to leave me, I could see a young Merlin dancing along at twelve weeks old on his first day in the park when the red may trees were in blossom; could see him, a few months later, fly up into the arms of a woman whose magnificently groomed blonde hair had impressed me so often and could remember how I watched, appalled, as he came away with it, shaking and worrying the wig while its owner stood by in shock; could see him a year later take his first trial race; could see him glorying in his own speed but submitting earnestly to the early morning training sessions around the asphalt paths. I remembered his delight in his own fields, free of constraint as he and Elke settled to their new life at the farm. Not once did he cast a glance at the stock and if Suyin and Pip still barely tolerated him, the other cats loved him to such an extent that when he arrived they would rush to rub themselves against him in an ecstasy of purring and follow him wherever he went.

If I went back to the city without him, people all over Kensington stopped me to ask about him and once, when I was refused an interview by a busy, well-known actor who also walked in the Park, I told his agent to say it was 'Merlin's owner' who wanted to see him, and the interview was granted immediately. He grew into a big whippet and even when he was in racing form, he weighed about twenty-six pounds. Racing was something he loved more than anything, not just for the actual running but for the whole ritual of starting bells and traps and having his muzzle put on, jumping up to put his face into it as soon as I took it out of the bag. He knew that racing bag well, with its set of numbered silks, the coat to stop him getting chilled, the massage glove and the bottles of muscle liniment.

We took him to see some racing when he was still a pup, although he wouldn't be ready to take part until he was at least a year old. There weren't any strict age rules then, but racing too early can put a strain on the heart of a growing dog. The marvellous thing about pedigree whippet racing is that it's usually done for the honour and glory and the sheer enjoyment of seeing your dog come up through the bunch and win. The whippets love it even more than their owners and, while a race is going on, they go berserk trying to join in. I did a programme once on whippet racing and got amused complaints from owners all over the country when their dogs, hearing the starting bell on the radio, went completely wild.

The first little club we joined was a gloriously haphazard affair. It met on a field bordered by huge elms in Berkshire and the 'track' had to be mown by hand before we could begin. Everybody had a picnic, family groups sat under the trees gossiping about whippets while children and dogs cavorted around and every now and again we watched a race. The dogs were slipped by hand and the 'bunny' (a battered football with fluttering rags attached) was drawn up on a winch operated by a car battery. At the end of the day, every dog present could join in the last race, even the spaniels and terriers who'd been egging on their kennel companions with the rest of the crowd.

When he was about fifteen months old and we judged that his muscles had been hardened up by the light road work we'd been giving him, we took Merlin to the more organised Surrey Club, where he was to have his first trial race to see if he could behave on the track, for a dog that wants to argue and fool about is a dangerous nuisance.

At this club they had the luxury of proper traps and that was something else Merlin had to get used to. When the afternoon's proper racing was over and the rosettes and plaques had been handed out to the jubilant owners of the winners, we took Merlin down to the traps where a few other people had volunteered their experienced dogs to make up a bit of competition for the newcomer. These dogs were tired after their afternoon's racing, of course, but that didn't lessen the thrill when Merlin shot out of the traps like a veteran and strode home to finish first.

He won a lot of races after that and the Park routine was now a carefully controlled training session which meant getting up very early and plodding endlessly round the paths to make up so many steady miles per hour instead of our leisurely ambles across the grass. And oh, the special diets, the massages, the 'secret' recipes for racing tonics and all the other fascinating black magic which the owners discussed and repudiated and recommended as we waited our turn to take the dogs to the starting-line.

Merlin adored it all. He knew when we were going racing even before the bag was brought out and checked; he knew within a few miles when we were getting near the club and was clamouring to be let out. If he'd had a win he sat imperiously gazing out of the window on the way home, but when he'd lost he crawled onto my lap and wanted comfort while the Artist and I went over the race and the reasons why he might have failed and what we could do about it next time.

Sometimes we went further afield to other clubs, where the owners and their dogs were a bit more beady-eyed and serious about racing and one glorious day, when the Albertine roses filled the villages with perfume, we went to Middle Wallop to take part in an inter-club competition with the New Forest. Now they were a very professional lot and their dogs were hard-muscled and keen. Bernard Venables, the artist and writer, his wife, Eileen, and their three children were with us to watch Merlin race. There was quite a crowd present because it was a charity fair and our racing whippets were part of the attraction. There was even a little tote to raise more money.

It soon became apparent that the Surrey Club was outclassed. Race after race went to the New Forest and the gloom amongst the Surrey supporters was terrible to see. Merlin was due to race in the last but one and, to our dismay, he'd drawn the New Forest champion, Jack's Boy. There were two dogs from each club in every race and to make things worse, partnering Jack's Boy was a dog which had been known to beat even him.

The Venables and I stood watching while the Artist walked Merlin down to the traps. I tried in vain to explain the situation to the three children, who'd been looking forward all day to watching Merlin win. The Artist glanced across at us as he went down the track with Merlin dancing on his lead, and shook his head hopelessly. The dogs went into the traps, the New Forest supporters wore a smug look and the Surrey lot gazed sorrowfully at the starter. They were like raving maniacs a few seconds later as Merlin hurled himself out and roared up the track to come in a good first. The Venables children looked at me accusingly for my want of faith.

Jack's Boy, who was a truly great dog, beat Merlin at the next championship meeting, but the day Merlin saved the Surrey honour, the cheers and the kissing and the scent of Albertines and the fact that the tote had to pay out quite a bit of money to the one person who'd had enough faith to back Merlin are still with me when I look at the engraved plaque we took home, glorying all the way.

If his public life was often full of honour, Merlin's private affairs were rather less successful. It was through him that I met David and Pan Wade. A photograph of Merlin in the *Radio Times* had inspired David to write and ask if it would be possible for my whippet to serve the Wades' little lurcher bitch who was about to come into season. Normally I wouldn't have consented, but when the eminent radio critic of *The Times* speaks, scrabbling freelances listen. A bout of 'flu on my part meant that one way and another, Merlin and I didn't go to see the Wades and their bitch until the very last day on which it was likely she could conceive.

Merlin was entranced by the seductive little female waiting for him in the Wades' garden at Chiswick and he spent a lot of energy showing his appreciation by doing a kind of soft-shoe shuffle around her, giving her the full range of his vocabulary, expanding his chest and gazing adoringly into her eyes. He didn't seem quite so interested in the fact that she was holding her tail to one side in readiness and was obviously very anxious to get down to business.

The Wades and I were equally inexperienced in the mysteries of handling mating dogs and, believing that the dogs themselves were quite capable of sorting things out, repaired after half an hour's bemused supervision of their antics into the kitchen, where a sumptuous tea of cakes and fresh scones was laid out.

The kitchen windows were large and, as we ate, we could watch the dogs in comfort. The trouble was, the dogs could also watch us. While the bitch continued in her efforts to make Merlin take her seriously and stop dancing effetely around her front end, he, deprived of his audience, faltered. He left the bitch, an agonised expression on her face by now, quartered the garden carefully, lifted his head, observed us through the window popping food into our mouths, stopped to stare at us with one paw raised, disappeared from sight for a moment and then trotted into the kitchen, sat down by the table, honking reproachfully, and demanded his tea. The bitch almost wept.

Another member of the Surrey Club saved the day by being rushed to Chiswick to mate the bitch while I retired with Merlin, replete with scones, his virginity intact.

Merlin's greed was his one great fault, although until the day he raided Magnolia's grave, he'd never actually been a scavenger. For the thousandth time, I looked down at his still body and cursed myself for not remembering that in spite of his great intelligence, he was after all a dog, and dogs love well-seasoned rubbish. Now his one fall from grace was killing him.

There was a gentle bump at the door, which opened a crack for a small, black nose to appear. It was Misty, a delicate, pale, brindled bitch, one of Bea's pups which were now grown up. We still had four of them: Gloucester, Boy, Misty and Squiff. All in all, with Bea, her brother Bran and the pups (as we still called them) the whippet pack numbered seven. 'Do you breed them,' one visitor had asked, 'or do you have them like other people have mice?' Which was rather intelligent of him because whippets do tend to multiply in your life.

I've known a lot of people, unremittingly determined to have only one dog, who have acquired a whippet and within a year a second. If they are very strong-willed they'll stick there, but the odds are that before long they'll be just as inventive as the rest of us in making up excuses for having yet another and another and another.

Whippets, as I was to learn very early on, are not just miniature greyhounds. To the unpractised eye they may have a similar shape, but in fact their backs have an elegant curve, whereas the greyhound's is straighter. If the arguments about training, diet and massage occupied most of the conversation amongst the racing whippet owners, the conformation, size and origins of these little dogs took up the rest.

The most commonly held theory is that whippets were bred by the northern miners some time in the last century so that they could have a small version of the greyhound to live with the family in their tiny cottages, to provide a bit of racing and to collect the odd rabbit for the pot. To get the size down, it is thought, they mixed terrier blood with that of smaller greyhounds. Which terrier it was nobody was quite sure, but my own favourite bet is that it was the Bedlington with its curved back and nippy movements and silky fur, for the whippet has all those things. In its character, the whippet has the gently affectionate nature of the greyhound, overlaid with the sharp intelligence of the terrier. But perhaps it was nothing to do with those northern miners after all: small dogs like whippets also appear in old tapestries or on the laps of Renaissance ladies in paintings, and many of them are obviously not of that other more ancient breed, the little Italian greyhound, which resembles more truly the large dogs.

Whatever their background, whippets are addictive. The perfect house dog, it can curl up like a cat, keeps its fur impeccably clean and, wonder of wonders, hasn't got a pervasive doggy smell. When not defending you and your property, the whippet spends a great deal of its off duty hours asleep. But offer to go out and you have instant, explosive movement, beautiful to watch and exhilarating to be with. Their critics say they are too thin, but in actual fact they're more likely to be just very fit, and their lean ribs are counterbalanced by their bulging muscles. They do indeed feel the cold when they're not moving fast, mainly because they lack that second layer of insulating fur which most dogs have, but whippets are the most accomplished actors and if they think a fit of shivering will get your sympathy and your lap, they'll shiver to the gallery like anything. Unlike human actors, however, they have no professional jealousy (unless it's on the racing track) and when Bea and Bran came to share our household and my affections, Merlin accepted them calmly.

The pups hero worshipped him and all that day, while he lay in a coma, one after another they tiptoed in and out, putting their noses against his and retiring to their communal bed, where they lay mournfully and silently together. Midnight came and went and still Merlin lay without moving. I'd shifted him many times to stop the fluid draining into one lung, a danger when an animal is immobilised on one side, but not once had his eyes even flickered. At last I nodded into sleep too.

A loud, peremptory honk woke me. Merlin was sitting up on his couch, looking at me with bright, clear eyes. He stretched his neck towards the water with which I'd been moistening his tongue all through the day and night. I passed the bowl over to him. He drank it all and honked at me enquiringly. I picked him up, still wrapped in a rug, and went out with him into the cold, clear dawn.

I steadied him onto the grass where he peed for a full minute, gave a wavering stretch and came to lean his head against my knee.

'Don't you ever give me a fright like that again!' I told him, and felt the tears pouring down my cheeks. 'What you're going to get now is a thundering great dose of paraffin to flush the rest of that muck out of you, and then I'm going to sort that pig out once and for all.'

To this day, if you say 'dead pig' to Mrs P, she goes quite pale. All that morning I stuck to the gruesome job of disinterring what remained of poor old Magnolia after all that time, parcelled it up into feed sacks and carried them down the hill escorted by clouds of attentive flies. The smell was shocking and permeated the whole farm; the dead sheep had been as nothing to it. Even about a litre of Jeyes' Fluid didn't help much. I didn't care, because whenever I faltered momentarily in my task, the joy of Merlin's miraculous recovery and the thought of him, weak but already discussing the menu with Mrs P in the kitchen, would have sent me with my frightful load right to the top of the Fans themselves. As I worked on, the cries of the squabbling gulls as they circled round the distant tractor, which was still crawling up and down the opposite slope, echoed from the hills like a song.

That night I was still on a high as I inspected Doli to see if she had begun to bag up properly. There was no great difference and yet....

'I'll be a while before I come in to supper,' I told Mrs P. 'I think I'll just give the looseboxes a good scrub out.'

'Oh, come on,' she said. 'You know Bertie says it probably won't be for a couple of weeks yet. And if you don't get some sleep, you'll die on your feet.'

'I don't know,' I said. 'She's got a funny look in her eye.'

'Doli's always got a funny look in her eye,' Mrs P snorted.

'I still think I'll get the looseboxes ready, though,' I said. 'I meant to do it yesterday, but what with everything, of course I didn't. I doubt if I'll get any sleep anyway.' I took the rest of the Jeyes' Fluid and went out to scrub the floors and walls of the loosebox once more and get bales of fresh straw stacked up in readiness. The box would be needed only if there was a problem with the birth of the foal, and I hoped it would be born out on the field where the risk of infection was less and Doli would have plenty of room to move around.

By the time I was finished, the fact that except for a short doze, I'd had nothing in the way of sleep for the past forty-eight hours was beginning to tell. Stiffly, I walked down the field to Doli, who was cropping the moonlit grass. Seeing me, she lifted her head and whickered gently. And then she yawned three times. Now one thing I've learnt in my constant staring at my own animals is that frequent yawning is sometimes a sign of stress or pain or imminent birth. Of course they also yawn when they're tired, but that is something else again. When an animal yawns a lot, I always get one finger poised on the alarm button.

Doli yawned again. I groped under her and felt her udder. Sure enough, it was bigger and thick blobs of wax were dripping from the end of the teats. It was going to be another all night watch.

208

At four o'clock, with the stars already dimming in the sky, I went out for the tenth time to see if Doli was showing any sign of going into labour. I didn't open the gate, not wanting to disturb her, but she sensed that I was there and came ambling up the field towards me. We stood there companionably for a while until Doli turned and began casually cropping the grass.

'You old fraud,' I said cheerfully. 'Nothing doing, eh?' I went back inside to get some sleep on the couch by the fireplace, setting the alarm clock so that I would wake in an hour, just in case.

I woke from a dream of long, rolling breakers and a white, deserted beach and the haunting cry of gulls. For a while I lay with my eyes closed but the cry of the gulls went on. I sat up and saw them circling round and round outside the window. The sound of them came down the chimney like a shout, a very urgent shout.

'Gulls? They must be waiting for the tractor. What the hell's the time?' I muttered as I scrabbled off the couch and picked up the clock. The alarm had gone off unheeded, the time was already half past six and the sun was bright outside.

And Doli? I could see her standing rigidly still in the middle of the field as I fumbled desperately with the gate. Beside her, swaying on its long legs, its coat the colour of a newly minted penny, was a foal.

It was a filly and I called her Gwylan, which is Welsh for Seagull.

# Chapter 20

'What you *should* call her is Sidonie Vicious,' Bertie declared.

'She's not vicious,' I protested.

'No, but she's very, very fick,' he said. 'You shove a safety pin through one of her ears and paint a few purple stripes down her mane and she'll be the complete punk foal. Look at the way she's standing there with her big mouth open!'

Gwylan shut her mouth, sidled over and affectionately pinned her critic to the wall with her big behind.

'Get off!' he spluttered. 'Give her a tickle. Quick!'

I rubbed Gwylan's stomach obligingly. She simpered at me and relaxed her limbs into rubber, weaving her head foolishly from side to side.

Bertie straightened up and adjusted his canvas hat so that it came forward over his brow and collided with the top of his round spectacles. 'Just what I said.' He nodded at the foal. 'A fick punk what mugs people.'

At twelve weeks old, Gwylan was already enormous and a perfect Cleveland bay foal to look at. It was as if Doli had had no part in her production. Apart from her looks, she'd also inherited from Bert his complete unconcern for obstacles of any kind, and walked into and through any she happened to encounter. Already in her short life, Bertie had paid several visits to patch up the inevitable damage to her legs, while I despaired over the fences and learnt to be very tidy. Doli did her best to steer her foal away from all the places which she, as an experienced and watchful mother, knew would do her no good, but Gwylan continued to plough her way through life and was running me up some pretty horrendous vet's bills.

On the day she was born, it had taken Doli and Gwyneth and me a whole day of striving to get the new foal to understand which was udder and which was nothing more productive than a large piece of her mother's flank. I'd finally had to milk some colostrum off and give it to her as a drench, which she resented noisily. She then returned to her favourite dummy with a reproachful look. Doli, who was full of milk, stood patiently letting it down so that it actually streamed out onto the straw of the loosebox as Gwyneth and I, sweating with the heat and the effort, held the foal's nose against the welling teats. Gwylan kept her mouth firmly shut. If we opened it for her, she just kept it open.

Apart from the fact that the foal had had little in the way of nourishment since she'd been born twelve hours before, Doli had not yet shed her afterbirth, which was still hanging in a long ribbon behind her and threatening to strangle Gwylan as she blundered around her mother. The suckling of the newborn animal helps the mother's womb to contract, but it got no help from Gwylan. The flies had been taking a malevolent interest in the afterbirth for some while and, although I knew it wasn't too desperate yet, I can never really relax until I see it properly expelled. Retention of the afterbirth can lead to some very nasty complications and, if left unattended for too long, even to the death of the mother from metritis.

'I think I'd better come over and shove a few injections into them both,' said Bertie when I rang him. I returned to the loosebox to have one final try at persuading Gwylan which part of her mother was nourishing and which was not. She remained obdurately unconvinced by my explanations. The sound of a car grinding its way down the hill brought me up off my knees under Doli and, as I straightened up, Gwylan stared at me through her big doe eyes.

'Look, you silly idiot,' I said, 'for the last time, that *there* is udder!' I gave her a final shove in the right direction. Dawn never came up more thunderously than it did on Gwylan's face. At the precise moment when Bertie came to lean over the half-door, she applied her lips to one of Doli's teats and suckled as if her heart would burst.

'Nothing wrong with that then, is there?' said Bertie airily, while I contemplated murder. Right on cue, the rest of the afterbirth slid out, complete in all its parts.

From that time on, Gwylan spent the greater part of her day plugged into the milk supply. The odd clumsy sortie into the pond or the fence aside, she passed the rest of her time asleep. There was little of the energetic exploring of the power of her gangling limbs which Moelwyn had indulged in; just a lot of lying about and dozing. Foals (and indeed all young things) do spend a great deal of time in sleep, but as she grew older, Gwylan's passion for a nap grew almost into a permanent state of mind. The rest of the stock learnt early on to give her a wide berth, for Gwylan's sudden collapse on the ground was as unpredictable as her sleep was sustained. Doli began to have a hunted look. An over-conscientious mother, she would never leave a sleeping foal unguarded and neither would she dream of grazing when she was on duty.

As time went on and her gangling daughter demanded more and more milk and continued to sleep it off, Doli snatched quickly at the sweet summer grass for the few moments her daughter remained vertical. No human mother importuned by her implacably desperate offspring in the most public of places could have said 'What? Now?' more eloquently than did Doli's expression as Gwylan subsided to the ground between one stride and the next. I was assured by Bertie that there was nothing wrong with the foal physically. She was just a slow developer.

Nevertheless, the sight of Doli standing patiently immobile beside the dreaming foal for so much of the day began to worry me. I was even more worried when I saw her grazing quite alone at the end of the field one morning at about eleven. Of Gwylan there was no sign at all.

'Now don't panic,' I was muttering furiously to myself as I hurried through the gate. 'Doli wouldn't leave her if she was in trouble.' The sight of a bright copper rump lying on the ground by the fence sent me flying across the field, but as I got nearer I stopped in wonder. Gwylan was asleep as usual, but beside her lay Dolores and the foal's head was stretched luxuriantly across the goat's flank as if on a pillow. Dolores, the terror of the kids, who could barely tolerate her own offspring, was on foal duty and Doli, who had disdained my offers to take over the watch, had accepted her services confidently enough to leave her foal a field's length away. I stayed and watched them for a long while, saw Doli come back once or twice to check that all was well and then continue her grazing, saw Dolores accompany the foal to her mother to suckle without any resentment from Doli and shook my head in amazement when the goat actually persuaded the foal to have a mad little gallop with her round the field.

They became a familiar sight, Dolores and Gwylan together. At night, when the goat was inside, the foal whickered at her through the door which opens out onto the field and Dolores shouted reassuringly back. In the morning she pushed past me impatiently, collected the foal from her mother's side and, with what seemed like earnest enquiries as to how she'd passed the night, took her over to their favourite spot for the foal's nap while Dolores got on with her cudding. It was only when autumn began to chill the air and Dolores had other things on her mind, like keeping an eye out for a passing billy goat, that the bond between the companions began to relax.

It was just as well it had for, as the idyllic days of summer faded and the bright flame of the rowan berries blazed on the little tree at the end of the garden, I began to say good-bye. There had to be a limit to the number of times the cavalry could come galloping over the hill at the last moment and why indeed should I expect to preserve my little fantasy world when there were people far more in need than I was? No matter that I had a group of animals, trained broadcasters every one of them, waiting in readiness for the day when they could illustrate the programme which, obsession though it had become to me, had still not been accepted.

My couple of years of fumbling about on the farm hadn't qualified me to pontificate about life in the country, but it had knocked the gilt off the fond dream which so many media people seem to have about the beauty of the simple life; it had shown me what a complicated life it really is and given me a deep respect (mingled with a bit more cynicism about the self-styled 'experts') for those who strive to make small livings out of the mainstream of agriculture.

I'd also learned about things like the life expectancy of a pair of real, working wellies, the intimate secrets of a septic tank, the way in which dust and damp combine to make instant antique mud and the impossibility of banishing either from an old cottage. I'd learned that far from being the quiet, leisurely amble through the seasons which popular legend would have us believe, country life is a wild scramble to beat the weather, the wind, the needs of your animals and the trespass of everyone else's. Neither was there too much of that solitary bliss, even in a place as remote as mine, for neighbours know your business earlier than you do, people on holiday treat your yard as a turning place and take the opportunity to use you as a map-reading service, public phone, water supply and even a camping site. Believe me, if ever I really wanted to be alone, I'd go back and live in the middle of London. There, at least, you can hide behind the aspidistra if you don't want to answer the door. In the country, even the most casual caller, reassured by the presence of your transport betraying you on the yard, can be remarkably obtuse and persistent in their efforts to flush you out.

The single most important thing I had learned, though, was that everyone who actually survives country life has a story to tell. I no longer wanted to do a programme about the happy peasant tilling his soil; I wanted to get on tape people like the men who drive the massive machines along tortuous lanes and down suicidal slopes to collect the garbage from remote villages and farms; or the postmen who struggle through floods and snow and over icy roads to get the latest circulars safely delivered. I wanted to record the odd-job men like Robin Spedborough, or the country builder freezing up his ladders on dizzying roofs, exposed to the full force of the wind. I wanted to talk to the Gwyneths and the Myrddins of the countryside as well as to the earnest newcomers battling to make their rural dream come true and fighting valiantly against disillusion. I wanted, too, to search out the individuals like Gerald and Imogen who abound in the country, where they find room to be themselves.

Then there was the whole fascinating world of the various

breeds, rare and otherwise, each inhabited by dedicated personalities like Beryl Rutherford, each with its own long history, so often made by the particular character of the part of the country where they thrived best. Above all there were the small questions, hundreds of them, which, I'd realised as I was asking them, are often not considered important enough to put in a book, and the answers are usually found by experience or from a neighbour. I suppose that was what I really had in mind – a programme which was like a conversation with a country friend.

As I worked and worried and walked in the wood, ideas for the programme multiplied. At the same time, however, the memory of me as a professional broadcaster was fading fast, along with my credibility to the producers. That meant it was getting harder and harder to sell any ideas, let alone this one for a series as ambitious as I originally had in mind. So, as the programme took firmer shape in my mind, it became more and more obvious that I could no longer afford to stay in the place which would have given it birth and been the foundation of its continued existence. My earnings had dropped to a level which wouldn't even service the mortgage and the overdraft, let alone start paying them back, and, even if I'd been employable in any other capacity, things had already gone too far.

That they had been able to go as far as they had was due solely to the faith of Mr Chapman of Lloyds Bank, Knightsbridge. Before you are impressed with that address, let me assure you that my account and I had followed Mr Chapman there from Kensington. When I was being badgered by the building society to get the repairs done to the cottage before they would give me the rest of the money I was to borrow from them, I'd approached Mr Chapman for a bridging loan. Till then my meagre earnings had been stashed away in a place where only my personal attendance would produce any cash. In this way I put a curb on my impulse to spend, because the place was in Kingsway and, by the time I'd thought about taking the journey there and back, my urge to buy what I shouldn't be buying was cooled. But with such heady things as bridging loans and mortgages to deal with, the time came when I needed a proper clearing bank.

Mr Chapman, as well as doling out my loan and persuading me to put my financial affairs on a more regular footing, proved

215

to be a man of much wit and understanding. He took a fatherly interest in the farm, directed me to another building society with more reasonable rates and generally helped me to manage my money affairs. Even when I deserted London and the possibility of earning reasonably well, his faith in my fortunes didn't diminish. Well, not much anyway.

Mr Chapman once told me that he knew I worried far more about the bank's money than they did. He was right there. In spite of his encouragement and his determination that I should try to hang on to the farm until better days, that overdraft was like a sore in my mind. The thought of it went with me everywhere and if I slept, I woke to its hideous reality night after night. At last, with the broadcasting world closing its doors firmly in my face, I had to put it to Mr Chapman that the only possibility left to me of earning a living at the farm was to borrow yet more money. With this I could convert the cowshed (which, apart from being a very solid building, has spectacular views) into two holiday flats, finish the work on the other cowshed beside the house and go into the tourist trade. There was also a chance that I might get a grant to do this.

I betook myself to London and the plush surroundings of his office opposite Harrods. Mr Chapman was just as affably welcoming as if I'd had a deposit of millions instead of a steadily mounting overdraft. He listened carefully once again to my ideas and finally promised that if I could get a grant as well, the bank would lend me the money I needed. There was only one blight on our meeting: the phone rang on his vast desk and the kindly face in front of me grew stern as he spoke to the unnamed caller. He listened for a while and then said curtly, 'Well, I'm afraid things have got out of hand and I really must ask you to do something at once about reducing the loan considerably. I shall expect to hear from you in a day or so. Good afternoon.' He put the phone down firmly and then turned back to me and smiled, 'Now, what were you saying?'

It was without any real conviction that I continued to outline my plans. In my mind, I had become that caller who had evoked such a change in my kindly bank manager. Knowing that any building has a way of being delayed and of getting more expensive, and realising that my debt would go on rising, I could see ahead of me the spectre of the bailiff, Mr Chapman no longer friendly, the animals forced willy-nilly to go to market and the besmirching of all the happy days of the past by the awfulness of being 'sold up' publicly. Far better to leave now before things got out of hand and I could at least sell the animals privately and leave the valley with dignity.

That day I had lunch with a great friend, Jack Sassoon, who ran the little secondhand bookshop at the top of Kensington Church Street. As well as having an evil sense of humour, Jack writes ridiculous stories about his tame vampire, Fred, to entertain his friends and sends us rude cards for Christmas and birthdays and any other thing he can think of. He is also a man of great culture, knows just about every book that's ever been published in all its editions, is an international authority on Japanese art, worships cats and is beloved of everyone who knows him. He endeavoured vainly that day to cheer me up. Finally, to distract me from my mournful meditations, he produced a card, a reproduction of a Chinese painting. 'It's a lucky card,' explained he who doesn't believe in such things. 'See, there are the lucky twins, the fungi of longevity, the tiger.'

I took the card from him distractedly and glanced at the back. 'It's in German,' I said. 'What does it say?'

'A poet inspired by a dragon,' he replied. 'Dragons be lucky too, you know.'

'Not for me in Wales they aren't,' I said miserably, but I put the card in my wallet. It's there still, tattered and torn, but I keep it to remind me how I felt that day when even Jack's civilised nonsense couldn't cheer me up and because it's a symbol to me never to give up hope.

As if to emphasise my sense of loss, it was apparent when I returned home that the swallows were preparing to leave. Before I'd gone to London, the groups sitting on the wires had grown larger and larger. The sound of their excited twittering echoed the dead summer, all the joy I'd had from the two little broods in the cowshed, the dream-like swooping of their wings across the hay field and the irritable chittering of the parents if by some chance I inadvertently shut the door of their shed.

That afternoon, I was standing wretchedly under the ash tree, gazing out across the beloved view, when the noise on the wires seemed to grow and grow until the air was full of it. I glanced up and saw the wires black with the silhouettes of swallows. Dancing

before them were single birds, who trod the air and swung out in great long arcs and came back to hover before the ones on the wires. 'Like scouts,' I thought.

At once, as if on a signal, all the swallows rose into the air and, still singing, circled around the cottage, higher and higher. It seemed in that moment as if they were being joined by hundreds more coming from every side of the valley so that the sky above me was black with the tiny, swirling bodies. As a cloud, they began to drift towards the southeast. The twittering throng met with a hovering buzzard, broke formation but re-formed and kept on beating forward. I stood there until it seemed that the last straggler had caught up and I was alone with the ash tree. Soon, I would be going too.

I had gone to London on Tuesday. On Wednesday the swallows left. On Thursday I can remember only blank depression. On Friday there was an airmail letter left on the mat by the postman whose knock I hadn't heard.

Mr Chapman was cautious when I rang him to ask the current exchange rate between the Australian dollar and sterling. 'Why do you want to know?' he enquired.

When I told him, he was silent for quite a while and then he didn't seem sure whether to commiserate politely or to laugh. He was still trying to make up his mind when I put the phone down and went outside. Merlin and I sat on the hill with Blossom for hours and hours. I was trying to get used to the idea that it was all safe, that the totally unexpected legacy the letter had announced would wipe out the overdraft and the mortgage and keep all of us for at least another year.

But if the last, unexpected windfall which had saved Doli had had no strings attached, this one came trailing grief behind it.

I hadn't known my father well, in fact I suppose I hadn't seen him above a dozen times since he and my mother had parted when I was too young to remember much about it. When we had met, we'd found absolutely nothing whatsoever in common; his world and mine had not touched even on their furthest perimeters until, in the past few years (lonely years for him), my life with the animals on the farm with the unpronounceable name so far away had somehow stirred his imagination. We had started to write to each other, beginning at last tentatively to repair the damage of the long years of indifference. That his last

218

thoughts had been enough of me for him to change his will was as much in my mind as the fact that financially I was in the clear and the past years of worry were over.

They weren't, of course. I may no longer have had to worry where the money for the next feed bill was coming from, but the months ahead were to prove the most difficult of all. I faced them alone because Mrs P finally went back to Australia, thinking that at least now I could afford to buy help if I needed it. Apart from a brief return by Meta Bonney, though, I didn't get anyone else, deciding that at last I would try to pass the final test of unremitting solitude and see if I could bear it. A winter of blizzards and a springtime full of animal disasters came and went, but this time, when I emerged, I had the satisfaction of knowing that I could manage most things alone if I had to. By the time my mother returned seven months later, I felt far more in control of myself and my future than ever before in my life.

Oddly enough, the one thing I did jettison that winter was the idea for a programme about making a small country living. So when, on a day in high summer when the valley should have been blazing with sun but was instead immersed in thick, seeping fog, Michael Bowen, the Network Radio Editor from Bristol, came to see me, it was to talk about a couple of features which had little to do with the country. Over lunch I mentioned with a laugh my old obsession and sketched in a few of the ideas I'd once held so precious.

As he left, Michael turned to me and said slowly, 'How long would it take you to write me up a proposal for that country programme you were talking about?'

It was December and the gales were already tearing through the valley again when, for the first time for over a year, I went to a city once more. The noise of the traffic was far more terrifying than the screaming of the gale I had left behind me. Only when I sat in the quiet, professional calm of the studio, waiting to record the pilot which was the next step towards acceptance of the programme so long dreamed of in vain, did the old, familiar touch come back.

I adjusted the headphones and Michael's voice crackled sharply in my ear. 'We'll go ahead in one minute from now. All right?'

219